KEY

1. SALEM HOSPITAL
2. HIGH SCHOOL
3. COMMUNITY
    FUND BLDG.
4. NEW HEALTH
    CENTER
5. DOCTOR'S ROW
6. RAILROAD STATION
7. CITY HALL
8. BD. OF HEALTH
9. ESSEX ST.
10. DERBY ST.
11. HOTEL
12. BD. OF HEALTH
     HOSP.
13. ELECTRIC CO.
     PLANT
14. BAKES HOSPITAL
15. LAFAYETTE ST.
16. BRIDGE ST.
17. NORTH ST.
18. HIGHLAND AVE.
19. CHESTNUT ST.

N

Mass.

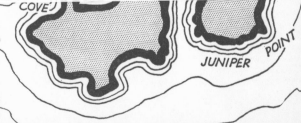

COVE

JUNIPER POINT

COMMUNITY ORGANIZATION:
ACTION AND INACTION

Published for
The Institute for Research
in Social Science
by The University of
North Carolina Press

COMMUNITY ORGANIZATION: ACTION and INACTION

By *Floyd Hunter*
Ruth Connor Schaffer
Cecil G. Sheps

CHAPEL HILL
The University of North Carolina Press *1956*

To Katharine Jocher

Preface

THIS REPORT may be considered a study of a self-study. The general objective of the research described in these pages has been to locate a community in which people were active in relation to health needs and to observe systematically and record the processes by which decisions were reached, plans were formulated on the basis of these decisions, and action programs were initiated and carried out to meet health problems of a community.

This study represents an empirical and interdisciplinary piece of research of processes of stratification and social action. It was made possible by a grant from the Health Information Foundation of New York to the University of North Carolina's Institute for Research in Social Science. The officials of the Foundation and the University group felt that research into the processes of community self-study, through giving clues about community organization which can be utilized in meeting local health problems, might be of considerable significance to many laymen, social scientists, students, community organizers, and community health educators.

Between March 7 and June 1, 1952, three members of the University staff met frequently to work out a tentative plan of research. The co-directors of the project were Floyd Hunter, Associate Professor in the School of Social Work, and Dr. Cecil G. Sheps, Research Professor of Health Planning. Ruth Connor Schaffer was appointed research fellow. Mrs. Schaffer served as full-time field observer in the community for one year beginning June, 1952. Harry Martin and Ester Hunter carried out specialized research assignments in relation to the project. Mr. Martin, a graduate student in sociology, made an intensive study of the participation of medical practitioners in community activities. Mrs. Hunter, a graduate student in anthropology, observed community participation patterns of one of the larger ethnic groups, the Polish, in the community. Emily Wilson and James Dinsmore were graduate assistants who handled data gathered in the community by the field workers.

During the first two weeks in March, 1952, letters were written to all of the secretaries of community councils and chests in every urban community with a population of between 40,000 and 70,000 in the mid-Atlantic or New England area from Maryland to Maine. Directors of public health programs, in a broad sample of communities, and secretaries of state medical societies also received letters from the project staff. The letters contained a statement of purpose and asked for help in locating an urban community, within the population range, which was active in relation to solving health problems. The letters emphasized a particular interest in the size of the community, what was happening in relation to health, and asked for the name of one person in the community whom the staff might contact in connection with the final selection.

Approximately seventy replies were received and evaluated. Mr. Hunter, Dr. Sheps, and Mrs. Schaffer visited six communities which seemed to meet the qualifications set up. After due consideration, the selection of a research area narrowed to an interest in Salem, Massachusetts.

Salem had a recent history of a successful screening program in relation to one of its health problems. In 1950, under the auspices of the Community Fund, Community Council, Board of Health, and the Tuberculosis Association, a city-wide X-ray program was conducted with over 20,000 persons participating. The Salem Community Council, in February, 1952, set up a special committee to study and make recommendations concerning a permanent health committee or council. A visit to the community and a discussion with thirty leaders in the health and welfare field showed that Salem might prove a fruitful selection. In May, 1952, the Community Council, as well as civic leaders in Salem, invited the Institute for Research in Social Science at the University of North Carolina to use Salem as their study community.

After numerous staff conferences, a general frame of reference was set up containing the postulates and hypotheses to be used in the study. A wide variety of factors for study were examined and taken into account. A social structural picture of Salem seemed necessary if the staff was to understand the activities of persons related to the self-study. Consequently, background material related to population, vital statistics, history, socio-economic patterns, community location and function, and patterns of formal community organizations were gathered in the early stages of study. General bibliographies containing information on self-studies and community organization for health were compiled for study and reference.

Before going to the field it was also felt that the general frame of reference for study should specifically encompass an analysis of health organizations and a qualitative picture of health facilities—local resources, relationships with state health resources, positions of health organizations within the organized community, and a reconstruction of community activities leading up to the self-study to be undertaken by the Salem Community Council. This frame of reference was utilized in studying the processes of self-study.

It was felt that field observers should pay particular attention to a structural analysis of generalized prestige patterns, power relations, and decision-making processes.

A plan of participant observation was projected to enable Mrs. Schaffer to record individual and committee actions, to classify the degree of involvement of people in the study process, and to evaluate and classify problems turned up in the study. Patterns of action leading to recommendations for community action were of particular concern in this phase of the work.

Preliminary thought was given to the mechanics of analysis of field data and the final writing of the community study report.

With an eye to social change and with a predisposition to observe action in the Salem community, the research staff of the Salem Health Study recognized that all observation would need to be guided by definite hypotheses. The sponsoring Foundation had hypotheses it wanted tested and the University staff was in agreement with testing two major hypotheses, namely:

1. Cultural changes occur with least conflict and confusion along lines of established community patterns.

2. A community can solve most of its health problems through action programs if:
   a. its citizens have available to them an objective picture of their health situation;
   b. its citizens have a knowledge of other communities' experiences in solving similar problems; and
   c. it has competent, democratic leadership.

These hypotheses were based on a postulate which implied that the process of "self-study" is an effective means of insuring positive social change. How well this postulate and the hypotheses resting upon it were borne out will be disclosed in later analysis.

The phrase, "self-study," posed problems from the beginning of the research process. In negotiations with the Foundation's research department, there were several long discussions over what might be meant by self-study. Two questions dominated the discussions: (1) does self-study mean that no outside help could be sought by a community studying itself? and (2) would the presence of a research team in a community which was attempting self-study distort the whole process, i.e., would a community act differently when it is aware of being observed than when it is actually "going it alone"?

The first question was more easily disposed of than the second. It was agreed that a community might normally seek some outside assistance in a course of self-study. That is, it might seek the experience of other communities and outside health organizations in developing study schedules and methods of procedure. The difficulty in attacking the second question lay in the fact that it was recognized that no very accurate measures could be set up to determine the influence the research team might have during the study process. It was finally determined that the research team would take a passive role in any study groups that might be formed in the community. The difficulties of such a position were not minimized, but it was felt that the research team, by recognizing its role and spotting those instances in which there were demands by community members for more than passivity, could hold stimulus to a minimum. The working definition of self-study upon which research activities were based was as follows:

A self-study is a social process whereby (1) a situation is observable in which a definite number of individuals or a definable group within the community becomes aware of community health problems, and (2) these individuals or the group begin an exploration of health problems in order to isolate them and come to some solution, and (3) major stimulation for exploration, definition, and activity during the process of study related to given problems comes from within the community structure, rather than from outside.

Eight additional hypotheses to be tested in the community study were developed by the University group. These were:

1. Salem, Massachusetts, goes about solving its problems related to health in a manner that would conform to its general pattern of problem-solving on a community-wide basis.

2. Community functions are delegated to specific functioning groups in the community.

3. A relatively small proportion of the total population will be involved in the "self-study."

4. A few leaders will emerge in the study process who will be primarily instrumental in furthering the study.

5. Matters of community-wide "policy" in relation to health problems will inevitably involve the community "power structure."

6. Health organizations will have greater interest in promoting and extending the study than other community groups.

7. Members of the study committee will, in general, follow their traditional role expectations.

8. The formation of the study committee will be subject to the general economic, political, and social processes that bear upon the parent sponsoring body—in this instance—the Salem Community Council.

These hypotheses emphasize the structural-functional approach to social analysis. They imply that an adequate appraisal of the actions of any group studying health problems and health organizations must take into account a community-wide range of social facets in order to interpret specific data. Thus, the research staff was alert to a broad range of data. With each observation made within the study period, the staff was consistently asking itself such questions, as, "Where does the organization fit into the whole community scheme?" "What is this man's position in relation to the group with which he is identified?" "What function does this specific action serve in relation to another set of actions?" "What connection is there between this fact and the health study?" Seemingly isolated facts and events were recorded in journal form, and in some cases they remained enigmatic, but in most instances definite patterns of relationships between data began to appear.

A system of processing the field data was set up before field work began. It was felt that conceivably there would be three types of data gathered: (1) interviews; (2) journals consisting of field personnel's behavior which might influence the self-study process, memos on community movements, "hunches, hypotheses, generalizations," and field work suggestions; (3) published materials dealing with the social structure of Salem relating to health such as newspaper clippings, pamphlets, and books. Arrangements were made to code and file all interviews and the running journals which were to be kept by staff members in the field. All material sent from the field was to be coded, clipped, and filed in the appropriate position within the code for classifying data.

In order to perfect the plan of study an advisory committee was selected from the University of North Carolina to scrutinize the work of the staff before entering the community. This committee consisted of Gordon Blackwell, Director of the Institute for Research in Social Science; N. J. Demerath, Professor of Sociology; Arthur E. Fink, Dean of the School of Social Work; Dr. E. G. McGavern, Dean of the School of Public Health; Dr. W. P. Richardson, Professor of Preventive Medicine; Rupert B. Vance, Professor of Sociology; Elizabeth Kemble, Dean of the School of Nursing; Dr. William Fleming, Professor of Preventive Medicine, and Dr. John Wright, Professor of Public Health Administration.

Entry was made into the community the first week in June, 1952. The first month was spent in gathering background data on the community and in interviews with the executives of the health and welfare organizations of the community. The staff felt that the summer should be spent in gathering data on historic Salem, the ways in which Salem had faced community problems in the past, and, in general, to determine leadership patterns and practices. A portion of the summer was spent in studying the power structure of the community. During preliminary interviews a careful record was kept of the names of leaders suggested by the interviewees. At the end of a month and a half the names of approximately two hundred community leaders were placed on a list. A panel of active citizens was set up to judge the list of names representing leaders in every field—church, government, civic affairs, and business. A final list of 40 top leaders in these various categories was the result of panel judgment. A schedule was then prepared to be administered to the 40 men and women selected. The schedule was devised to determine who was considered the most important leader in the community and to determine who the top ten leaders of the community were. This technique of determining power structure enabled the staff to gain insight into the community which proved valuable in later interviews and in the interpretation of data gathered on the self-study process.

The month of August, 1952, was utilized in investigating health problems and institutional structures in relation to health. During the year 1952-53 periodic visits were made to the community by the co-directors of the project.

The Salem community has a number of nationality groups within its boundaries. While it was impossible to study each of these groups in detail, Mrs. Hunter, during the summer of 1952, intensively studied the Polish community in order to relate organized activity of this group to other ethnic groups and to the community as a whole.

During the summer of 1953, Mr. Martin studied the participation patterns of Salem physicians in relation to community activities.

Salem was founded in 1626 and has played an active part in the early historic events of our country. Today it preserves more historic landmarks, relics, and articles of colonial interest than any other community in New England. The population of Salem is approximately 41,000 as of the 1950 census. While an extraordinary effort has been made to preserve the historical character of Salem, mercantile and civic interests have managed to make a wedge into community life. People in Salem found industrial employment at the Naumkeag Mills, the home of Pequot sheets; Jack Brothers, Incorporated, the world famous manufacturer of games; Sylvania Electric Products, Incorporated, and Electro Corporation, two of the nation's more prominent manufacturers of electronics equipment. Salem has 24 churches representing almost every denomination. Approximately 80 percent of the population is Roman Catholic. There are large French Canadian, Irish, Polish, and Italian neighborhoods.

Various social agencies in the community had organized a community council which was the organization that invited the research team from the University of North Carolina into the community. In 1952 this council organized a committee on health and intended to make a community self-survey of the health problems of Salem in the fall of that year. The committee on health of the community council was expanded and finally had 14 members representing business, professional, and civic interests.

One of the major reasons for selecting a community with a population between 40,000 and 70,000 was the fact that communities of this size often have formally established patterns of community planning. This proved to be the case in Salem and made the task of observation less difficult than it might have been in a smaller community where greater demands undoubtedly would have been placed upon the staff for guidance in the processes of organization.

Community cooperation with the University of North Carolina study was excellent. Methodologically, the staff had a few problems attempting to establish and keep a passive role in the community. There is always a temptation to direct and to organize and to emphasize problems and problem areas when they are not seen by the lay persons. Over and over again the staff had to define its role to various representatives of organizations. After the self-study process began, however, the staff was able to take a relatively passive role in observing the community in action.

Floyd Hunter
Ruth Connor Schaffer
Cecil G. Sheps

Contents

COMMUNITY ORGANIZATION:
ACTION AND INACTION

CHAPTER 1

First Views

SIXTEEN MILES above Boston, along the north shore between Boston and Gloucester, Massachusetts, lies a restless community, Salem. Situated around an old and atrophied harbor, Salem is a study in contrasts of the old and new, the beautiful and drab. By-passed by the major trunk highways, served by the antiquated Boston and Maine railroad, strangled by growing suburban satellites, fighting a rear guard action for the retention of commerce and industry, and wracked by gnawing internal problems of an ethnic and religious character, Salem retains a proud, if somewhat unreal, independence as a community. The unreality of its independence lies in the fact that contrary to the wishes of many in Salem it is a part of the nerveless, sprawling, amoeboid, metropolitan area of Boston.

As Salem declined in the nineteenth century as a shipping port, Boston grew. As Boston grew, it never politically captured and absorbed the satellite cities growing at its outer borders. Consequently, today it is tightly hemmed in by a ring of cities expressing civic independence within the metropolitan region of which Salem is now a part.

Between the historical boundaries of Salem and Boston, and linking them, lie the independent community of Lynn and suzerainty of Swampscott. Surrounding Salem, in a land and population vise, are the communities of Marblehead, Beverly, Peabody, and Danvers. In this complex, urban situation the mounting costs of congestion, the competition for land, labor supply, water resources, and the struggle for markets are grossly apparent. The difficulties of trying to

1

meet problems on a community-by-community basis are obvious and almost insurmountable. Thus, many of the problems of the Salem community are external. Many, on the
other hand, are internal.

Salem, founded six years after the historic Plymouth land-
ing, was for several years the capital of the Massachusetts
Colony under Conant and Endicott. Here in 1633 Roger
Williams unrelentingly preached and criticized the acts of the
government and was banished. Here was passed in General
Court a law forbidding any Jesuit priest to enter the Massachusetts Colony under penalty of banishment for the first
offense, and death, if he should return. Here, too, the terrible
"witchcraft" delusion of 1692 brought Salem undying shame
as word of the execution of 19 people resounded in an already
apprehensive world.

With transition and growth Salem's golden age was yet to
come. Ranking next in size only to Boston, New York, Philadelphia, Baltimore, and Charleston, all of which had excellent
harbors, great rivers, or more extensive inland waterways,
Salem, lacking natural advantages, exceeded them all in the
amount of its world-wide, ocean-going commerce during its
great commercial era. It is purported that Salem had com-
menced American trade with more different ports in Africa,
South America, Asia, and the islands of the sea than all other
American ports combined. It has been customary to account
for Salem's success in terms of the intelligence and courage of
its captains and merchants. The romantic appeal of the period
and of the men whose industry encouraged whole sections of
the trading world to believe that the United States must surely
be but a part of a small New England port could hardly escape
the imagination of the historical novelists who have repeatedly written of it. Seamen, captains, and merchants were of
one mind: the accumulation of wealth. The change from one
status to another, from seaman to captain, was straight and
easy for men of intelligence and energy. Freedom was un-
paralleled. There were no trade, business, or labor laws, and
no commercial treaties. As far as the government of the

United States was concerned, captains could go where they wished abroad, carry whatever they wished, and bring back whatever they pleased. Fine residences, many designed by the famed McIntyre, were built by the sea captains about the town common and later along Federal and Chestnut Streets. These handsome homes were furnished with elegant treasures collected from all corners of the earth. Chestnut Street is often referred to as the most architecturally perfect street in the United States today. Salem grew and flourished as a shipping port until the War of 1812. With the close of the war and smothered by the famed Embargo Act of 1807, Salem ended her epoch supreme and began anew.

The Salem of Hawthorne's youth was a different Salem. The freedom which typified the shipping era had gone. While intermarriage between French Huguenots, one or two German immigrants who found their way to Salem's shore, and a half dozen Irish families with the native stock had been perceptible in the eighteenth century, it became less and less frequent in the nineteenth century. Social mobility became more rigid. With the passing of time industrialism encroached upon the dignity of Salem. By the end of the nineteenth century it had become a city of factories huddled about the glories of antiquity.

As wars and revolutions wracked Europe, the population altered, imperceptibly at first, as people sought peace and opportunity in the new world. Drawn closer and closer together, the original stock of New England stubbornly held to its heritage and clung to the memories of its past, allowing the newcomers little or no place within the community structure. Nevertheless, as the transplanted of other nations took root, that influence made itself felt. In Salem, however, an ever narrowing circle, clannish, proud of its blood, kept itself aloof from foreign infiltration. It still survives in declining numbers on Chestnut Street. Behind the unchanging, beautiful McIntyre porticoes with their iron gateposts many an old name is dying and a new name is taking its place.

Meanwhile the foreign population lived a busy, as well as prolific, life. To Salem came the Irish and settled, as if in simulation of the past, in the old, time-worn section near the harbor. With much industry and the passage of time they acquired entry into local politics from the domestic and industrial jobs previously delegated to them. (Salem's mayor at the time of this study, Richard J. Corcoran, was of Irish descent.) Tempted by the occupational opportunities offered by the textile industry, the French came from the far-distant Canadian cities of Quebec and Montreal. At first they partly replaced the Irish and competed with the latter for the inexpensive housing offered in the old sections. Finally the French Canadians settled in an area above the harbor about the mills. For many years they spoke only their native tongue, a mixture of French, Indian, and English. Even though they have worked side by side with other national groups and have tended to adopt a few cultural patterns of those about them, they maintain a group cohesiveness through the retention of French fraternal organizations, churches, the support of French newspapers and radio broadcasts. To Salem more recently have come the Italian and the Pole. A more detailed treatment of the Polish population will be presented in a later chapter.

In the town where for many years only one church and one manner of worship were tolerated and where the reaction to Catholics and Catholicity were attested by law, temples have been erected whose names speak volumes. There are the Church of the Immaculate Conception and St. James Church—both predominantly attended by Irish Catholics; St. Mary's for Italian Catholics; St. Joseph's for French Catholics; the Church of St. John the Baptist for Polish Catholics; St. John's Ukrainian Church for Greek Catholics; and St. Nicholas Russian Church. A new Jewish Synagogue has recently been completed. In many respects the foreign population of Salem celebrate marriages, births, and deaths according to the beliefs of their fathers in the Old World.

The descendants of the early founders hold membership in,

but seldom take the trouble to worship at, the First Church Unitarian, rebuilt for the fourth time in 1826. Besides the First Church there is a Second Church Unitarian, two Methodist churches, two Episcopal churches, two Baptist churches, two Congregational churches as well as six additional religious groups including "store-front" fundamentalist sects.

Approximately 80 percent of the city's population is Catholic, 16 percent Protestant, and 4 percent Jewish. These figures are not comprehensive of the fact that there are a relatively large number in each group which might be classified as unchurched. It may be noted that 80 percent or 33,504 individuals attend 7 churches while 16 percent or 6,720 individuals attend 16 churches.

The Salem of 1953 consisted of an area of 8.2 square miles and a population of 41,880, of which approximately one-third were of French Canadian descent and one-third were of Irish descent. The next largest ethnic group was of Polish descent.

The manufacturing industries are diversified. While once confined to cotton and leather processing, now incandescent lamps, radio and TV tubes, games, and machinery have been added to the line of products. In 1953, Salem had seventy different lines of manufacturing representing 150 factories.

Until recently one of the principal industries had been the Naumkeag Steam Cotton Company. During what is commonly referred to as "the great fire of 1914," its plant was destroyed as the flames swept across most of the city to the water. Since the fire the company has re-erected its buildings entirely in reinforced concrete.

In spite of the fact that the plant facility of Naumkeag was one of the largest and one of the most modern in the community, the industry late in 1953 completed the process of moving from the city. A portion of the Naumkeag's interests in Peabody, Massachusetts, was first sold and the plant moved to South Carolina. For a longer time than the city fathers care to remember they have attempted to retain the mill interests in Salem. The continued movement of plants throughout New England to the South predicted the futility of their attempts. Salem, like other New England communities, has a stranded population of unemployed mill workers.

Local industrial development has seen the establishment of two electronics companies—Electro Company and Sylvania Electric Products Company. The latter is the third largest incandescent lamp manufactory in the country and the second largest manufactory of radio tubes. Jack Brothers, one of the largest and best known manufacturers of games in the world, is an old Salem concern.

In 1950 the New England Electric Company built a large power plant on the shore of Salem harbor. Plans were in process for an additional unit of similar size. The magnitude of the project in terms of tax receipts and without local government expenditure for auxiliary services, such as fire protection and new access streets, was being pleasantly felt in terms of a reduction of the local tax rate.

This then was Salem at the time of study: a community striving to find its place in the modern industrial world in the face of strong pressures which continued to make it look longingly back into the past. A part of the internal problems faced by Salem was due to the fact that some of its leaders had been content to live in the past. However, the things of which they had been proud were embattled, encroached upon, and in some cases, in a state of decay beyond repair. Some of the leaders in the social life of Salem had withdrawn from active participation in its civic life and had built for themselves a pleasant society within a society. Because of the land poverty of the city in terms of desirable new residential areas some had moved their homes to nearby communities in which such sections were available, but they retained business interests in Salem.

In light of what has previously been said, it might be assumed that the authors believed Salem was disintegrating as a community without hope of survival. This would be no more true than if we had opened our story with a flattering account of the virtues and strengths of the community—of which there were many. Few communities the size of Salem disintegrate and die in our American culture. They do change, however, and it is the process of change with which we are concerned in this account. Community problems presage change, and by observing how a community goes about solving its problems one may plot trend lines of future development.

Salem, the Salem of today, was in the first stages of an exploration of its health problems at the time of the first visit by a member of the University of North Carolina research team; that is, there was discussion among several members of the community council related to the desirability of extending a process of self-study to include general health problems. Planning had not gone beyond the general, informal talk stage, but upon receipt of our letter of inquiry about communities that might be "moving in regard to their general problems of health," the director of the community fund and the director of the department of public health, with others, saw the University proposal as an opportunity to stimulate activity within the council and specifically within the health section of the council.

There was some evidence to indicate, during exploratory discussions with community leaders in the council, that the council health section was being strengthened after having been dormant for some time and that this council section would probably engage in some sort of self-survey whether the University group entered the community or not. Thus, the University group reasonably assumed that it would be able to make a study of a self-survey. This assumption has been borne out.

While it was clearly stated from the beginning of the negotiations with community council leaders that the University group would not in any sense direct the efforts of those who might be involved in the self-study program, it was also recognized that the mere presence of staff members in the community would act as a stimulus in the whole process—positively or negatively, as the case might be. The leaders tentatively understood this and apparently were not bothered by the question. As a matter of fact, they were pleased to think that their independence of judgment and direction of their own affairs were not to be encroached upon by outsiders. At a later stage in the study process, the sincerity of the staff in this regard was to be tested, as will be seen, but the resolution on the part of the staff remained firm throughout the study. Aside from the stimulation of our presence, the results of self-study must be regarded as those created by Salem citizens. The staff engaged in no backstage manipulations to secure results. There needed to be no *pretense* that community leaders were acting on any motivations other than their own. The Salem leaders acted on their own in relation to the heart of this report, the self-survey.

There is, however, a broad range of materials contained in this book that were not gathered by the self-survey committee of the Salem community. As was pointed out in the preface, the University research team felt that, in order to observe action in the community, various social structures would have to be isolated and identified in pattern form. This idea largely underlaid the plan of work. It was taken for granted that the University group would need to do basic social research, particularly during the preliminary stages of study, in order to relate persons in action in the community to a meaningful pattern of institutional groupings, associations, clubs, cliques, and the like. Knowing this, and further knowing that the observations made would finally be written up for the use of others, the research team explained to council leaders in general terms that team members would be looking into many areas of community relationships, but that such work would only serve to orient the staff to generalized community behavior patterns and would not be concerned with seeking out or defining health problems in the community. The staff further explained that it was being taken as axiomatic that Salem groups organizing themselves around health agencies are functional groupings of people related to other social organizations of the community—that health agencies are not isolated from the operations of industrial and commercial organizations, church groupings, prestige, power, policy, and political structures. Consequently, it seemed desirable to the staff to do some investigating of these matters during the period in which the self-study group organized for its operations.

The position of the staff, again, was understood by the community leaders of Salem. The preliminary investigations were carried out without incident and with considerable individual interest and cooperation given to the staff by scores of people in the community. Without this type of preliminary investigation and without the understanding and help of community members in the process, the team is convinced that the "study of a study" would have been impossible.

With the exception of arranging to meet members of the community council for the preliminary discussions, the research team spent no time in organizing the community for its self-study. One reason for selecting a community the size of Salem for study was that it has established lines of communication and relatively fixed patterns of organizing to accomplish study tasks. Organizing committees, delegating responsibilities, choosing personnel for specific purposes, and the like, are not strange activities in a community of 40,000 people, and the skills of local citizens along these lines could be relied upon, relieving the research team of any such responsibilities.

Acting upon its own and independently of the self-study committee, the University team gathered data that will be presented in the chapters to follow which relate to basic social structures in the community. Observations made by the staff observer in the self-study committee will comprise the central portion of this book. The latter exposition presents a specific community structure, a committee, in action and acting in relation to larger social structures of Salem. The final chapters of the book will embody a critique based on the major hypotheses of the study. This portion of the writing will also be couched in terms of community organization for health services. The whole writing represents a complete view of a community as seen by members of the community and as observed in an interdisciplinary scheme laid out by the research team.

Obviously if all of the data gathered in the study were presented, the telling would make a tedious recital. The materials selected for presentation are intended to be illustrative and to tell as complete a story as possible. The facts given here represent ordered facts, but hopefully not distorted ones. One unavoidable distortion, however, must be mentioned.

In describing the actions of people, the social scientist is always faced with a dilemma. Should he use the names of the people, the community, and the organizations he describes, or should he disguise names and places in order to offend none who might not like their actions to be known? To use proper names, in many cases, may be a matter of distaste. To refuse to use them tends to distort materials. Communities that have been studied and described under pseudonyms, by sociologists, are often widely identified, and the pains of producing the disguises seem futile, if not ridiculous.

In this writing we have changed the proper names of persons, although every precaution has been taken to avoid muckraking personalities or reporting materials that might be hurtful to any individual. Gossip and mere hearsay are not repeated. The whole purpose of the writing is to reveal processes of action rather than to build or belittle personalities. The manuscript has been read and criticized for factual statements by responsible representatives of the Salem community.

CHAPTER 2

History, Ghosts, and Totems

A KNOWLEDGE of the history of social distinctions was an important element in the community system of Salem. An acute knowledge of history was a thread of consciousness that held together the upper reaches of society. This knowledge was not confined to the assessment of the witch trials or the founding date of the community—facts generally known to students of American history—but it extended into the minutiae of family histories, places of residence, and social and civic development. History was one device for welding some groups into a cohesive whole and for keeping other groups at a distance.

Objectively, Salem is a modern community. It has a scattering of fringe industries, road signs, hamburger stands along the incoming highways, traffic snarls, old houses and new houses, noise and confusion that characterize the commercial and living arrangements of any community of its size. But like all communities it is divided into neighborhoods that represent a variety of social distinctions. A quiet backwater removed from the bustle and turmoil of urban living is an area known as Chestnut Street. Those who live on this street look back nostalgically to a day when Salem was less dedicated to mass material progress and more dedicated to the refinements of Puritan virtues.

Hawthorne's brooding story of *The House of Seven Gables* with its ghostly suggestions was well laid in Salem. It would not be correct to say that the upper prestige persons of Salem were ghost worshippers as the term is applied to primitive culture, but there was a cult of ancestory operative within the

11

community. Images of recall is the term we shall apply to the process of using ancestors in lending social prestige to a person. Many of the recalled images were "ghosts" of Salem's past.

Recalled images is a term that also may apply to living relatives as well as to dead antecedents. In most social gatherings in the elite groups of Salem, the recall of famous ancestors or living relatives was a pastime that was inescapably connected with such meetings. The process of recall usually started with such a statement as, "Oh, Mary, did I ever tell you the story of Grandfather Jones on a bear hunt?" Even if the one addressed had heard the story many times, she was almost bound to reply negatively, particularly in the presence of strangers, since she, too, may have a story of a famous ancestor she will wish to repeat presently. As ancestors are recalled, one can almost feel their presence. They become real persons whose past actions give clues to present-day behavior. Some such sessions have an almost seance quality about them, if one may allow for a slight exaggeration. Images recalled may, in unusual circumstances, be described as bordering on rascality, but in the main they have quasi-heroic qualities.

Within the Yankee group, the group that holds the upper prestige positions and the majority positions on the corporate boards of the community, the recall of ancestors may go back several generations. For example, the Pierce family can recall a great grandfather who served in the cabinet of George Washington. This, of course, was a trump recall in any Salem gathering. The Phillip Reeves, through Mrs. Reeves, could go back to General Glover. Others could make connections with various Boston families of fame such as the Adamses, Lowells, Cabots, and Lodges. In each instance of such recall, the speaker's prestige was upwardly influenced within the company addressed and in the process of time there grew up an aura of respect for the persons who could, by proxy, claim the virtues and despoil the vices of famous progenitors.

The social significance and function of this process is obvious when one contrasts the type of images that could be recalled by the dominant group with those of sub-ethnic groups. The Polish community member who, by some stretch of imagination, might find himself in a company of Yankees would be loath to recall the shade of his grandfather who came to Salem by steerage passage and whose only later distinction was that he tanned hides. The social history of Salem has been written about the Yankee grandfathers who hired the immigrant grandfathers who tanned hides, built factories, cleaned fish, and moved produce. History was kept alive by the process of recall described here, and it provided a basis of inclusion and exclusion socially. It was all bound up with "proper" conduct on the part of forebears—proper in the sense of acceptable work, religion, ethnic background, and to some extent ethical and moral behavior.

Most professional workers recruited, as so many were, from a class of forefathers who did manual or skilled work, also found it impossible to compete with the dominant group in image recall, and their social position was invariably downgraded in the interviews held with leaders during the process of study of community social patterns. Within the pattern of stratification, the professional workers fell below the elite groups in both power and prestige. In general, they recognized their position by paying deference to those above them and receiving recognition from those below them in educational and economic achievement. Education had brought them some measure of social position. They are upwardly mobile, and if the historical process holds true, some of the children of the professionals may through education and proper marriage ties reach positions of top prominence in the community. The stratification structure in Salem was not closed, but it was extremely rigid, and none whom we encountered fully broke into the upper circles in the space of one generation.

Exclusiveness of space, materials, and persons provide totemic reference for Salem's social gradations. The historical objects, old houses, antiques, books, letters, and the like are associated with certain persons and families exclusively. These persons, consequently, take on totemic characteristics associated with deference, reverence, and awe. Social groupings are organized around the inanimate symbols of prestige as well as around persons, and such groups furnish measuring devices for the social class system of the community.

One set of organizations of this character is the exclusive sewing circles of the community.

In a dinner conversation with a group of community leaders, in the home of a man of good social connections, one of the women laughingly said,

"We must tell our visitors about the sewing circles!"

There was some bantering back and forth between the men and women present, subjecting the sewing circles to some ridicule, but there was also a seriousness in the trend of talk. One of the men jokingly asked the ladies,

"You don't really sew at those meetings, do you?" And before one of the women could answer, another man joined in and said, "Of course they don't sew. They hold meetings late in the afternoons during the winter in these poorly lighted old houses so that they couldn't hit the eye of a needle even if they tried!" This remark amused the other guests, but when the laughter died down, the hostess said,

"You can laugh all you want to, but the sewing circles *are* important in Salem, and I'll tell our visitor how really important they are when you are not around."

A follow-up on this bit of information revealed that the Salem sewing circles, at least three of them, the "Thread and Needle," "Busy Bees," and "Cheerful Workers," constitute social prestige groups in the community. In a functional sense, they are extremely important groups in the society structure of the town. They provide a social measuring device for townspeople in determining who is the "right" kind of person and who is in social limbo.

Each of the sewing circles is limited to fifty members. To be included in a circle, the individual under consideration must meet several crucial tests. She must be asked to join. One does not apply for membership. She must be a resident of Salem. She must not be the type who dyes her hair. If she is a daughter of a member and has been presented in the annual assembly, she is almost automatically asked to join the circle of her mother. If she is the wife of a minister of one of the ranking protestant churches, she is asked to join a circle even if she is a new arrival in the community. The circles compete for such members. If she is a community newcomer, and if there is a vacancy in one of the circles, created by death usually, and if the lady is known through former school connections, such a person may be asked to join one of the circles. All of this, provided her husband has proper business or professional connections in the community and the couple is considered "attractive" by other members of the circle. If a woman passes all of these qualifications she is "in"; but not all pass, and often there is much feeling on the part of those who are excluded.

Writing about the development of the sewing circles, James Phillips has this to say about them.

Female society of the nineties rested securely on the basis of Sewing Circles. Even in those days the sanctity of antiquity hung around the "Cheerful Workers." None of the young people could remember when they began, and thought there must always have been "Cheerfuls." Nobody ever knew just when they started, but there was a general impression that they grew out of a group which sewed for the soldiers during the Civil War. But even if the "Cheerfuls" were not in the first blush of youth, they were full of life and energy. They met regularly, sewed for charity—just what I don't know,—and at rare intervals invited the other societies to a party, and what a party it must have been! Young fry were not invited, and it was spoken of discreetly in their presence, so we knew little about it. Men were also anathema, and were never invited.

Next in order of antiquity came the "Busy Bees," a group of cheerful young matrons in those days, which included our Mammas and were much nearer our comprehension than the venerable "Cheerfuls." The "Bees" were distinctly more human in those days than the "Cheerfuls," but their dignity was far less. Most of the founders of both were still alive, and they did not feel the need of new blood. If a new lady came to town and did not offend anybody, after she had been looked over carefully, she might be drafted as a "Bee" or a "Cheerful," as her status seemed to indicate, but there was no rushing for candidates, and the policy of taking in daughters was far in the future.

The ranks of the Society were, however, yearly increased by growing debutantes who were not sewed into any circle, and just what was to be done with these blooming and attractive young women. Their Mammas realized that they should be organized socially, and the obvious probability of marriage as the destiny for most of them brought the practical idea of a cooking club, so a cooking club was born. Whether they ever made a loaf of bread was not even known to the outside world, but certain activities were. They gave parties to which men were invited, and they did not cook the food served to them. They also presented each member, as a sort of marriage certificate, a prize or reward of merit, call it what you will, on her wedding day, with a replica of a Paul Revere pitcher. The ranks of the "Cookers" soon filled up and none were taken in after about 1893 or 1894, so the problem of what to do with the unorganized females of the late nineties again pressed upon the social planners of the day. The more demure girls of that day refused to serve under the motto that "the way to a man's heart was through his stomach," and again took to the more refined art of sewing. One cannot tell, of course; they may, under arched eyebrows, have just reasoned that a scarf, a necktie case, or a set of shoe bags made a more lasting impression on the wayward male than just a welsh rarebit. Anyway the "Thread and Needle Society" came into existence, partly as a protest against exclusion from the "Cheerfuls," "Bees," and "Cookers," and partly as an offensive and defensive alliance against the male population of the town, and they were the dominant organization of the female society of the late "Nineties." [1]

In a conversation, one evening, with a group in the home of a family living just outside Salem, the hostess remarked, "Living outside Salem has its repercussions in social life."

1. James Phillips, *The Essex Institute Historical Collections,* Vol. XC, Salem, Massachusetts (January 1954), pp. 34-35.

The conversation which followed revealed the present-day potency of the circles as exclusion devices.

Another woman present, a leading young matron in one of the sewing circles, asked her what she meant. The gist of the conversation that followed was in this wise:

The first speaker, the hostess, said that for a long time she had wondered why she had not been asked to join a sewing circle. Her guest replied that the sewing circles were open only to people who live in Salem. The hostess took exception to this and cited a couple of examples of persons who belong to the circles but live outside the town. The guest countered this by saying that these persons were members of a sewing circle before they moved from the community. It seems permissible for a person to move away and still retain circle membership.

The hostess insisted that she knew of a person who was born outside of Salem and had lived outside all her life and still belonged to a circle. The guest, upon learning the identity of the woman, said that this was an exception to the general rule, because the person named belonged to a family that had traditionally belonged to a Salem circle. It seemed evident that the hostess was not completely satisfied with the answer and that her tacit bid for membership had been rejected. She turned the conversation by saying,

"My first two years in Salem were the most horrible experiences of my life. I thought I would never get to know people and I thought Salem was the most hide-bound place, socially, of any community I had ever lived in!" She went on to say that she had grown up in Brooklyn, New York, and that, in spite of the jokes that are made about Brooklyn on the stage and over the radio, it really is a fine place and has a very active and good social life.

Her guest responded by saying that when people first come to Salem they often do not like it. Other people do not know them—what kind of persons they really are—and in the hostess' case, none of them had realized for a long time what an *attrac-*

tive person she was until they had seen her operate so effectively on a civic committee. She then asked if the hostess did not feel that she is now well accepted in the community, and the latter answered in the affirmative.

Placing people on civic committees is sometimes a second best way of admitting them socially. Many of the civic committees and agency boards of Salem have socially prominent people on them. This factor often leads to the confusion of power and social prestige, as we shall presently see. Before dealing with this related topic, let us examine the family patterning of some of the sewing circles. Here it may be shown that family connections effectively tie together the status organizations under consideration.

Representatives of the major sewing circles helped to diagram family relationships existing among these groups. Blood and marriage relationships have genuine meaning in providing organizational solidarity in these circles. Some disappointed women have started competitive circles; for example there is an "X" circle, but it is relatively new and cannot be compared to the three major groups. It seems possible that the "X" circle may eventually meet the same fate as the "Cookers." It may be forgotten.

Once a member is admitted to a circle, she is required to produce three garments a year. Often she has a dressmaker do most of her work. The garments are usually given to a worthy charity. Rarely is a member dropped, but sometimes she may be for non-attendance when she willfully refuses to come.

The sewing circles purposefully have been described at some length. They represent a social measuring device used by certain members of the community to maintain group solidarity and group dominance. The dominance of the Yankee group is maintained in part by the exclusion of other ethnic groups from sewing circles. To the outsider looking at the sewing circle pattern of organization, the importance of the circles might be minimized, but for those living in the community and close to the centers of prestige and power, the sewing circles have a real function in group organization.

Definite connections between members of the power structure and the sewing circles were made by the research team. We shall presently discuss the power structure in more detail, but it may be stated here that of 40 top power leaders studied, seven of them were related to members of the sewing circles. Such links, standing alone, may not be of primary importance, but as one ties various groups together through establishing active relationships the pattern becomes meaningful as a whole. Such linking was a basic research task in this study.

The study team was concerned with the problem of relating social status to social action. It was felt that the most direct way of relating these two variables was to make as many connections as possible between formal and informal groupings in order to describe the social system of the community in action. The team wished to short-circuit the more elaborate process of obtaining status data utilized by Lloyd Warner in his Yankee City study and at the same time obtain data that would have a bearing upon status and social action.[2] The community designated Yankee City was located, we understood, within a few miles of Salem. The population characteristics were comparable, and many of the statements made to us by Salem people had counterparts in Warner's more elaborate study of class structure.

Other prestige groups observed during the process of study now may be briefly mentioned. There is no athletic club in Salem, nor any downtown men's club that can serve as a luncheon meeting place. There is, however, a loose tradition that has grown up for various businessmen to eat in a restaurant owned by a Greek named Moustakis. At a rear table of the restaurant, six or eight men can be seated comfortably at a time. During the lunch hour there is a tendency for some of the well-known merchants on "The Street," as Essex or the main street is called, to gather at this table. As the lunch hour proceeds, professional men, lawyers, accountants, real estate

2. W. Lloyd Warner and Paul S. Lunt, *The Social Life of a Modern Community* (New Haven: Yale University Press, 1941).

men, and finally bankers may join the group or take the places of men who have finished eating. There is a shifting pattern of membership of this group, but through habit on the part of members, the key pattern is relatively stable. Not all men, by any means, who represent the commercial and professional interests of the community eat at Moustakis'. The restaurant is, however, recognized as a place where gossip is exchanged and an eye is kept on important happenings. Other restaurants serve a similar function, of course, but none are quite as well known as the Moustakis' "clearing house."

It was observed by the research team that none of the operators of the larger industrial establishments of the community ate at Moustakis'. The country club, the yacht clubs, the hotel dining room, or restaurant facilities within or nearby their plants served them. Thus the men at the apex of the social and power hierarchies of the community habitually eat their lunches in isolation from the men who importantly underpin them. The formal luncheon clubs bridge this gap somewhat by overlapping membership attending weekly luncheons, and on specific occasions the men of lesser influence may attend luncheons called at one or another of the outlying clubs habituated by those of higher status. More private matters of business or civic decision could not be discussed, obviously, in the public restaurants.

Another kind, the informal communications group that tends to hold things together, is contained within the society ranks but of itself it is not prestige bearing. There is a "telephone chain," or gossip chain, within the upper social group that has three or four major members. The leading member is a woman who was looked upon with some discomfort by the upper social group. She is a source of information on all happenings of the neighborhood in which she operates. Her function, we were told, was to inform others in the prestige neighborhood of items of interest so that talk should not go beyond certain bounds. Thus, in this way and in other important ways already discussed, the community is held in social balance.

Within the social system of values in Salem there is a recognition and tacit agreement, on the part of many, that this or that person or group is desirable as an affiliate. Some of the factors implicit in this value system have been illustrated. Persons of "proper" background, in a familiar and historical sense, are up-graded in social worth. The associations, clubs, neighborhoods, and other items of social location patronized by the leaders of tradition are deemed worthy and desirable both by those who belong to them and by persons who are excluded from them but who may have some hope of joining one or another of the prestige groups on their own grounds and terms. Gradations within the system provide places for most members of the community who may wish to join with others in formal or informal association. Associational substitutes, parallel to the prestige organizations, also flourish. An associational substitute has been illustrated by the example of the "X" sewing circle. As in any community, and as an added example, those in Salem who "cannot make Rotary," a high prestige luncheon club, may join a club of parallel function but of lesser prestige.

If community lines of prestige were too sharply drawn or if there was no way in which to bridge the gaps of higher and lower social prestige, it is obvious that communication between groups would be narrowed to unworkable proportions. In order to function as a total order, the community must, and does, provide countless overlaps of associational interaction. Health agencies, along with innumerable welfare, religious, and cultural groupings of people, provide a means by which prestige lines are partially breached and community-wide communications established. Perhaps a thousand persons in the Salem community belong to the major association groupings which provide general locales of inter-communication within the community system.

Agency boards, innumerable committees, and mass membership organizations from the P.T.A. to the T.B. Association provide common meeting ground for hundreds of Salem citizens. Yet, here again, in spite of the democratic tendencies of such associations and regardless of their worth as communication devices, the prestige factors of history, social exclusiveness, and narrowed social values come into play. A latent function of any organized group lies in its operation as a medium of social control. Within limits, every association in Salem is graded on a rough prestige scale by its members and by those outside its membership.

Thus, concretely, within the social value system of Salem there is real meaning attached to some of the following facts. Mr. Newberry belongs to the board of the Essex Institute; Mrs. Bentley belongs to the Woman's Friend Society; Mr. Barrow belongs to the T.B. Association, and Mr. Douglass belongs to the hospital board. These associations are prestige bearing, and their members have prestige. Some of them have more prestige than others, and those "in the know" can quickly grade these persons and associations. The mediums of social organization mentioned are a part of the network of social controls extant in the community and are necessary adjuncts of community order. They tend to be dominated by persons who are socially elite or who border on being so. What these persons do and the values they hold are held up to the population in general as being desirable. Few openly question the assumption of worth attached to these persons and organizations and their function of maintaining order.

The elements of prestige broadly presented in this chapter are functional to schematic arrangements of power in the community, and in the next chapter we shall develop this idea more fully. It may be noted here, however, that power and prestige may not be synonymous.[3] Some persons in the community who were rated high by others on a prestige scale were down-graded in a power rating and vice versa.

Within a narrower range of activities than those of the total community, the various health organizations are aware

3. Robert Bierstedt, "An Analysis of Social Power," *American Sociological Review*, 15 (December 1950), p. 731.

of the existence of community prestige factors and some utilize them advantageously. The North Shore Babies Hospital, the Salem Hospital, and the T.B. Association are recognized as associations that draw volunteers from the elite classes. This fact assures financial and moral support from these sponsors and assures the population *en masse* that the associations are "properly run and are worthy of general financial and moral support." The newer associations, such as the Heart Association or the Association for Cerebral Palsy, work at garnering support from the same status-bearing groups, but their newness militates against them. In the latter instances, as in the former but in greater degree, sponsorship of the agency on the part of any individual tends to enhance his social position community-wise, i.e., associational membership is a two-way affair. One lends his prestige to the association and it, in turn, lends the individual greater prestige than he before possessed. Persons on the fringes of the upper prestige groups may take positions in the newer associations, clearly recognizing that their own social position is thereby elevated. In these ways and in many others, perhaps, agency membership is functional in a system of prestige values.

Some of the other important ways the community is held together as an operating unit will be outlined in our chapters dealing with associational groups, institutions, and health agency personnel. Here we are mainly concerned with community prestige factors.

It must be said that the research team was not unaware of the fact that some of the elements brought out here in relation to social prestige may tend to give more weight to this whole factor than it deserves. Thousands of people in Salem seem relatively unaware of this factor, or if they are aware of it they tend to discount its importance. There is an element of unreality in the social exclusiveness of some of the "better" families. Life for most Salem families is vitally bound up with earning a living, having some recreation with family, friends, and neighbors, and for them, the "fancy pants people" do not count—they think. We believe they do and in some of the ways we have suggested. They do because they are organized and close-knit for survival reasons, if for no others. By measuring their influence and their relationship to action events, one can, hopefully, see the community described in clearer perspective than would be possible otherwise.

CHAPTER 3

Persons Who Influence Decisions

IT IS A patent rule in community organization that, if things are to get done, one has to involve top flight leaders.[1] We assumed that, if action were to be taken on any recommendations that might come out of a community study of health, various leaders (at some point in the process) would be involved. Being strangers to the community, we knew little about Salem's general pattern of leadership, and, consequently, one of the first tasks of the University research group was that of determining the generalized patterns of power and decision structures of the community. At the same time and early in the study, patterns of social prestige, already described, were examined. Both of these pieces of research were intended to give the staff some idea of "where people fit" in the general community pattern and in relation to the self-study process.

Knowing that a dragnet operation of getting opinions related to leadership from every member of the community was impossible, as well as undesirable, the research team concentrated its efforts on getting opinions of people who were presumed to be close enough to community leaders to identify them. Persons identified with civic organizational work represent the types of persons who generally know their community well enough to give important leads related to individuals considered to be leaders. From this start one may be referred

1. The term "top leaders" will be used in this chapter in the same sense that community chest directors speak of "involving top leadership," i.e., leaders who are recognized as status bearers and who are considered to be "at the top of the heap."

to persons who may operate outside of the formal organizations and who also know the community leadership patterns well enough to give additional names. Such initial interviewing was serial in nature and inconclusive, but it is a part of the exploratory process utilized to move toward a systematic appraisal of the names given at this stage of work.

During the early stages of interviewing associational and other types of leaders in the serial process of interviewing, a total of 193 names was given to us as being those of persons who might be considered leaders in various categories of civic endeavor. Given to us were 59 names in the business category, 23 names of religious leaders, 31 names of persons active in civic affairs, 19 in political life, 43 names of professional persons, 13 names of socially prominent people, while the remainder were names classified as "general" leaders.

Nine persons of civic prominence were asked to judge these lists of names and select from them, on a percentage basis, a list of 40 persons who would be considered top leaders in the categories mentioned.[2] The "judges" were asked to select 12 names from the business group, 6 from civic affairs, 4 from the political group, 8 from the professional group, 3 from the list of socially prominent people, and 2 names from the uncategorized group. In each instance the judge was asked to substitute names of persons whom he might consider to be more powerful than any that were listed. After the lists were judged, the staff went over them to get a composite opinion of the judges. Forty names, receiving the highest number of votes, were utilized in preparing a questionnaire to be administered to the list of 40. These persons represented a *cross section* of top community leadership, but because their names were drawn from several categories this does not mean, as we shall presently demonstrate, that the 40 were co-equal in power.

2. The judges included a businessman, a banker, two religious leaders, a woman prominent in civic work, and four professional persons who were secretaries or directors of community organizations representing large memberships or community followings. Two of the organizations were in the health field—one publicly and the other privately financed.

In order to verify further the judge's opinions, nine more persons were asked to rate the original composite list of 193 names on a power scale of from one down to five. These latter judges were also asked to rate all persons on the larger list according to their social position. The social rating was done on a scale of one down to three. We were told that persons either belonged to two upper social groups in Salem, or "they did not rate at all." Thus, the number one social rating meant that a person belonged to the so-called "400" of the community. A number two represented the "country club set," while a number three was outside both of the former categories. While we were fully aware of the fact that an extended downward rating of social position could be made, we were satisfied that the three categories would suit our purposes.

Finally, to assure ourselves that we were somewhere near the center of a nucleous of power and decision makers, we worked out some of the "clique" relationships existing between some of the leaders identified in the top listing of 193 names. With this preliminary work done, we were ready to interview the 40 persons who were considered by their community contemporaries to be in policy-making positions.

The interview schedule administered to the 40 leaders was designed to get information about the individual leaders: whom he would choose as a top group of ten leaders out of a list of 40; whom he would choose as number one leader; how he had related himself with other leaders in the past; and, what he, as an individual, considered Salem's two most important community problems. On the last question, he was asked to illustrate how he had been active in relation to the problems cited. A summary of the answers of the 6 women and 34 men interviewed revealed the following information.

The 10 top leaders emerging in the interviewing process belonged predominantly to the industrial and business group of the community. Seven of the top 10 could be so classified. One each from the civic, professional, and religious groups were also among the 10.

Of these 10, 8 were Protestant, one Catholic, and one

Jewish. In the total list of 40 persons the religious ratio was 27 Protestants, 11 Catholics, and 2 persons of the Jewish faith. This ratio may be contrasted with the over-all community population: 80 percent Catholic, 16 percent Protestant, and 4 percent all others.

Among the 40 leaders, 28 of them were born within the state. Fifteen of the 28 in-staters were born locally. Four persons on the list born out of the state were foreign born. Two of the foreign-born persons made the top 10 group of leaders. One was born in Poland, the other in Canada.

The median age of the 40 leaders was 49.6 years, a figure that compares favorably with other studies of community decision-making groups.[3] From data at hand, it would appear that the prime age for policy making leadership is in the neighborhood of 50 years. Below this age men are liable to be "comers" in power ascendancy. Older men may be declining in their activities power-wise. There are notable exceptions to this observation, particularly on the side of men past 50 years of age.

Of the leaders, 29 out of 39 answering the question owned their own homes. Four of the church leaders did not own homes and a few of the professional persons did not. Nine leaders owned their own businesses or a major portion of its stock. Eleven had property in excess of their businesses and homes. The fact of property ownership does not prove anything standing alone, but contrasted with an employee group studied in Salem it may have some significance.

In order to contrast the answers of the 40 leaders with a group of people outside this "inbred" listing, a 10 percent sample of personnel was drawn from a medium-sized business establishment of approximately two hundred employees, and the same questions were asked of this group as were asked of the leaders who made top billing in the straining-out process

---

3. In general, the data collected in this study related to power structure conforms to a general pattern worked out in four such studies done in southern cities between 1951 and 1953. See particularly, Floyd Hunter, *Community Power Structure* (Chapel Hill: The University of North Carolina Press, 1953).

of leadership selection. Of 19 persons interviewed, from the president down to the janitor of the corporation, only three persons owned their own homes, one owned a piece of land, and one had an interest in the corporate enterprise. Thus 15 percent of the latter group were home owners contrasted with a 75 percent home ownership factor in the top leadership group. According to 1950 census figures, 40 percent of Salem homes were owner occupied.[4]

Membership on corporate boards is another measure of the influence of a person, and among the top leaders 22 persons held an average of 4.6 memberships. Fifteen held no such memberships. Of the 22 corporate board members, 16 of them held board officerships on an average of two boards each. The employee test held one corporate board membership and one officership.

Within the list of 40 community leaders, questions were asked to determine degrees of acquaintance between them. Table 1 contrasts the answers received from 35 leaders who answered the question and from the corporate group who were asked the same question related to the 40.

TABLE 1

Degree of Acquaintance Between 35 Top Leaders
and 19 Other Members of the Community

Kind of Acquaintance	Number Known by 35 Leaders	Number Known by Corporate Group
Socially	4	1
Well known	18	2
Slightly known	9	2
Heard of person	2	9
Not known	2	26

One person on the list of 40 was related to another top leader by marriage. Thus more than half the top leaders "knew each other well" or better. The group of corporate employees had little personal knowledge of the group of top

4. U.S. Bureau of the Census, *U.S. Census of Population: 1950*, Vol. 3, Chap. 6, Table 3, "Characteristics of Dwelling Units, by Census Tracts" (Washington: U.S. Government Printing Office, 1952), p. 98.

leaders. In some cases, the latter group "knew" the leaders by hearsay or by having read their names in the local newspaper.

Another test of relationship between top leaders was made by asking each to identify the number of associations he had belonged to with others. In the group of 40, the number of organizations to which they belonged with each other averaged 18. The majority of the organized groups were civic committees. Only one person in the employee test group belonged to an association with a person on the top list. This association was a political group. Thus it can be safely said that there is a high rate of interaction among the 40 leaders and practically no interaction between them and the employee group. This does not necessarily mean that there are no lines of communication between the leaders and a group of people that may be termed followers, but the communication is obviously not of a personal nature.

A few more figures may be given before we attempt any detailed interpretation of how the persons on the list acted in relation to each other in getting things done. On the question related to community problems, the following items were given and answered by 39 leaders as indicated:

Type of Problem	Number of Times Mentioned
Parking	14
United Fund appeal	13
Elimination of railroad station	9
Water supply	8
Improvement of social services	6
Improvement of health services	5
Improvement of schools	4
Industrial development	2
Traffic control	2
Chamber of commerce development	1
Liquor licenses	1
Historical restoration	1
Religious issues	1
Salaries of elected officials	1

Two-thirds of the leaders interviewed were active in some way in relation to solving three out of every four problems listed. Those who were inactive indicated, in the majority of cases, some interest in certain problems, but they were passive in relation to them.

The research team had at least two ideas in mind in asking the leaders about community problems. First, it was of interest to know what major problems existed in the community. Second, without posing questions on health, it was of interest to see how many of those interviewed would spontaneously mention health problems.

It will be noted in the listing that the most pressing problems mentioned by the leaders were not related to health. The improvement of the water supply perhaps may be considered indirectly related to a health improvement measure, but the improvement wanted in Salem was to enlarge the water supply. Thus, the improvement of health services, mentioned only five times, falls into sixth place of importance in the opinion of those persons who were willing or able to answer the question related to general community problems. This is not to say that health problems do not exist in Salem. They do. And we shall presently see what some of them are, but the leaders at this stage of the study were either unaware of the problems or had dismissed them as being relatively unimportant. All of this, of course, relates to problems of health education and approaches to this important subject.

It is well known that social agencies and health agencies sometimes make surveys to determine community needs. Much work goes into these surveys year after year in innumerable communities. Many of the studies are filed away for future reference, while the communities in question go about doing the things some members really want to do. In other words, there is always a priority for community action along certain lines. In Salem it was evident that the community leaders, at least, were interested in solving five problems which were to them of greater priority than health problems.

If the premise upon which this chapter is based, that is, "if things are to get done, one has to involve top leaders" is true, then it becomes highly important to know what the top leaders are doing and to figure out how one can divert their attentions to what health and welfare leaders may think should be done. Much of this process of diversion comes under the general heading of "health education," or "program inter-pretation," as the case may be. It is evident also, that if one is to involve top leaders, he should be sure that he knows who the top leaders are. Leadership selection, as any community organizer knows, is a tricky thing. Top leadership in a given field, such as health, may not be top community leadership. There are levels of leadership. Top leaders may be moved by top leaders, but they may remain passive in relation to propo-sitions put to them by second- and third-echelon persons in the community.

In Salem there was, and there had been for a long time, movement in relation to the top problems mentioned. That is to say, there had been meetings, private conversations, studies, pressure put on the city council, publicity releases, and the like, in order to solve the parking problem, the multi-ple fund appeal problem, the water supply problem, and other top priority problems. Some of these had been subject to various attacks for many years. For example, the question of water supply had been under consideration for more than twenty-five years. During the course of our study, this latter problem was solved—not because of our study, but because the discussion and study of it had come full term and the time for action had arrived. The water supply problem had become an open political question. Some of the city politicians were using the issue involved as a political vehicle to enhance their own political fortunes.

Some of the most influential leaders of Salem have worked on the problems of highest priority for varying periods of time. As indicated in the water problem, the community does not move precipitately even on major problems. With the pos-sible exception of a real crisis situation, the community lead-ers tend to take their time in coming to decisions that mean change. The traditional pattern of action in the Salem com-munity would indicate considerable conservatism in this re-gard. This fact is not particularly novel, nor is it peculiar to

Salem. Established patterns of decision making in other communities reveal the same dynamics.

For those in positions of power and upon whom decisions rest, several factors have to be taken into account in relation to shifts in community policy. First of all, there is the question of the allocation of time, money, and materials. When any new proposal is up for consideration, inevitably the questions are asked, "Who is behind this thing?" "How much is it going to cost?" "What will it do to my business, or my agency, or my reputation?" as the case may be. In every community there is a loose delegation of responsibility to certain groups or specific individuals to provide preliminary answers to these questions. For example, a question related to the improvement of welfare services probably would have been referred to Joe Colbert, director of the Community Fund, for an initial opinion. Mr. Colbert might have given an immediate and satisfactory answer, provided the question did not involve either a major shift in present agency program adjustments or a radical realignment of welfare expenditures. If these latter conditions were present, Mr. Colbert would have consulted with members of his board of directors, informally first of all and then formally should the question involve matters of public concern. There are many other steps that would be taken that are familiar to community organizers, but the point here is that a delegation of responsibility in the field of welfare was recognized and socially routinized in Salem. So it is with matters pertaining to health, recreation, economic development, political organization, or any other matter of general community concern. The whole process is related to the establishment of community order.

Certain persons within the community of Salem have become recognized as decision makers within definite spheres of action. This situation has been demonstrated by the fact that a large body of leaders, the list of 193 mentioned earlier, was able to choose persons from various fields as being more powerful or more firmly established as decision makers than others on the list. Some figures have been cited to show a relationship among 40 of them. The statistics, however, do not tell the whole story. A qualitative analysis of the persons on the list is necessary to round out the pattern that we wish to establish and at the appropriate time relate to the health study group.

In a strict sense of the term, the 40 persons designated as top leaders cannot be called a "group." It is highly unlikely that all of the 40 have ever sat down around a table and figured out what might be good for Salem. Yet, it is quite likely that no major project was ever put over in Salem in recent years without a substantial number of the 40 becoming involved in one way or another in the project. Individual members on the list of 40 were representatives of pyramids of power and decision, and as such they helped to provide a balance between many competing and conflicting forces in the community as well as being key figures in cooperative ventures.

Within the list of 40, there was recognition on the part of individuals that some on the list were more powerful than others. Thus, when the top 40 were asked to choose a top 10 from the list, certain names were repeatedly chosen. The top number of votes in the leadership poll went to Ralph Douglass, operator of a large business establishment dealing in coal and fuel oil. Mr. Douglass received 26 votes for a place in the top 10 from 38 persons expressing choices. Two persons on the list received no votes at all. An array of the 40 persons, arranged according to their type of leadership and the votes received from the highest number to the lowest is shown in Table 2.

This listing reveals that the largest number of votes was received by persons whose civic identity was related to industry and commerce. The middle group was largely composed of persons related to professional, religious, and political activities, while the bottom strata were composed of persons largely identified with civic and social organizations in the community.

TABLE 2
Number of Votes Cast by 38 Leaders in Choosing Ten Top Leaders

Leader	Type of Leader	Number of Votes Received
Ralph Douglass	Industrial	26
Edgar Macon	Banker	23
James Foley	Industrial	21
Carlton Gage	Religious	20
Duncan Coker	Industrial	18
Joseph Abramson	Commercial	15
Mrs. William W. Burroughs	Civic	15
John Plunkett	Banker	15
Christopher Dowd	Industrial	14
Stewart Phills	Professional (M.D.)	14
James Poole	Industrial	14
Joseph Colbert	Professional (welfare)	13
Herbert Parsons	Industrial	12
Paul Carletno	Professional (education)	11
Edward E. Doolan	Religious	11
Richard J. Corcoran	Political	10
Carl Fulton	Professional (newspaper)	10
David Baynes	Political	9
Robert Joyner	Banker	9
Isaac Katz	Religious	9
David Michaux	Religious	9
Grant Archer	Professional (education)	8
Robert Hallett	Professional (lawyer)	8
Donald Lackland	Civic	8
Thomas Barrow	Industrial	7
George Marley	Commercial	7
Daniel Hilton	Professional (lawyer)	6
Margaret Lassiter	Professional (M.D.)	5
Lucien Gosset	Political	5
Anna Resnick	Civic	5
Donald Arlis	Industrial	4
Donald Lattimore	Political	3
Albert Moise	Civic	3
Thomas C. Newberry	Social	3
Mrs. William Adkins	Civic	2
Mrs. John Garrett	Civic	2
Joseph Starnitski	Religious	2
Edward Sears	Social	1
Mrs. Keith Bentley	Social	0
Russell Perry	Unspecified	0

An analysis of the pattern of choices indicated by the top ten on the list reveals that more than half, 55 percent, voted for others within the top ten group. Another 25 percent of the votes of the top ten went to persons in the upper half of the list, 16 percent to the third quartile, and the remaining 4 percent went to the fourth quartile. Thus top leaders tended to vote for top leaders.

Analysis of the votes of the bottom ten leaders suggests that they tended to vote upward, that is, they voted for persons who received more votes than they, but they did not vote as heavily for the top ten as that group did within its own ranks. The lower ten cast 42 percent of their votes for the top 10 contrasted with the 55 percent given by the top leaders to themselves. The lowest gave 26 percent of their votes to the second quartile, 23 percent to the third quartile, and 9 percent to their own group.

These ratings and the suggestion of strata within the top leadership grouping conform to patterns found in other community studies in which some leaders are considered "first rate," "second rate," "third rate," or "first string," "second string," according to popular terminology.

When one moves outside the list of 40, the choices of top leaders take on another pattern. The employee test group chose as the top ten leaders two persons in the field of business (persons connected with the plant in which they were employed), two politicians, four professional people, and one religious leader. Their choices, with three exceptions, would appear to be made among persons who receive considerable publicity in the local press, but who are not considered top leaders by those who know the inner workings of the power pattern. This group ranked Ralph Douglass in fourteenth place rather than in the first place position he occupied in three different tests we utilized in determining his position. They did choose Carlton Gage, Dr. Stewart Phills, and Christopher Dowd within the range of their top ten choices, giving Dr. Phills a slightly higher rating than he received from his peers, but approximately coinciding with top leader ratings given the Reverend Gage and Mr. Dowd, the industrialist.

In making leadership choices various individuals spontaneously gave their reasons for so doing. Notes were kept by the interviewers and a summary of the reasons may be listed. The order of the listing to follow is not according to any relative weights but is merely an array of factors. Thus a man was considered for top power billing if:

1. He belonged to a recognized power clique. He is given additional weight if he was a clique leader.

2. He had the will to exercise power and leadership. Many men possessed a potential of power, but they did not choose to exercise this social prerogative.

3. He had a moderate amount of wealth or property. Great wealth did not coincide with power wielding.

4. His relationships with major civic associations was such that either within them he exerted influence or influenced their direction by acting through key leaders within them. Often the top leaders delegated civic associational work to a lesser man within a corporate hierarchy and kept in touch with community affairs through him. This latter fact was well known to the associational personnel, and therefore deference was given the corporate proxy.

5. His community residence was "satisfactory." Newcomers were often subjected to a trial period, and length of residence had some bearing on his acceptance. The place of his residence also was a factor in his social acceptance. Newcomers who settled in the community with high status in corporate enterprises often found ready acceptance in business associations. Their social acceptance tended to follow, in these latter cases, the social position of corporate executives of similar position, and in some cases a man carried his "family background" with him from community to community. Social status, as will later be demonstrated, did not coincide with power standing.

6. He controlled a number of employees. All other factors equal, the greater the number of employees, the greater was the power of the person.

7. He had "control" of a corporate enterprise. Local control, through ownership first, or management second, helps to raise a man's rating in a power scale. Management of an outside corporation gives the local manager power in conformity to the size of the enterprise and in relation to the power of decision the local manager possesses.

8. He is of "prime" age. If he is too young, he may be a "comer." If he is too old, he may be discounted in the making of community decisions; however, some men become elder statesmen and are consulted on most matters. As before indicated, the prime age of men of power seems to be, on the average, in the neighborhood of 50 years of age.

9. He is closely allied with major economic or political enterprises. This is particularly relevant for the professional man.

10. He maintains good press relations. This includes the ability to keep out of the press and put others forward as public figures. In the latter case, those "in the know" are aware of the "fronting" situation, and carefully watch the "front man" to ascertain what the "number one man" is doing.

11. His personal qualities are in conformity to standard community conduct. This does not mean that he has to be a paragon of virtue, aggressive, or shy, or of any particular personality stamp, but his general behavior must be accommodated and accepted.

12. His social clubs and church affiliations are in conformity with his life station. These factors are subject to wide latitude, but they remain factors and are more important in some communities than in others. Hobbies and types of recreation may have some bearing on a man's acceptance by other leaders. Yachting, for example, in Salem is considered far superior to other types of recreation and many of the leaders engage in the sport. It is not a primary requisite to

leadership, but it seems to help establish some of the leaders and is symbolic of prowess.[5]

13. He has an adequate rate of interaction with other community leaders. The "lone wolf" enterpriser might be a powerful individual within a particular industry or business establishment, but if he has no interaction with community leaders on civic matters, his own community power of decision is delegated, per se, to others. Many men were of considerable independence in matters of decision, even on community affairs, but there had to be some give and take in arriving at action decisions, and if a man was too biased or stubborn in most situations, he finally was disregarded or largely discounted in community issues or projects.

No man embodies all of the attributes listed here, but the factors suggested did influence the choices of men of power and decision in Salem. There are a few negative factors that may also be mentioned—factors that tended to rate men downward in the scale of power or that kept some from making the top list.

A man lost in power rating if:

1. He was known to be a follower of another in such manner or degree that his opinions could not be considered his own.

2. He took on responsibilities for a community project and it failed.

3. He made an unsuccessful bid for public office.

4. His personal qualities were objectionable to top leaders.

5. He was considered a "controversial figure" by top leaders.

6. He belonged to an ethnic group that did not have approbation of leadership groups.

Taking every tenth name, beginning with the first name, on the list of 40 in the rank in which they appeared in the

5. Thorstein Veblen, *The Theory of the Leisure Class* (New York: B. W. Huebsch Co., 1922).

leadership poll and weighting them according to the factors given above, reasons become apparent for the rank order.

Ralph Douglass rated high on most of the positive factors. He belonged to several potent community cliques and was a leader in the top clique mentioned by interviewees. He had a driving interest in exercising leadership and power. He held a top position in one of the leading industries of the community and had a good income from his work. He had belonged to the major associations of the community, taking active part in their work. At the time of the study he was withdrawing from some of the community groups in favor of regional and national activities. He was furnishing men under him in his business to take his place in some of the associations and was keeping a hand on some of the decisions that were made in them through manipulating men close to him in business. For example, from what one of the researchers was able to observe, hear, and read about Mr. Douglass' second man, Mr. James Andes, it seems quite likely that Andes will assume growing importance in community affairs, but it is generally known that the latter will not move independently of Mr. Douglass' judgments. A recent up-grading of Andes within the corporate structure of Mr. Douglass' business and within the community structure and Mr. Douglass' withdrawal from certain activities made other upward shifts possible.

Mr. Douglass had been in the community for at least twenty years and had taken an active part in social life, living in a desirable location. He was considered a generous host. The fact that he did not make the upper circles of society, because he was relatively a newcomer in the area, did not detract from his usefulness as a community leader. His social position will be more fully discussed in a later chapter.

Although Mr. Douglass did not control the largest number of employees in the community, his corporation enlisted the work of more than two hundred persons, and he had a wide range of authority in relation to them. He owned a portion of stock in the outside, nation-wide corporation that controlled the local company. He was of "prime age." He was a good mixer and had many personal characteristics that were looked upon with favor by his fellow businessmen and townsmen. He engaged in yacht sports and was considered a "man's man." He made his own decisions, but in conformity with the interests of his business primarily and with the interests of his business associates secondarily. This was considered good practice in Salem.

Mr. Douglass had never run for public office, but he had been quietly effective in his relations with elected politicians both before and after their election. His press relations had been excellent.

The tenth man on the ranked list is Dr. Stewart Phills. Dr. Phills was a professional leader. He was considered the top ranking physician in the community and for many years was chief of staff of the hospital. His power within the medical profession had been undisputed, and he had been looked to by other community leaders for cues to action in the general field of medicine and health affairs related to hospital care.

Compared with some of the industrial leaders, Dr. Phills would not have as wide a scope of community decision. He had tended to limit his interests to health matters, and he did not wish to engage in many of the purely economic and political activities of the town.

Dr. Phills was a man of wealth, of good social position, and he was in the class of the esteemed leader. His advice was sought on many matters and was generously given. He did not seek publicity, but he got considerable mention in the local press. His personal qualities were unimpeachable and molded in good Yankee tradition.

Dr. Phills had been active in many worthwhile civic movements and took part in the community self-study. His advice was sought before and during the study by community leaders, and a part of the acceptance of the study within the community, and particularly among the leaders, can be traced to his initial decision that the study would be "worthwhile and beneficial." He kept an interest in the study and served on one of the continuing committees. He was not an extremely active participant, but the fact that he was willing to lend his support to the project lent general community credence to it. Dr. Phills was a symbolic person, symbolizing cautious integrity and professional skill and knowledge. It is quite possible, according to what we know of the Salem community and from what we have heard of Dr. Phills, that if he had not given his approval in relation to the health study it might have created considerable difficulty for those concerned with it.

The twentieth man on the list, Isaac Katz, was a Rabbi. He, with other ministers on the list, represented a cross section of religious interests in the community. In this representative sense, Rabbi Katz was also a symbolic person functioning in relation to the religious community as Dr. Phills functioned in relation to medical practitioners. In the case of Rabbi Katz, however, his functions as a leader were limited in large measure to the Jewish community. He and other religious leaders, priests and ministers, acted in concerted community enterprises representing a semblance of solidarity. It cannot be said that Rabbi Katz was, in his own person, a man of power, but like all other leaders he was a part of the power structure and the group he represented was partially linked into the total power scheme by him and by men like him. He was instrumental in carrying his community along, or expressing contrary views, when major projects were up for consideration on a community-wide basis. Like other professional religious leaders, Rabbi Katz would rate relatively low in some of the power criteria outlined in relation to top leaders which we shall not repeat in detail. He was dependent in his community decisions on other powerful lay leaders within his congregation, and top leaders in the community at large knew that usually when Rabbi Katz spoke, he was conscious of opinions that had been carefully considered by leaders in the Jewish community. Other professionals in the community stood in the same relationship to top leadership whether they were in the professions of education, health, welfare, or in many cases, law. Rabbi Katz was outranked on the leadership list by Joseph Abramson, a Jewish merchant.

The thirtieth person on the ranked list was Anna Resnick. Mrs. Resnick was of Polish descent. She can best be described as a marginal person between the large ethnic group of Polish citizens and the general community. Her interest in becoming a part of the larger community, rather than confining her social life and civic activities to Polish circles, removed her from the latter group to a certain extent. On the other hand she was not fully accepted in certain social circles in the larger community. She was thus a marginal person between ethnic groups. Such a person was useful in community life, however, since she acted somewhat as a liaison person between the groups. She was a good personal friend of Mrs. William Wallace Burroughs, an extremely active civic association leader who rated much higher on our list than Mrs. Resnick. Mrs. Burroughs, supported by Mrs. Adkins on the leadership list, acted as a kind of sponsor for Mrs. Resnick in getting her engaged in numerous civic enterprises. Both Mrs. Burroughs and Mrs. Resnick took an active interest in Republican politics, but they were more or less on the fringes of the inner workings of local and state political organizations. By hyperactivity these women gained a feeling of importance and they served as useful sounding boards for the larger interests. In their many activities and by much discussion with others they would pick up bits of information that were freely passed on to other leaders who were interested in knowing what was going on. They were considered by the persons we interviewed to be genuine civic leaders, but a civic leader is not, per se, a decision maker. Civic leaders, by and large, are down the scale in relation to the leaders in industry, commerce, and politics. Mrs. Resnick was no exception to this general rule.

The fortieth and last name on the list of 40 was Russell Perry. Mr. Perry's name was added to the list of top leaders from a small group of general leaders and as a test to see whether he would be picked by any of the other 39 persons on the list as a top leader. None so picked him. He received no votes at all in the poll. He was a bank employee and had served on a YMCA committee or two, but he was not in the running with some of the other leaders in the major categories examined. He was a minor political official, serving as chairman of an official licensing board. Mr. Perry recognized the fact that he was placed on a list of persons with whom he was not generally connected and stated in the interview with him that he wondered why he was put on the list. Several other persons on the list asked the same question. This fact helped to assure us that there was a recognizable group of leaders and that the majority of the names were those of persons recognized as leaders in various categories of leadership.

Identifying leaders involved the construction of static classifications. No person or group is ever completely static. Their social positions change, but they tend to change slowly in most cases. Thus, the facts brought out here in relation to the power status of various persons is a static picture. It does not, and is not intended to give, a view of these persons in dynamic relation to each other. In a later chapter an analysis of how projects are decided upon and action carried out in relation to them will be discussed. Here and in the succeeding chapter we are in the process of identifying persons and telling where they fit into the social patterns of the community. The static position of some of the ethnic groups is observable in a leadership poll.

The religious leaders of five of the larger ethnic groups are represented on the leadership poll, namely, Yankee, Irish, French, Jewish, and Polish. The order in which the names of these groups is presented is the order, in descending rank, in which the leaders received votes. The relatively small number of Italians in the community did not have a religious leader represented on the list of top leaders. From interviews and observations in the community a pattern of social stratification and social deference would follow the pattern of votes received by the leaders of the ethnic groups cited here. It may be noted that the French and Jewish leaders received the same number of votes and were ranked roughly half way down in the total list.

Our observations of the Salem community would indicate a top leader—from the point of view of a person a community organizer would wish to involve in a program pointing toward community action—to be of Yankee stock, a Protestant about fifty years of age, an owner of a large corporate enterprise, a person who is willing to assume community responsibilities, a person who has good connections with the associations of prestige in the community, and one whose social position is at least in the second rung of prestige. Another important prerequisite would be that he has the confidence of, and deference from, the many differing political and ethnic groups in the community. Obviously, all of these qualifications are hard to find. Perhaps Ralph Douglass, named many times by his contemporaries as a leader, came as close to meeting the ideal qualifications as any Salem person. But Ralph Douglass was a busy man and his time was devoted to so many things in connection with his business that he did not figure very prominently in the self-study. This was true of several other men who may be termed decision makers.

As any community organizer knows, when the very top men are not available for community work, one goes down the scale and picks up leaders as near to the top men as one can get. This was done in Salem, perhaps not consciously, but the persons who were most active in the self-study, while active within the power structure, were, with one or two noteworthy exceptions, persons who would be second and third level persons of influence.

As the self-study got under way several persons were named to a committee, as outlined in Chapter 8. Out of 14 persons who were most active on the study committee, 13 may be classified as professional people. Mr. Epley of the Salem newspaper was a business representative. Four of the professionals were medical doctors who could not be put in the same class with Dr. Phills, a top ranking physician previously mentioned. The other professionals were recruited from health, welfare, business, and religious organizations. One woman who is classified as a civic volunteer was the additional committee worker. As we have observed in the ranking of leadership votes, neither professional nor civic volunteers consistently rate top positions in a stratified power scale. This does not mean that the professional and civic workers are unimportant in the power or control structure of a community, nor that the people in these categories are personally inferior to those who hold the top positions in the decision-making process. It merely means, we would infer, that some scheme of stratification is functional to the community as an operating social system.

The role of the professional and civic person is one of handling technical matters with knowledge and assurance within a given area of competence. The top decision makers, the men who must be consulted before tax rates are changed or large sums of private donations may be raised to put civic plans in motion, are dependent upon the professionals for their technical skills and knowledge, as the professionals are dependent upon the top leaders for "the green light" on things they know should be done.

Four of the persons who operated on the self-study committee made the list of 40 top leaders: Carlton Gage, the top-ranking minister in the community; Joseph Colbert, the Community Fund Director; Paul Carletno, Superintendent of Schools; and Dr. Margaret Lassiter, a civic-minded, retired physician. In the order in which they are listed here they were ranked in fourth, twelfth, fourteenth, and twenty-eighth positions in the leadership poll.

What a man *does* places him in the total power structure. How he acts in relation to other persons within the structure ranks him in the strata. The professional leaders who worked on the self-survey and who made the top listing of 40 leaders were *doers*. They were well known for their civic interests and could be depended upon to give careful thought and much time to any project in which they became interested. As top leaders within the professions they represented they helped

to influence decisions. They helped to determine "what will go
and what will not go." But decision making is a relative matter, and some persons tend to have more to say, "when the
chips are down," than others in final decisions. The persons
mentioned here were dependent upon others in the latter
case, and in the chapter on "how things get done," we shall
delineate further the relationships between the professionals
and top leadership.

In relation to a consideration of leadership patterns an attempt was made to determine to what extent physicians in
the community would recognize persons who are reportedly
leaders. Accordingly, respondents were asked: "In your
opinion, who are the most influential and powerful persons
in the community; that is, who are those that get things
done?" Thirty-three persons supplied 29 names in response
to this question. The following 9 individuals received two or
more mentions:

TABLE 3

Community Leaders Chosen by Physicians

| | Mentions | | |
Name	Number of Mentions	Rank by Physicians	Rank by Leaders
Mayor Richard J. Corcoran	13	1	16.5
Ralph Douglass	7	2	1
James Foley	6	3	3
*John C. R. Barden	5	4	*
Duncan Coker	4	5.5	5
James Poole	4	5.5	10
Congressman David Baynes	2	8	19.5
*Former Mayor Harrigan	2	8	*
Judge Daniel Hilton	2	8	27

* These names did not appear on the list of 40 leaders.

Comparison of this list of persons with that of the self-
rankings of the forty leaders in various areas of community
activities (see page 35) is highly suggestive. The latter was selected from a list containing 40 names (including their own)

which had been pre-judged as top leaders in several spheres of community activity. Each person on this list then chose the ten persons whom he considered to be at the top among Salem leaders. The physicians, on the other hand, had no such list but were simply required to name individuals.

The physicians named 12 persons on the list of 40 leaders, and 7 of these received 2 or more mentions. The most obvious difference between the two rankings was the placement of Mayor Corcoran in first place by physicians and in sixteenth place by the leaders. Ralph Douglass and James Foley, local industrialists, were ranked first and third, respectively, by leaders and second and third by physicians. Edgar Macon, a banker, second on the leader list with 23 choices, received only one mention from the physicians. Those persons appearing on both lists but receiving only one mention each from physicians were as follows: Joseph Abramson, Christopher Dowd, the Reverend Carlton Gage, Edgar Macon, and Thomas Barrow. The first 4 of these 5 men were among the top 10 choices of the leaders. Thus the physicians named 12 persons previously judged as among the top 40 leaders in Salem, and, in doing so, chose 7 out of the top 10, although 4 of these received only one mention each.[6]

These results are suggestive but do not warrant rigorous interpretation. They do constitute an independent judgment as to who community leaders are and thus lend support to our efforts to isolate top community leaders. However, the data do not justify the interpretation that, by and large, the physicians recognized community leaders in the several spheres of community affairs. It will be noted that four of their top nine choices are politicians and the remaining five are industrialists which leaves out all other spheres of activity. Moreover, 25 percent of the respondents questioned on this point frankly

6. The physicians' mention of John C. R. Barden, an industrialist, supplied the name of a top leader in Salem affairs who was not mentioned by the original panel of judges but who was mentioned many times by top policy makers in the community. Phillip Reeves, an attorney, was in the same category.

admitted that they were not familiar with the names of community leaders.

Forty-nine of the physicians were asked: In your opinion, what are the primary problems facing Salem as a community? The purpose of this question was to obtain some idea as to: (1) what the physicians would consider as community problems, (2) how these would compare with problems suggested by a group of community leaders, and (3) what problems of health would be mentioned.

Eight of the respondents were unable to suggest any problems which they considered outstanding. Those problems receiving two or more mentions from the remainder of the group were as follows:

Problems	Times Mentioned
Health problems	21
Loss of population	16
Loss of industries	10
Traffic problems	8
Insufficient housing	8
Poor educational system	6
Need for new school buildings	3
Need for new industries	3
Grade crossing removal	2

A breakdown of the health problems is informative. Only three problems received more than two mentions: need for additional hospital beds, five; financing the hospital, two; and a need for free dental care, two. The other eleven problems mentioned were as follows: need for a health education program, better care and management of the aged, need for a health center, better sewage disposal, general improvement in public health, improved restaurant inspection, need for an eye care program in the schools, elimination of waste-dumping in North River, need for a medical building, need for a second hospital, and a study of medical fees considered too low relative to other places in the state.

Problems mentioned by the community leaders are listed on page 30 above. Comparison of these two lists shows that the first three problems for the leaders were (1) parking problems, (2) United Fund appeal, and (3) elimination of the railroad station. While for the physicians, beyond their concern for health problems in general, the three top specific problems were (1) loss of population, (2) loss of industries, and (3) traffic problems. Thus, in the top three problems for both groups only one common problem appeared—traffic or parking difficulties. The problem receiving the greatest number of mentions by the physicians was not mentioned at all by the leaders, and the second place problem of leaders was not mentioned by the physicians. Loss of industries, the second place problem for physicians, was not specifically mentioned by the leaders. Other than traffic problems, those receiving more than one mention by both groups were related to health, schools, and to the need for new industries or industrial improvement.

No hard and fast conclusions may be drawn from these data; however, these differential perceptions of community problems do prompt several observations and questions.[7] First, the leaders tended to mention problems susceptible to, and currently under, direct attack, whereas, the problems mentioned most by physicians were generally less susceptible to such attack.

The concern of the physicians over population loss was interesting, especially when it is recalled that Salem's population has varied very little during the past four decades. In fact, it gained some 600 persons between 1940 and 1950. Actually, the concern appeared to involve certain qualitative aspects as much as, or more than, it does number. This is inferred from two facts: first, five of the persons mentioning the loss of population (three were pediatricians) were concerned with, as one of them put it, "How can we keep the young people?" And

7. In considering these differences it should be kept in mind that the physicians were seen a year later than the leaders. Possibly the main difference resulting from the time lag would be the number of mentions on the water supply problem. This was a community problem at the time the leaders were seen which had been practically resolved when the physicians were interviewed. This problem received eight mentions from leaders and one from the doctors.

second, a number of physicians expressed the opinion that the better educated or "higher quality" people were leaving the community. The economic factor in this interest is self-evident.

Health problems, as would be expected, received many more mentions from physicians than they did from the general community leaders. When the health problems suggested by the physicians are examined, one is impressed by the wide range or variability of the problems. Only one problem got more than two mentions—the need for hospital beds. Does this mean that a need for additional hospital beds was the number one health problem of Salem? Actually, several physicians maintained that the community had no health problems; this judgment was based on the absence of epidemics in the community.

In an attempt to get an appraisal from the physicians of their activity in community health affairs a large number of them was asked: "Do you think the medical group in Salem is doing about as much as it should or could in health matters?" The responses may be grouped as follows: 16 positive, 8 negative, and 8 equivocal.[8] The positive responses tended to be brief and to the point, such as, "Oh, sure, definitely"; "They are excellent"; or a simple, "I think so." The negative and equivocal responses were somewhat more extended; for example, two negative replies were: "They do not devote enough time to the education of the community—it is always the same doctors who are speaking"; and, "I don't think they are doing too much, I don't know what's holding them back. I suppose no one has pushed them into anything." From the equivocal group: "I don't know enough to give a sensible answer"; and, "Remarkably well; the medical man does not look too far beyond his work. He doesn't do anything negative but possibly not enough positively."

These results are in essential agreement with, and support,

8. This total includes just over 60 percent of the staff physicians and just under that number of non-staff physicians. Response types were about equally distributed in both groups.

the view posited above—that there is a lack of consensus among the physicians as to their role in community health affairs. Certainly, the opinions given do not indicate a clear majority regarding the group's actual performance in matters of health in the community, that is beyond their individual practices. In short, the responses to the question did not indicate a well-defined, collective orientation or interest toward the problems of health on a community-wide basis.

The physicians cannot be classified, as a group, as community power leaders and policy makers, but like other professional groups they have recognized delegates who tend to speak for their whole group on those matters that affect individual physicians and their practice of medicine. As with other professional groups, individual practitioners are aware of the generalized pattern of community power and authority even though they may not participate directly in the over-all processes of decision making.

CHAPTER 4

Persons of Lesser Influence

A s a community system, we have observed that Salem divided into dominant and subordinate ethnic groups. The dominant group within the community was the Yankee minority. Smaller in numbers than the Irish, French, and Polish ethnic groups, the Yankee group dominated them socially. As this pattern of dominance and subordination was manifested early in the study, it was decided that one of the subordinate ethnic groups would be selected for intensive study. The Polish group was chosen.

Several reasons were behind the choice of the Polish community for investigation. In some ways it represented a medium community. The Polish was neither the oldest nor the youngest ethnic group there. It had not surrendered many of its ethnic characteristics nor had it remained completely aloof from the community at large as had been the case with the French group. On preliminary investigation, it also was evident that the Polish leaders were achieving some recognition in politics and in the professions but they had a long way to go to achieve as much in these areas as the Irish group had. On the whole, the Polish people in Salem were on the move literally and figuratively, and this interested us. They were moving out of the purely Polish neighborhood into the community at large and they were moving up the status ladder by the route of achievement.

It was decided that the same type of preliminary and exploratory study would be made in the Polish community as was being made in the larger community. That is, it was determined to investigate the outlines of Polish community leadership and ascertain how this leadership generally related itself to other leaders in the community at large. We were interested in getting this base-line information so that we could observe how Polish leaders might be chosen to serve the self-study committee on health.

In going about the task of constructing leadership patterns within the Polish community, it became apparent that there were three types of leaders recognized within the community even though the first inclination of the people there was to deny that there were any leaders at all but that everyone in the Polish community operated on an equal basis. The three types of leaders that were isolated may be characterized as elected leaders, informal leaders, and self-appointed leaders. In order to get a pattern of the effective working relationship among such leaders, they and others in the Polish community were asked to describe how they had gone about organizing and executing a major project within their own community. The project they chose to describe was that of the school building fund. Basically, the people had organized themselves to raise a fund for building a parochial school. In this process, the types of leaders we have indicated were seen in operation. After defining our leadership term a little more precisely, we shall outline the organization of the school building project in the community.

By elected leaders we mean those persons who are put in positions of leadership to serve as members of committees or organizations and who have been chosen to serve either by receiving votes from committee and organization members or who have been appointed to serve on these by an officer.

Informal leaders are those persons who are consulted about important decisions but who do not hold official positions within any of the organizations designed to promote and execute community projects.

Self-appointed leaders are those who think of themselves as leaders, put themselves forward, and volunteer their services before the group asks for volunteers.

Any of these three types of leaders may serve as a bridging

leader between the Polish community and the community at large. The bridging leadership function is that of acting as a liaison between persons.

In the initial interviews that were held with the people in the Polish community there was a general denial of the fact that there were any leaders within the community who would stand out in relation to others. It soon became apparent that this was not true in spite of the egalitarian motivations behind these assertions. We found that the leadership within the sub-community followed the general pattern of subordination and superordination of groups elsewhere. There were elected leaders and self-appointed leaders and most important of all, for our purposes, there were definable persons who could be characterized as bridging leaders. In one of the interviews with the Polish parish priest, he said that there were several persons within the community who could be described as "those who could perform the function of bridging the gap that exists between the Polish and Yankee communities." In other words, the bridging leader is a liaison agent between his own sub-community and the larger functioning community. The leader who performs the function of representing his ethnic group in civic, welfare, and health committees initiated by the dominant Yankee minority are considered bridging leaders. In such committees the leader of the Polish community may meet similar bridging leaders from the French, Italian, or other ethnic sub-communities.

A bridging leader's usefulness is maximized for the community at large when the leader truly represents the aspirations of his people. The person who is put forward as a bridging leader and who "goes over to the other side" loses his usefulness to his own group, and eventually he is of little use to the dominant group. There was a general misconception within the dominant group in the community at large as to who the real leaders were within any of the ethnic groups. The dominant power group in the community tended to pick as leaders within the ethnic communities the priests of the foreign groups. It was quite possible, as we shall show in the

Polish community, that the priest was not the real leader or a top-rate leader, but a leader in a given subgroup. Consequently when Yankee members of a city-wide committee picked one of the priests to serve, they did so out of ignorance or because they felt the priest was able to accommodate himself easily to such service as he might be asked to perform. Often the persons asked to serve on city-wide committees, unless they are elected or appointed from within the ethnic community, are looked upon with suspicion within their own group.

After indicating briefly the type of sub-community in which the Polish leaders live, we shall describe three or four of them in relation to the school bond project, previously mentioned. We shall pay particular attention to the position of the Polish priest in this account since the priest is usually considered by the dominant group in the community to be a bridging leader.

Many people in the Yankee community speak of the area in which the Polish people live as "Derby Town." Actually the slightly derogatory name derived from the fact that the Poles live on and around Derby Street. To the casual observer, Salem's checkerboard composition of various languages and different elements of cultural heritages is not too apparent. Most of the construction of all houses is of wood frame type, two or three stories high. Most houses have no front yard but have fenced in back yards. All of them give one the impression that they have been there for many years. Some are more spacious than others. Some have elaborate stoops. Some are freshly painted and others have camouflaged their rotting wood with a covering of imitation tar paper brick. Some have little garden plots at the side of the house or in the back. In spite of these small differences, there is an integration of housing style in the prevailing colonial form. Derby Street, which was looked upon as a run-down section by some members of the community, runs parallel to Essex Street, the main commercial thoroughfare in Salem. Derby Street ends at the water front. It was once the exclusive neighborhood where the sea captains' homes were located. The community antedated the now famous Chestnut Street area. The sea captains long ago moved to Chestnut Street and other outlying areas, and their homes were occupied successively by the Irish and then the Polish who displaced the former.

Several years ago a wealthy Yankee woman who wished to "provide constructive recreational facilities for Polish children" was instrumental in utilizing the income from the House of Seven Gables to support a settlement house. The Polish people have never openly said so, but from information that we gathered, it was apparent that many of them have resented the fact that this settlement was established to "uplift" them. The neighbors in the immediate vicinity of the House of Seven Gables resent the many visitors and tourists who come to see the place and congest the very narrow streets in the area utilized by the inhabitants for ingress and egress. Some of them have threatened lawsuits to keep the tourists out of the area.

While one can see tow barges going in and out of the harbor from the well-kept lawn of the House of Seven Gables, from this vantage point one can also see the smokestack from the local mill—not a very beautiful sight, to be sure. The neighbors of the House resent statements they sometimes overhear visitors make to the effect that "these beautiful sea captains' homes are now in the slums and are being allowed to deteriorate."

The Polish people with whom we talked did not think of themselves as living in the slums and prided themselves on the age and construction of their "old homes." Most of the houses we visited had well-kept interiors. It is true that some of the houses in this area have been covered with imitation brick at which some of the upper-class Yankees point with horror. In any event, the image of the community held by the persons who live there and by those who live outside of it differs.

Through a process of self-selection, we were able to interview a number of Polish people who were considered to be leaders within their community. Little by little as one person after another, who had been singled out as a leader, told us what their group was doing, what they were expecting to do, and specifically how they were acting in relation to raising money to build a new parochial school, the Polish people began to emerge as a functioning sub-community in the larger community. The raising of money to build the Saint John the Baptist Elementary Parochial School was considered the most important project in the whole community by all of the leaders interviewed in the Polish community. The project was set up to raise a half million dollars.

The old primary Polish school, also named Saint John the Baptist, was located in a narrow street off Derby Street. It was not big enough, at the time of study, to house the Polish school population.

Walking from Derby Street toward the docks, one passes by the schoolhouse and the building next door which was used as living quarters by the nuns who teach in the school. The latter house, like the schoolhouse, was in bad repair. Dr. Flack, one of the three practicing Polish physicians in Salem and a leader in the school fund project, said, "Anyone would know that it is a shame to have a school that looks like a torn down wreck. Sometimes I feel that I could go and burn it down and it wouldn't be a sin." There were many people in the community who agreed with Dr. Flack and the launching of the school project had good community backing. Dr. Flack, as chairman of the business and professional subcommittee for the Saint John the Baptist School building fund exemplifies the professional leader of the community.

The professional in the Polish community brings to a position of leadership prestige acquired through education.[1] There are still proportionately few professionals among the Poles in Salem. The majority of persons are occupied in skilled and semi-skilled positions. There are also a few small business operations.

1. Albert J. Murphy, "A Study of the Leadership Process," *American Sociological Review*, VI (October 1941), p. 674.

From the list of 66 names of potential leaders gathered at the beginning of the sub-community study, 10 of the persons listed were professionals: 4 lawyers, 3 physicians, 1 high school teacher, 1 dentist, and 1 priest. The scarcity factor added to the prestige of the professional people and some of the professionals were recognized by Yankees active in political and community affairs.

Professionals who accept positions of leadership are often bridging leaders. One of the main functions that Dr. Flack had in relation to the fund drive was to approach bankers and businessmen in the larger community and get money from them. He was quite willing to do this since he had other kinds of contacts with these men, but he did not believe that he would get too much response. He felt that most of the money he would raise would be from canvassing professional people within his own community.

Dr. Flack was chosen as a leader by his own people, partly because he was "the least controversial professional figure within the community." Some of the other professional persons within the community, functionally related to Dr. Flack in the fund raising scheme, were much less controversial than he. The factor of controversy is particularly related to the Polish priest of the community, Father Joseph Starnitski, who came into Salem at the end of a bitter church controversy. When the parish priest, the predecessor of Father Starnitski, died, the Polish community was split into two groups. Each of these groups contended that it had a right to negotiate with church leaders to help select a successor to the priest who had died. Each group advocated a different successor to fill the vacancy. The church was picketed, leaders on each side made radio speeches, and the split within the ranks of leadership within the community was noised abroad in the larger community. Neither of the two groups won what they wanted and the bishop appointed Father Starnitski as an alternative. One of the groups was partially satisfied by the selection of Starnitski and these came back into the church and took part in community activities. Only a few of the other group made a similar move.

Thus, when the business and professional fund-raising committee was organized, an undertaker in the community who was an active business leader and a neutral, relatively speaking, was asked to move that Dr. Flack serve as chairman of this group. This move was designed to heal many of the wounds left by the controversy. It was felt that a relatively neutral chairman could pull the various groups together in the fund-raising venture. Dr. Flack assumed the chairmanship of the committee even though he was not considered to be the most outstanding leader in a community of his peers.

A person who was recognized as the number one leader in the community by those who responded to our leadership poll was an attorney, George Stefanow. Mr. Stefanow was a less controversial figure than Dr. Flack. He was a person who was involved in Democratic politics and had served in an appointed capacity on one of the commissions authorized by the last Democratic governor in the state. Mr. Stefanow's influence within his own community was recognized in some quarters in the community at large, since he had been appointed a member of the board of trustees of the Salem hospital shortly before our study was begun. In spite of this nod of recognition to such persons as Dr. Flack and Mr. Stefanow, who represented real leadership within the Polish community, the majority of the larger community leadership tended to prefer Father Starnitski as a bridging leader to represent the Polish people on community-wide projects. An indication of Father Starnitski's real position in relation to this community lies in the fact that, when leaders in the Polish community were asked to choose the number one leader, Father Starnitski received a very small number of votes while Stefanow received the majority vote.

In answer to the question, "If you had to choose a person from the Polish community to represent your community on a city-wide committee in Salem, whom would you choose?"

Father Starnitski again received very few votes while Stefanow received a majority vote. On the other hand, when these same Polish leaders were given a list of community leaders of the larger community (the 40 persons who were considered to be top leaders in the over-all community power structure), Father Starnitski's name was chosen. Since his name was the only Polish name on the list, this may account, in part, for popularity in this particular poll. Father Starnitski's name was on the list of 40 because in the process of selection in the community at large he had been chosen as a leader by the Yankees. He was chosen as a leader from the list of leaders of the larger community because there is an awareness on the part of these persons of the ethnic community that the priest can serve as their spokesman since the dominant group, the Yankees, consider him to be the most important leader in the Polish community. By the status and prestige accorded to him by the dominant group, but not necessarily by his own group, the priest is a potential bridging leader. In Father Starnitski's case he was recognized as a spiritual leader but was not ranked as a secular leader within the community.

The above observation disagrees with one made by Warner which runs as follows:

The priest in the Irish Catholic Church . . . is not subordinate to the Irish community in any respect. He derives his secular leadership, not from the local community, but from the authority passed down to him from the papacy itself through the diocese bishop.[2]

The Polish priest is in the same hierarchal position as the Irish priest, but in this instance we found that, though he was recognized as a leader in sacred functions, he was not recognized as a leader in secular functions within his own community. His role as a secular leader was not affected by "the authority passed down to him from the papacy itself through the diocese bishop."

2. W. Lloyd Warner and Leo Srole, *The Social Systems of American Ethnic Groups* (New Haven: Yale University Press, 1945), p. 171.

Because Father Starnitski was not recognized fully as a secular leader within his community he had not taken an open and leading part in the organization of the various committees related to the school fund. On occasion, Father Starnitski made suggestions, and he said that actually it was he who suggested the organization of the business and professional group to weld together some of the dissenting factions within the community. Father Starnitski believed that many of his flock had much to learn and that they were rather slow to take up some of his suggestions.

The way in which some of the members of the Polish community spoke of their priest would indicate that they were on a good give-and-take basis with him. He was considered much less authoritative than persons in his position are rather widely believed to be. Dr. Flack, the chairman of the professional fund committee, said that he had asked Father Starnitski "not to interfere and to keep out of the meetings of his group because he thought that this would contribute to a higher degree of success of the meetings." After one of the meetings of the school fund, Father Starnitski said to Dr. Flack that he had almost broken in upon the meeting to which he was not invited because he wished to announce that he had just received notice of having been made a Monsignor. After congratulating Father Starnitski on his new position, Dr. Flack said to him, "I am glad that you humbled yourself and didn't interrupt the meeting. You are a better man for that!"

Father Starnitski served on the War Fund Board in the larger community during World War II but resigned after he realized that his community and ethnic groups other than his own criticized him for accepting this position when a Yankee offered it to him. He had not cleared with the organizations within his own community. He said that now unless he was appointed or asked by the Polish community to serve, he did not accept invitations to act as a part of any committee in the larger community. This same clearing procedure is adhered to by other ethnic groups who send representatives to committees in Salem at large.

The fear of not being truly representative of the group was expressed by a Polish woman who had married a Yankee aristocrat several years before this study and who for a long period of time had not participated in Polish community activities. This woman, the only member of her community who then lived on Chestnut Street, said that a high official within the state had once offered her a position of importance to "represent her people," but she felt that "her people" would not have wanted her to represent them since she had lived for so long outside the boundaries of the Polish community. After much inner conflict, she had refused the governmental appointment. On the other hand, this woman had been asked to collect money for the school fund. Her position was recognized by the Polish leadership, and through her identification and residence among the Yankees, she was a leader, albeit a different kind—a bridging leader. Those who organized the machinery for collecting the money for the school building project knew their community, and they were going to utilize everyone possible and various types of persons in various positions of leadership to gain their objectives.

Other bridging leaders, who were intimately associated with some of the professionals, but who represented different types of activity, may be classified as general business leaders. Many of these persons were called upon by the Yankee community to collect money within the Polish community for various drives, such as the Community Fund or Red Cross. Some of them were contacted by politicians who came into the community at election time. Their business connections made them obvious targets for people who wanted a quick entree into the sub-community.

One of the Polish leaders who was closely identified with this set said, "We know those politicians and fund raisers! They are not interested in us but in what they can get out of us. The old people who didn't know any better used to take what they had to say, but a lot of us know better now."

There was considerable evidence of much conflict within the Polish community over the question of how much the group should stick together as a Polish group or how much it should try to move out into the larger community and be completely a part of it without regard to their ethnic origins. Some of the people within the Polish community recognized that they were exploited economically and politically by the fact that they stuck together so closely and did not have daily contact with members of the larger community who might be instrumental in "taking them in and getting them a break." For those who believe that community integration is allied to individual success, one of Salem's garage owners is a comfort. This successful businessman Americanized his name, joined the country club, and took his children out of parochial school because the nuns insisted upon teaching them to pray in Polish. In spite of having violated so many of the mores of the ethnic group, he had not been totally rejected by it. This is proof to many that these ways of action are legitimate. This particular man contributed good sums of money to many Polish charities and was expected to give handsome support to the Polish school project in spite of the fact that his children would not attend the school.

Another side of the argument for "sticking together" is that some people, notably persons who might be represented by a man like George Stefanow, feel that this is "the only way out for the foreign groups." These people believe that the way to gain strength is to become politically powerful. Political recognition, said one of the older members of the community, has been an issue for sixty years in the Polish community. As a way out, political activity has represented to many the notion of *full* representation in community activities. Many of the persons interviewed were surprised that they were being taken into account in any measure in relation to the health study because they were rarely consulted on community matters with the exception of political affairs. Their very numbers gave them political strength since they represented approximately a fraction less than one-fourth of the population of the community.

The lives of leaders within the community in relation to professional, business, fraternal, and church groupings, have given the community an inner strength that is taken into account by external forces. It also allowed the Polish community to handle many of its internal problems. The problem of fund raising that we have outlined sketchily will be handled, in the main, within the Polish community itself. When it looks outside of the community for support in this project, it will do so with some hesitation and with some regret. Some of the leaders felt that members in the larger community should help support the school fund drive because the Polish people have been called upon so often to help community-wide drives. There was a feeling that there should be a give and take relationship here, but there was also recognition that there were many prejudices in the larger community that the Polish group was forced to overcome. They said that members of the larger community failed to understand that one can be "politically an American, socially, a Pole, and as good as anyone else." Often in conversations with the Polish people, they wanted to make sure that the listener knew what a "good" Pole is. He is, "honest, courageous, has a great deal of feeling, pays his doctor bills, and is not aggressive." They felt sure that people in the other ethnic groups of the community said that Poles are the opposite of these things. Prejudice was shown by the Yankee group when they discussed the Polish people by using stereotypes, and, on the other hand, reverse prejudice was shown when the Polish people talked about the Yankees and used another set of stereotypes.

Stereotypes and expressions of prejudices used in the situation are employed as defense mechanisms and as a tool to maintain cohesiveness. They also discharge hostility. Hostility was shown, for example, when the Polish people said, "The Yankees are dying out anyway so why should we pay any attention to them"; "They have all the money"; "They are nothing but a sleepy group." The Yankees, in their turn, used expressions of prejudice and stereotypes when speaking of the Polish group, calling them "aggressive and tight knit." The Yankees do this to reinforce their power status, to maintain cohesiveness for their own group, and to discharge hostility. The discharge of hostility by the Yankees against the Polish group or against any other ethnic group is a mechanism used to eliminate the threat of losing the dominant position they now enjoy in relation to the ethnic groups.

The Yankees are threatened by what the future may bring in relation to their own numbers and the numbers within the ethnic groups. This threat has an historical background stemming from the gradual displacement of the sea captains' families from certain areas of the city by the foreign people, the Irish, who began infiltrating their neighborhoods.

In spite of the fact that Polish children were thrown into daily contact with Yankee children in attending school, some of the social distances persisted. Deutsch and Collins have explained this phenomenon by saying that persons may need each other in a formal situation in which the "niceness" is related to the situation and not to the persons involved.[3] In other words, while some of these students, Yankee and Polish, go to high school in large numbers, they carry to the school situation the same structural division in which they live in the community. They are controlled more by their outside social situation than they are by the personal relationships set up within the school situation. Polish adolescents, therefore, tend to associate with Polish adolescents in a community and the Yankee adolescents associate with persons in their own group.

Such a situation of prejudice and social distance within the community makes for personal and community problems.

3. Morton Deutsch and Mary Evans Collins, "The Effect of Public Housing Projects Upon Interracial Attitude," in *Readings in Social Psychology* by C. E. Swanson, J. M. Newcomb, and E. L. Hartley, eds. (rev. ed. New York: Henry Holt & Co., 1952), pp. 592-93.

There are many Polish persons who resist the pressure to conform to the norms of their own group. They are the persons who are considered "deviants." The situation in which the ethnic deviants find themselves is a very complex one. They not only go through the process of disassociation, but at the same time they try to associate with the dominant group, the Yankees, a group that does not always welcome them.

The Polish deviant generally rejects the norms of the Polish community in preference to the norms of the Yankee community. Some members of the Yankee community also viewed such a person as a deviant and his situation becomes somewhat intolerable.

Some of the norms in the Polish community that characterize the behavior of the deviant personality are these: Americanization of the Polish name, participation in the community activities in the large community without an official appointment to represent the Polish group, residence in a predominately Yankee neighborhood, and lack of interest in matters that concern the Polish community.

Regardless of the difficulty of the role of the deviant personality, he is the person upon whom social change in the community must depend. The deviant personality who finds himself between two groups, a dominant and a dependent, has a very definite function in relation to social change. Though these persons are criticized by the ethnic group, they are at the same time looked upon with a certain degree of interest because such persons often acquire some of the status symbols that go along with "success" in our society. Some of these status symbols which are acquired by the deviant person and are watched with interest by those who have deviated from their group norms are: adequate income and capital goods, membership in status clubs, housing in desirable neighborhoods, and acceptance by larger circles within the community in which they live.

The change of attitudes toward the deviant on the part of

some persons may be summarized in a statement made by a Polish woman, who is a very active political leader within her community and who from her position has to be identified with the norms of the community. She said, "In reality, I do not blame a young orchestra leader within our community because he changed his Polish name to an American one. He has to make a living. No one could pronounce the name he had before and, consequently, he could not become well known." She also confided that one of the reasons why she had stopped school while she was in high school was that she had an extremely long Polish name and the children at school always made fun of her when she was asked by the teacher to write it on the blackboard. In spite of the advantage that her Polish name had given her politically within her community, she added that, if she were young again, she would change her name and then said, "If my mother were living, she would die to hear me talk like this!"

The persons who are considered deviants in the Polish community are rejected by their group in various degrees. There is no indication of a deviant having been totally cast out of his group. None of the deviants interviewed had rejected all of the norms of their group, nor had they severed all of their connections with all the members of the Polish community. They had become deviants by rejecting some of the norms of their group. None of the outstanding deviants occupied central positions of leadership in the Polish community, but their growing numbers presage social change within the sub-community and forecast a shadow of social change for the whole community.

Many of the things that have been said here about the Polish community could be said of the other ethnic groups of our acquaintance, but we did not have as close contact with them as with the Polish people. The failure on the part of the dominant group to recognize the real patterns of social organization of the Polish community and the other ethnic communities made it impossible for us to observe Polish leaders in action in relation to leaders in the larger community. The materials that have been outlined here were gathered to make such observations possible. The fact that the Polish leaders were not included in the self-study process would lend credence to some members of the sub-community that they are "very seldom asked to participate in activities related to the whole community," and "Salem is a house divided against itself."

CHAPTER 5

Public Health Services
and Other Facilities

M UCH PROGRESS has been made in guarding society against
disease. All levels of government—national, state, and
local—play important parts in preserving our health. The
protection of health has always been a state function, although until some sixty years ago the states did very little
in this direction since scientific knowledge upon which to
base action was quite limited. Medical science advanced
rapidly, and the great majority of the states have taken positive measures to secure some of its benefits for the public.

The emphasis of the Salem self-study on health logically
required us to focus our attention upon the place of the
Salem public health department in the community and its
relation to other social agencies, groups, and individuals
which might be involved in the study process.

The Salem board of health is over 150 years old. For most
of that time it has been concerned only with contagious
disease and environmental sanitation. It was organized [1] in
June, 1799, as the result of a petition empowering the inhabitants of Salem to choose a board of health for the removal
and prevention of nuisances. In the miasmatic theory of
contagion prevention was a natural corollary of removal.
Since the real objective of the board of health in abating
nuisances was to check epidemics of disease, its history and
development was highly influenced by the advances in treat-
ing communicable disease. As an important seaport the town

1. Unpublished records of the Salem board of health, 1799.

fell prey to most of the "plagues" of the eighteenth and nineteenth centuries. The board ruled on the treatment of the diseased, notably of those with smallpox, later of those with diphtheria and influenza. It also quarantined ships arriving from exotic ports and built a contagious-disease hospital which still stands. Like the city councils, the early boards drew membership from the most influential men the community had to offer—sea captains and financiers. With community change and the changes in attitude toward those who were politically elected or appointed on a local level, board composition altered. Since the position conveyed little prestige, it was no longer coveted.

During this study, the Salem board of health, as was legally required, was composed of three persons, one of whom was a physician. They were appointed by the mayor for a term of three years, subject to confirmation by the city council. No member of the city council could serve as a member, and the board was required to organize annually. A chairman was selected from its membership; and a clerk, who was a nonmember, was appointed. The powers and duties of the board were defined by law.

The board of health, subject to civil service laws, rules, and regulations, had the power to appoint an agent who acted as the administrative officer. During this study the board had as its chairman Dr. Max Katzenstein, a local practitioner, who played a prominent role in the Salem self-study of health. A retired businessman and a pharmaceutical salesman completed the threesome. The staff of the department consisted of an agent, two public health nurses, a sanitary inspector, a plumbing inspector, a garbage collection supervisor known as a working foreman, a crew of collectors, one clerk, three part-time people—a physician, a dentist, an animal inspector—and a superintendent of the hospital for communicable diseases.

The agent of the board, who in Massachusetts did not have to be a physician, was Dr. Henry L. Tracy. His role in relation to the self-study was of importance to this work and will be discussed in detail in the next chapters. Dr. Tracy was appointed in 1946. His appointment was preceded by the following newspaper editorial which indicated to some extent the diminutive concept of the job he was expected to do.

MAN WITH A CHORE [2]

There is one man in the city's service who finds himself, without a doubt, with a prodigious backlog of work. His schedule would be a full one but his diligence in prosecuting his important task will result in benefits for everyone who resides within the limits of this city. Dr. Henry L. Tracy, recently named agent of the board of health, will find his work cut out for him.[3]

Since last April until a fortnight ago the city was without a qualified person to check up on violations of the health laws. And the violations have been plentiful. There have been instances where on a Sunday morning at five o'clock residents in heavily populated areas have been awakened from their sleep by garbage collectors—not the official city collectors—driving their noisy trucks to houses and collecting an accumulation of decayed vegetables from hucksters who use their residences as storage places for this refuse. While circulating publicity material urging the removal of the rat nests from the city, the city for months has had no official clothed with the authority and with the time to make sure the conditions did not exist to encourage the city's rat family. Black market meat has been sold in Salem during the last few months under sanitary conditions which left much to be desired. Physicians have reported that many persons have been made ill by eating this meat.

It has been a miracle that epidemics of skin diseases and kindred ailments have not resulted from the careless manner in which tavern keepers have washed their glasses—or not washed them. Restaurant workers in many cases should be in some other line of business. Medical inspection is not mandatory. A powerful lobby at the Statehouse always defeats legislation toward this end because of the penurious stand of some restaurant owners. Higher class help would cost more money. Possibly our health authorities may one day succeed in enacting a city ordinance which will cover this.

2. *Salem Evening News* (Massachusetts), August 21, 1946.
3. This editorial was paragraphed by the writer.

All of which points to the fact that our new health agent has plenty of constructive work ahead of him. There is a civic duty for us all to help him to succeed. He can make himself the most important official on the city payroll.

Public health work today includes an intricate maze of activities. Many of these activities are still at the "policing" level, such as control of communicable disease and sanitation, while others are trying to strengthen preventive medicine. The Salem department carried on public health functions involving the services of nurses, sanitary inspectors, and a part-time dentist and doctor. Nursing services consisted of communicable disease control by means of immunization; maternity, infant, and pre-school hygiene; parochial school hygiene; and some tuberculosis control work in cooperation with the Salem Tuberculosis Society.

The two public health nurses involved in this program during the course of the research were Mrs. Evelyn McCarthy and Mrs. Elsie Miller. Both were graduates of the three-year Salem Hospital School of Nursing, though neither had public health nursing certificates. Mrs. Miller had additional nursing education in Boston, Massachusetts. Mrs. McCarthy, who had been on the staff for some time, confined her work to communicable diseases. This appeared to be a source of annoyance to Dr. Tracy, who felt that a nurse should be able to work in a multitude of areas and would have liked for Mrs. McCarthy to devote some of her time to school health as well as communicable disease control. Mrs. Miller, who was appointed later than Mrs. McCarthy, usually did school health work but was willing to work with communicable disease or any other job, including clerical, that the health agent assigned to her.

Much of the departmental program was sanitation. Several years ago the agent was saddled with the responsibility of garbage and refuse collection, for which more than three-fourths of his budget was devoted. The inspection staff of two concerned themselves with plumbing inspection, housing, school sanitation, rodent control, and food sanitation, which included inspecting milk, meat, and other foods and the inspection of food-handling establishments.

Commenting upon the efficiency of his inspection staff, Dr. Tracy once remarked that for a time the health department was fortunate in having an excellent inspector whose educational background was exceptionally good. His grade on the civil service test was in the nineties. Operationally, he went around to the various restaurants, took tests, and applied the usual checks involved in sanitary inspections. He seemed to be doing a very fine job. Then in 1951, or thereabouts, a civil service examination was again held for the position. A young man who made a grade of 70, but who had veteran's preference, took the inspector's place. Dr. Tracy argued with the public officials about the change but was nevertheless forced to take the new appointee. The new inspector was considered by the agent to be most unsatisfactory since he spent much of his time in the laboratory rather than in the field. During the course of this study the department held a food handler's course in which this inspector aptly shared heavy responsibility. It is not unreasonable to assume that the criticism of the second inspector by the health agent stemmed from his annoyance at the replacement of the first well-trained employee.

The department also employed an inspector of animals, who had the responsibility of diseased horses and dogs. Salem had been free of rabies for several years, and his work was hardly confining.

Dr. Tracy was an almost undemanding "task-master." While he expected his employees to fulfill their responsibilities despite insufficient personnel, he seldom pressured them. They were free to attend local or district health meetings, but their attendance was not urged. Occasionally the nurses were seen at district meetings held by the State Department of Health or at the Salem Community Council meetings.

The agent certainly did not exert any unwarranted control over his staff. He did not maintain a permanent system of staff conferences during which employees could learn of the problems or progress of their colleagues, exchange ideas, express grievances, or participate in the democratic administration of the department. Yet the department was certainly a democratic unit.

The staff consisted of representatives of the various ethnic groups prominent in the community, more specifically the Irish and French Canadian. None could be classified higher than lower middle class, and all of the employees of the health department were Roman Catholic.

In the three years that Dr. Katzenstein was chairman of the board of health before this study, he attempted to secure better inspection of restaurant facilities by the public health department and also attempted to change the function of the contagious-disease hospital to one caring for patients who were chronically ill, those who had contagious diseases, and those who were convalescent patients. He was not successful in either of these ventures partly because he was not politically wise.

As far as could be ascertained, he confined his activities to presenting department needs to the city council as a whole and to certain members of the city council who were supposed to be assigned to the public health committee. He found that the members of the council who were supposed to be interested in health problems actually evidenced very little interest. They would say that they believed the health department had a good program and that they were 100 percent for it. However, when it came to voting money to increase services or to change the functions of facilities, they would vote negatively.

In order to supplement their board of health appointments, the city council had established a council committee on public health. This committee seldom acted. When questioned concerning its movement, Mr. Edgar Coggins, former mayor of Salem, and Dr. Max Katzenstein, chairman of the board of health, responded as the following extract from the writer's journal will show:

Mr. Coggins said that the committee of councillors set up to work with the health board was completely inactive and had been for many years. "Most of these committees just do not function the way they are supposed to. They leave the details of health work to the board, to the agent, and to the doctor in charge!"

Dr. Katzenstein spoke briefly about the health committee of the city council and said that this committee, like all the other committees set up by the council, does not function. He said that the board of health does not call the city council health committee into consultation at any time and that, as a matter of fact, he does not even know who is on the city council health committee at the present time. On the one occasion that he asked for a meeting of this committee he met with little success in interpreting his views.

Although the health agent and board were free to work and participate in community health programs, it was apparent that they could do so only within certain financial bounds. Unfortunately, good programs are frequently expensive programs. Coggins once said that even though Dr. Tracy might understand the various health needs of the community he was unable to do much about them for financial reasons. There were other reasons involved which Coggins felt were too delicate to discuss since they were connected with the political system.

The Salem department of health interacted with other health and welfare agencies. Most of these were on the local level except for the State Department of Public Health, which is an important agency to the local health department and will receive a brief treatment.

The Massachusetts Department of Public Health is one of the oldest state health agencies in the United States.[4] Traditionally its function was an advisory one to the local towns and cities which had been delegated local responsibility in the health area by the commonwealth. Several supplementary operational services such as the basic supervision of the establishment and operation of water purification plants and

---

4. Wilson G. Smillie, *Public Health Administration in the United States* (New York: The Macmillan Company, 1949), pp. 13-15.

the construction of such public institutions as hospitals and schools, which were more effectively handled by the larger body, were carried on by the state.

In the commonwealth of Massachusetts, with its over-abundance of small local units, which accept or reject the services of the state, the town and city ruled supreme. Administratively many areas and fields were aware of the difficulty of attempting to offer facilities and services for limited population groups. This was particularly true in public health. The American Public Health Association, which determines administrative and operational standards for community health programs, has cited the impossibility of providing adequate services for a population base of less than 50,000. Salem fell almost 10,000 below this level, a fact which indicates the possible difficulty of efficient and effective operation.

An attempt toward the improvement of local health service was made by the state of Massachusetts through the establishment of the district health plan. The state was divided into arbitrary units of territory by the state health department. A district health officer for each jurisdiction was selected by the state health officer. This man was a deputy state health officer for each territory, was paid by the state, and was responsible to the state health officer. His duties were to represent the state health department in his territory and to advise with and supplement the work of the local health departments. Salem was located in the Northeastern District —a division with an excellent resource staff.

This type of organization frequently rendered valuable service to Salem during the course of this study. The district health officer was an expert in accurate and early diagnosis of communicable disease, was familiar with state law and procedures, and was called on constantly by the Salem department for solution of difficult, technical problems. While this plan did not give well-rounded adequate health service because of the large size of the health district, it did tend to centralize and coordinate health activities. On several occasions during the self-study process the local department requested aid from the district state office.

On the local level the health department was a member of the Salem Community Council. Dr. Tracy was co-chairman of the council's committee on health and attended the monthly meetings regularly. Dr. Tracy, his public health nurses, several of the social workers from the Department of Public Welfare, and the vice-principal of the Salem High School, were the only employees of the city who attended or had membership in the Community Council. The Council grew out of the activities of several Salem social workers and the interest of several prominent civic and social leaders. It provided a social meeting ground and problem action group for interested Salemites and sanctioned action in the health and welfare field. In essence it was a community work group representing the top-power leaders in Salem. While only a few of the Community Council members were classified on the top level, many Salemites, including Mayor Corcoran, the city councillors, and even Dr. Tracy considered the Council as "upper crust." While several Catholics participated in it, it was frequently described as a "Protestant do-gooders group."

Working in relation to the public health services, paralleling and strengthening them, the Community Council's voluntary agencies were a part of the Salem health complex, each dependent upon the operations of others. Many of the private agencies raised money to spread information abroad about the control and elimination of particular diseases. Their methods of operation were similar whether they were an association for those interested in cerebral palsy, heart disease, tuberculosis, or health conditions in crisis or disaster.

During the period of study in Salem, the Salem Association for the Prevention of Tuberculosis repeatedly came to the attention of the field staff. It was an agency well accepted by the community leaders. Its leading personnel was active in the self-study, and it typified the working of organizations of its general purpose. Consequently, a brief description of this association may serve to illustrate the workings of other useful private health associations.

The Salem Association for the Prevention of Tuberculosis was founded in 1912. It has grown in scope and changed its program over the years adapting itself to the improved knowledge on the part of the public and the increased understanding of the disease, tuberculosis, resulting from medical progress. It obtained funds from its annual Christmas Seal campaign and a budgetary grant from the Community Fund Association. It is a local organization and employed two professional persons, an executive secretary, Miss Schroder, and a full-time rehabilitation worker.

Probably one of its most important activities was in the field of health education. This service was directed at popular education through a speaker's bureau, frequent participation in radio programs, particularly the Health Forum of the Air conducted in conjunction with the Salem health department, and also spot announcements. In addition, there was a good deal of material prepared for radio, and pamphlets were distributed through industry to the public. This organization also carried on some professional education activities directed at the nurses of Salem through lectures to the undergraduates at the Salem Hospital Nursing School and to other nursing groups and through the distribution of professional literature to physicians.

Another important activity of this association was that of case finding, that is, attempting to find hitherto undiscovered and unrecognized cases of tuberculosis in the population. In 1950, together with the local health department, this association sponsored a very successful mass X-ray screening of Salem's population, with almost 20,000 people being X-rayed. This was financed by a contribution of $10,000 from state government funds and $4,500 from the Community Fund Association of Salem. During this study it cooperated with the Salem board of health in the conduct of a monthly diagnostic clinic service and a quarterly X-ray clinic for mass screening and the X-raying of contact and suspicious cases delinquent in their follow-up examinations.

Another and well-organized activity of this association was the rehabilitation service which was carried on by the full-time rehabilitation worker. The fact that this association covers Salem only seemed to have real advantages from the point of view of the tasks of the rehabilitation worker. This provided her an opportunity to give each family more care than they would ordinarily receive. As soon as a sanatorium admitted a patient from Salem the worker went to see the patient and described her function. She arranged for the patient to have aptitude tests, personality and intelligence tests. As a result of these examinations, it was then possible to recommend some training program to begin directly by correspondence, which would be useful in terms of that patient's rehabilitation. The program included following these patients after they were discharged from the hospital and for a period thereafter in order to make sure that they obtained whatever help and guidance was needed so that they could make a successful readjustment economically, socially, and emotionally to their home, work, and community situation. This process, of course, could not be carried to a successful conclusion without the cooperation of medical and professional staff of the sanatorium, the private physician, the board of health, the Department of Public Welfare, the employment agencies, the veterans' organizations, and many social agencies.

The above is but one example of the effective activity of this association by way of integration and coordination with other agencies. This cooperation was extremely close, particularly with the board of health, with special reference to its health education activities, its clinic, and its case-finding and rehabilitation procedures. On a personal basis, too, the executive secretary of this association and the health agent got along extremely well, worked together, planned their programs together, and, in doing so, met several times a week.

In the field of tuberculosis prevention and control, there was evident the problem of the growth of organizations covering a larger region or metropolitan area. Since the year 1924, 13 years after the founding of the Salem Association, there had been in existence a county-wide organization—the Essex County Health Association. It had its headquarters in a city bordering on Salem and as a county-wide organization was affiliated with the National Tuberculosis Association and the Massachusetts Tuberculosis League. A recent annual report stated that its purpose was to cooperate with these last two organizations and with "existing health agencies in the stimulation, promotion, and coordination of anti-tuberculosis and child health education, tuberculin testing, case finding, clinics, public health nursing, and rehabilitation. It also maintained a scholarship fund used for providing specialized training for physicians, nurses, or teachers in health education or public health.

Salem continued to support its own, older organization which, as stated, did an effective job. There was little doubt that the co-existence of these organizations—one small and local, the other larger and county-wide—had called forth discussion about their relationship to each other. This issue is likely to become sharper when the executive secretary of the Salem organization nears retirement. Her widely recognized effectiveness in Salem facilitated the state of co-existence of the two organizations which existed at the time of study.

Certainly as one looked at the panorama, healthwise, of Salem, the Salem Association for the Prevention of Tuberculosis loomed up as an important voluntary organization. In addition, however, there was a group of health organizations whose function in Salem was primarily one of raising funds such as the Cerebral Palsy Association and the Heart Association. There were also a number of social welfare organizations such as the Red Cross and the Society for the Prevention of Cruelty to Children whose activities embraced health functions from time to time.

In some instances the organizations collected funds locally

and dispensed them entirely through local services. In other instances funds collected locally were disbursed somewhere else in the state or the nation. There were also examples of health services which were provided locally but were financed on a state or national base.

One of the most striking problems and trends which affected all the health and welfare organizations of Salem was the fact that Salem was a relatively small community geographically surrounded by a group of similar communities. Already a number of the important and potentially important health activities affecting the citizens of Salem had come within the purview of an organization with a broader base, usually a North Shore organization, and sometimes even a state-wide or Massachusetts organization. Most of these voluntary social welfare organizations had a representative member at the Community Council.

Through activities in this council Dr. Tracy was able to develop important working relationships with agencies that beneficially supplemented his work.

Before the self-study of health began, the health agent was aware of certain problems or areas in which he hoped investigation would produce sizable community pressure for action. It is important to notice what these areas were when they were revealed in interviews and in newsprint. As far back as December, 1949, the *Salem Evening News* carried this article:

ALL PURPOSE HEALTH CENTER URGED
FOR SALEM BY DR. HENRY L. TRACY

In order that Salem might keep in line with present day trends in public health, Dr. Henry L. Tracy, agent for the Salem board of health, yesterday cited the need for an all-purpose health center under one roof, complete with clinics and laboratories, in a talk before the Salem Kiwanis Club in a session at DeKoff's Submarine Room.

Dr. Tracy told the Kiwanians that in the forward looking communities of Brookline and Newton such centers have been established where tests for certain diseases are being carried on free of charge to anyone who wants to come in. "The State Commissioner of Health, Dr. Geddings, has recommended these centers where the facilities are consolidated under one roof and to be in line with other visionary health departments of the State, I hope that some day Salem will establish one of these centers," Dr. Tracy stated.

Four months before the self-study began, Dr. Tracy expressed to the writer the hope that various needs might be met. He stated that he would like to see Salem cooperate with Marblehead, Beverly, and a few other surrounding communities in building an incinerator to care for garbage and ashes. He also had plans for improving the school health situation in terms of more extensive examinations, better dental care, and follow up services to determine the volume of correction.

In summary it can be said that the Salem board of health functioned under the control of the mayor and the city council. It was merely one of the many departments which continually pressed the council for additional funds, a better physical plant, or anything which would enable it, in the eyes of its director, to function better. Each department of a city administration is usually in competition with several other departments for any number of services. It is the responsibility of the council, and a responsibility which the public realizes, to guard jealously the city treasury. Some departments, whose functions are more easily recognized and on which the public has placed value, find it easier to satisfy their needs. With public opinion behind them, they are able to exercise more power than the others. The Salem health department was not in a position to exert much power. The general public does not entirely recognize the value of public health programs. Health is an intangible to them that is only understood in time of epidemic disaster.

In training, the board of health employees were perhaps the best that could be expected for the salary and prestige attached to their various positions. Within the organization they functioned with a large degree of freedom which was retained as long as conflict or problems did not occur. This was true of the agent in relation to the board itself and of the agent in relation to the more important political potentates.

Devoid of interest in the many areas of public health and caught in the grip of environmental sanitation, the health department in the eyes of the public was little more than a glorified police department. It is important to recognize that the department was attempting, within the bounds of competence, understanding, and political expediency, to provide the best possible service to the people of Salem. Its members were aware of many problem areas and had expressed this awareness publicly. The participation of its members in the self-study was but a reflection of their position within the total Salem community and their health department affiliation, particularly with the Salem Community Council, the mayor, and the city council.

CHAPTER 6

Physicians and Community Relations

UNDER EXISTING conditions of the organization of medical practice and service in the United States the physician is the keystone of the system charged with the function of health and health affairs in the community. Although the most vital and dramatic aspects of modern medicine are centralized in hospitals with their corps of technicians and auxiliary personnel, outnumbering physicians ten to one, it is the physician who is the symbolic and charismatic leader in the battle against illness and disease.

In view of the important and strategic position held by this profession which, for all practical purposes, our society regards as number one in occupational prestige,[1] the community may rightfully ask: Who are those persons fulfilling this role for us? Where and how do they fit into the various social structures of the community? Are there formal and informal aspects of the organization and practice of medicine which are reflected in the health care available in the community? How do the physicians view the community in terms of its general problems and the problems of health? In short, what relation, if any, is there between social structures of the community and the physicians? What effect do these factors have upon the practice of medicine in the community?

Many sociological factors intimately related to the practice

1. A number of studies verify this. For example, see Cecil C. North and Paul K. Hatt, "Jobs and Occupations: A Popular Evaluation," *Opinion News*, 9 (September 1947), pp. 3-13; John Hall and D. Caradog Jones, "Social Grading of Occupations," *The British Journal of Sociology*, 1 (March 1950), pp. 31-55; and Ronald Taft, "Social Grading of Occupations in Australia," *The British Journal of Sociology*, 4 (June 1953), pp. 181-82.

of medicine are frequently overlooked by communities which have resorted to the currently popular self-surveys in attempts to evaluate their health needs and resources. This discussion is directed toward an examination of some of these factors in order to delineate how, and in what manner, the general nature of the social structure and social organization, plus certain aspects of social control, are related to the practice of medicine. The latter concept, social control, will be the fundamental analytic idea, particularly in relation to the ideas of maintaining order within the medical profession ("policing") and establishing orderly intercourse with the community at large.

In specifying the purposes of social control H. C. Brearley says:

> The aims of social control, according to Kimball Young, are "to bring about conformity, solidarity, and continuity of a particular group or society." These purposes may possibly guide far-seeing statesmen or social scientists, but most individuals who endeavor to control their fellow men show little perspective in their efforts. Often they merely struggle to increase the acceptance of the modes of conduct that they themselves prefer. The preference may be based upon childhood training, insight derived from life experience, or the desire to exploit others in order to gain power—economic, personal, or political. Social control often perpetuates the accumulated wisdom of men long gone, but only rarely are living men and women cognizant of the significance of the cultural patterns they transmit or modify.[2]

The position taken here agrees with Hollingshead's statement that "social control inheres in the more or less common obligatory usages and values which define the relation of one person to another, to things, to ideas, to groups, to classes, and to the society in general."[3] In order to approach the problem and to illustrate these relationships, the medical

2. H. C. Brearley, "The Nature of Social Control," in Joseph S. Roucek (ed.), *Social Control* (New York: B. Van Nostrand Company, Inc., 1947), p. 7.

3. August B. Hollingshead, "The Concept of Social Control," *American Sociological Review*, 6 (April 1941), p. 220.

profession provides a good focal point. The discussion here will be confined, primarily, to a description of the ethnic and ecological distribution of physicians in the community, to certain features of the relationships between physicians and the community hospital, a brief survey of the social participation of the physicians in the community, and to certain modes of social control which more or less pervade the whole of the situations described. The data are based on interviews with better than 90 percent of the physicians, several lay leaders in the community, certain historical records, and approximately three months of observation. Only five of the total 56 physicians were missed in the interviewing. There was one refusal; the other four were missed due to illness, vacations, and inability to arrange appointments during the time allotted for the study.

Although no attempt was made to delineate precisely classes in the community, it is believed that to consider the hierarchy of ethnic groups as being closely related to the prestige and status hierarchy is a safe and useful assumption. It has been shown elsewhere that ethnic origin or background is of much importance in placing individuals in the social structure of this community. This also holds for the physicians.

The distribution of physicians in the community by ethnic origins was not in proportion to the size of each ethnic group. Yankees constituted 28 percent (primarily Anglo-Saxon), 30 percent were Irish, 16 percent Jewish, 9 percent French, 7 percent Polish, and 9 percent of unknown or other origins. The Yankees were Protestant and the Irish, French, and Polish were Catholic. Generally, this order of distribution corresponded positively to the status and prestige ranks of these groups in the community. However, the order of the French and Jewish groups was not clear. In terms of the population composition, Yankee, Irish, and Jewish physicians were over-represented, the Polish physicians were roughly proportional, while the French, the largest ethnic group in the community, were underrepresented. Although the number of Irish and Polish physicians was roughly proportional to the size of their groups, three Irish and three Polish physicians were not on the hospital staff, and most of these were graduates of unapproved medical schools.

The distribution and location of the offices and homes of the physicians tended to portray the social and professional status of the community's physicians and, undoubtedly, determined to some extent the social status of their clients. In most instances the offices of the physicians were in their homes which were located in the three most desirable residential areas of the city. Nearly 60 percent were located in the Chestnut and Essex streets area immediately west of the business center; about 20 percent were in the area around Salem Common near the east end of the business section; and approximately 20 percent were found in the French residential section of the community.

These three areas may be designated, relative to one another, as possessing high, medium, and low residential prestige in the order given. This ecological distribution is in agreement with Firey's conclusion in his Boston study that an affinity exists between the medical profession and areas considered to be previously of upper-class residence.[4] On Chestnut Street, for example, historically the home of Yankee blue bloods and the most exclusive residential street in the city, there were five physicians, while that part of Essex Street, one block away and parallel to Chestnut, was often referred to as "doctors' row." This street, which formerly shared a great deal of the prestige with Chestnut Street, had 16 physicians located within three or four of its short blocks.

Evidence of the influence of social and ethnic factors in the community was revealed in the ethnic distribution of physicians in these three residential areas. In the first or high prestige area Yankee physicians were in a majority followed by the Irish, Jewish, and French in that order. In the second or medium prestige residential area around the Common,

4. Walter Firey, *Land Use in Central Boston* (Cambridge, Massachusetts: Harvard University Press, 1947), p. 279.

Irish physicians were in the majority, Yankees second, followed by Jewish and Polish physicians. There were no Yankees in the third area, and French physicians outnumbered those from any other ethnic group. In all three of these areas there was an apparent tendency for those physicians to be excluded from the staff of the community hospital (hereafter referred to as "non-staff") and to be located on the periphery.

This pattern was a result of ecological processes; however, there was a degree of deliberate control of residential occupancy around Chestnut Street which stemmed from sociocultural evaluations. The residents of this street attempted to control property transfer in order to assure the presence of residents with "proper" social and cultural backgrounds. Four of the five physicians on this street were members of the Yankee group; the fifth was a Jewish physician located on the marginal end of the street near the railroad station and the post office. Even so, he was conscious of being an interloper. Shortly before this study a young surgeon of non-Yankee origin was able to get into one of the old homes on the street and set up for practice. This move occurred, however, without his having been admitted to the staff of the hospital, and in a few months he was forced to move to another community since he was unable to obtain staff membership. We have no positive evidence of a direct connection between this physician's "undesirability" as a resident and the fact that he was not admitted to the hospital staff.

In many ways the hospital is the primary nexus between the physician and the community and in many instances is a primary factor in intra-professional control. The hospital connections of the physician are a prerequisite and integral component of his social, economic, and professional status. Hospital connections not only afford him the many necessary facilities and medical services but are also the mark of professional acceptance by his colleagues, a source of prestige, and a factor in his social status in the community. Moreover, membership on a hospital staff is almost tantamount to professional and economic success. Exclusion does not necessarily preclude either; however, it greatly reduces their probability and makes the non-staff physician a marginal professional. And, undoubtedly, exclusion of any physician, for better or for worse, affects the level of health and medical care available in the community. With these considerations in mind we turn to a description of the hospital and physician relationships.

Historically, the 240-bed Salem Hospital was founded, supported, and controlled by the Yankees of Salem. All aspects of its existence were under Yankee control and direction. In many respects the hospital was a kind of "closed corporation." Members of the Board of Trustees were carefully selected from the Yankee population; funds to cover annual deficits were supplied or solicited only from persons within this particular group of citizens. With few exceptions, membership on the medical staff appears to have been available only by invitation to persons possessing the "proper" social and ethnic origins.[5]

About fifteen years ago the convergent forces of a complex of factors caused certain leaders among the Board of Trustees to realize that in order to maintain the hospital and keep abreast of advances in modern hospitalization these conditions would have to be changed. Among factors producing this realization were: (1) a decline in the number of individuals with personal fortunes who were willing to underwrite the hospital's deficits; (2) the increased costs of hospital operations; (3) a need for expansion of hospital facilities; (4) a lack of young physicians to replace an aging staff; and (5) pressures arising from various elements in the community

5. The importance of these extra-professional factors, such as ethnic background and family stability as means of professional control, are indicated by Oswald Hall in: "The Stages of Medical Career," *The American Journal of Sociology*, 53 (March 1948), pp. 327-36, and "Types of Medical Career," *The American Journal of Sociology*, 55 (November 1949), pp. 243-53.

against the exclusion from the hospital of certain well-trained physicians in the community.

Leaders within the hospital and the community report that, in order to cope with the problems demanding money, the hospital board had turned to the entire community to broaden its financial base. As a consequence of this move, pressures from the community arose to reduce the exclusiveness of membership on both the Board of Trustees and of the professional staff of the hospital. These pressures resulted in several persons from other ethnic groups being elected to the Board of Trustees and the admission of one or more physicians from most of the other ethnic groups to the hospital staff.

Prior to this shift in policy, several of the present members of the medical staff had been excluded for many years. In spite of these changes, approximately 20 percent of the physicians in the community (some of whom have large practices) were excluded from the hospital and could not care for their patients in the local facility. However, a number of these had hospital connections in nearby communities.

At least three reasons were given for the exclusion of these physicians and others who may have wished to practice in Salem. First, it was held that the admission of physicians trained in unapproved medical schools would impair the quality of medical services of the hospital. Second, the most frequently heard point, was the idea that admission of additional qualified physicians to the medical staff would tend to over-staff the various services and specialties and thereby be conducive to unethical and extremely competitive practices and conditions. The third reason given for exclusion centered upon a sentiment (or possibly device) that persons without former residential connections in the community should not be admitted to the staff. There was not, of course, complete agreement on all these points. One physician remarked, in regard to the third point, that if there were a decision between choice of a physician with the residential qualification and one who was without this qualification, but better qualified professionally, he would choose the latter.

Although no attempt was made to determine the general attitude of the community regarding this exclusion policy, there were apparent elements of unawareness, indifference, and an unquestioning acceptance of it on the part of Salemites. The attitude of staff physicians regarding the exclusion of persons from unapproved schools was one of general acceptance. Some, however, had difficulty in rationalizing the exclusion of qualified graduates from approved schools. In spite of the fact that they all enjoyed the protection afforded by the "closed" staff arrangement, several saw a dilemma in its supporting logic. For example, one physician expressed his opinion as follows: "They," he said, referring to his colleagues, "more or less justify the exclusion of other physicians on the basis that too many staff members will cause strenuous competition, fee splitting, and other undesirable practices. Yet they talk about free enterprise. This does not fit into this kind of thinking, and I can't see the logic of it all."

Though not always openly expressed, the attitudes of excluded physicians were characterized by irritation and frustration, modified, to a degree, by resignation. In instances where the prime factor for exclusion appeared to be based on ethnic or personal considerations, a measure of caustic bitterness was expressed. This was true of both the excluded persons and persons formerly excluded. These men considered their exclusion to have been, not only a penalty against them professionally and economically, but also a discrimination against their patients who were automatically barred from their community hospital as long as they desired to be cared for by their regular physician. A second attitude expressed by excluded physicians was: "If we are practicing poor medicine, why not help us improve by admitting us to the staff under supervision?" Apparently no effort has been made to solve these problems by either the community or the dominant medical group which tended to assume a kind of medical quality control for the community. The state medical society had approved a plan whereby physicians from unapproved medical schools may be admitted for practice to hospital staffs if their work is supervised; however, the local hospital staff had not seen fit to follow this plan.

In general this system had reportedly functioned satisfactorily for staff physicians and their patients. However, it obviously had served to exclude certain people in the community from receiving medical care in the community hospital, limited the number of practitioners in the community, and specified, to a certain extent, those who might choose Salem as a place of practice. The young surgeon mentioned earlier was an example of how professional and community factors may combine to exclude certain people. A second instance revealed the economic rationale of the professional group which supported the exclusion policy. The chief of one of the services in the hospital reported, at the time of an interview with him, that in recent weeks a number of doctors had called on him seeking possibilities of obtaining membership on the hospital staff. These requests presented him with a trying problem as indicated by a kind of apologetic agitation and the remark: "We really don't want their competition." Later he asserted that the size of his staff could be reduced by one-half and he could still provide services with a greater degree of efficiency and of a higher quality.

To get at the question of community participation, 60 percent of the physicians were asked if they could put more time into community life and affairs; 65 percent of this number felt that they could not and most of them gave lack of time as the main reason. A number of the respondents felt they could put more time into community life and had no particular reasons for not doing so. Three persons complained that they were not called upon by the community to participate more. In relation to this a number of leaders in community groups were questioned about membership and activity of physicians in their organizations. In every instance, except one, the inactivity of the physicians was excused on the grounds that they were too busy.

Memberships in various types of organizations and associations showed that 51 physicians averaged 2.9 memberships each, exclusive of religious and professional organizations. When the latter were included the average rose to 6.9 memberships each. A total of 21 offices, including directorships, chairmanships, etc., was reported. Of these 11 were in local chapters of the various health associations and other such groups, 8 in community groups of local origin, and 2 in local civilian defense activities.

Several noteworthy facts emerge from a closer examination of the data on offices held. About half of the 21 offices were in organizations whose activities were directly or indirectly related to various aspects of health; and more than half were directorships or of an advisory nature. Better than 60 percent of the offices were held by Yankees and just under 20 percent were held by Irish and Jewish physicians, respectively. The Yankee and Irish composed about 30 percent each of the total number of physicians. Therefore, in offices held, the Yankee group is over-represented while the Irish are under-represented. Jewish physicians constituted only about 15 percent of the total but held as many offices as the Irish. Possibly even more striking is the fact that one-third of all the offices were held by only two persons in the Yankee group. These data again emphasize the superordinate role played by the Yankees in the community.

The physicians took little direct part in local politics. Their interests tended to be directed toward state and national levels. This does not mean that they were not interested in local political affairs. They were interested; but it must be realized that there were certain factors which deterred and inhibited physicians from expressing a more personal and active interest in community politics.

Politics on the local level descends, at times, to a rather low plane of chicanery, mud slinging, and vilification of character. The number of physicians who were willing to undergo this was small. Secondly those political affairs most vital to the interests of the profession, as indicated above, revolved around general policy making and legislation at state and national levels.

The possibility of alienating patients by taking an open and positive stand on controversial political issues was a third factor which deterred individual physicians from being active in local politics. Better than a quarter of the respondents gave this as a reason why physicians should not participate. One doctor expressed the attitude by saying, "I don't think it is good; the more neutral you are, the better the practice. You can't antagonize people." A fourth reason suggested by several of the respondents was contained in the view that it is difficult, if not impossible, to do two jobs well; and it is more important for the doctor to do his job well than to engage in politics. The time factor also entered in. Most physicians considered themselves to be very busy men; however, it should not be overlooked that the habit of many physicians of evading participation in community activities on the plea of being too busy is possibly the most abused and overworked excuse in the repertory of American doctors.

Five physicians reported that they had been requested to run for the local school board but all refused for one or more of the reasons given above. Two of the physicians were, at the time of the study, active members of the community's school and health boards: Dr. Max Katzenstein was the chairman of the board of health—an appointive office; and Dr. Gilbert Riley, non-staff physician, was a member of the school board—an elective office. Dr. William Adkins served a four-year term on the school board several years ago. Dr. William A. Stribling, a resident of the neighboring and fashionable residential community of Marblehead, was recently defeated in a re-election attempt for a seat on the health board in Marblehead. Dr. Stribling had served on the board for a number of years and his defeat came about, according to reports from several quarters, through the efforts of his disgruntled constituents. The disfavor seems to have arisen from the appointment of a health officer who was highly qualified in all respects, except for the fact that he was not a Marbleheader.

From this survey of the physicians' participation in the several spheres of community life it is evident that they do not actively engage in the affairs of the community to any great extent. This gives rise to a number of general questions: Is this inactivity due to indifference, apathy, or to the fact that physicians are too busy to participate? Is it possible for them to participate actively in certain parts of community life without debasing their prestige or neglecting professional standards or duties? Is it fair to urge them to become more active as has been done recently? [6]

Historically, the physician has been expected to be a leader in his community. Andrew Peabody once said, in a commencement address at the Harvard Medical School in 1870, "the physician, equally with the clergyman, has before him, apart from the stated duties of his profession, a sphere of public service for which a well-trained and well-furnished mind alone can fit him." [7] He then proceeded to enumerate a number of areas of community life in which the physician should participate. Was this a realistic expectation then? If so, is it still realistic? This may be a question which both the profession and the community may have to evaluate.

All these questions cannot be answered here. There may be a modicum of indifference toward greater community participation on the part of some of the physicians. However, it would be difficult to distinguish this indifference from the feeling of being too busy or from the view that their time

6. The American Medical Association and some state medical societies have urged physicians to recognize and assume their "broad" responsibilities to the communities in which they live. See *Doctor Patient,* publication of the California Medical Association, 1950, p. 15 (no place or publisher given). For a more recent expression of this concern see the statement of Louis H. Bauer, "The President's Page," *The Journal of the American Medical Association,* 151 (January 31, 1953), p. 350.

7. Andrew Peabody, *What the Physician Should Be* (Cambridge, Massachusetts: Bigelow and Company, 1870), p. 12.

is too valuable (both to the community and to themselves) to be spent in the often lethargic process of community meetings. Certainly, the number of memberships in community organizations by the average physician is well above that which could be expected for the average citizen in Salem.[8] It appears that before a charge of "default" could be lodged against physicians in this matter of participation in community life a closer examination of their professional and private role commitments and expectations must be made.

As for the cost of the physician's inactivity to himself and the community, only surmises may be ventured. Certainly, most American communities could use additional leadership and possibly the physicians are a source not sufficiently tapped. As for the physicians, it may be good for them as individuals and as a profession to be more active in community affairs. Yet it may be impossible for them to participate more without implicating themselves. For example, if they should become too active, the public might view their most honest and sincere efforts as an attempt to advertise themselves as individuals. On the other hand, they may interpret community efforts to solve certain health problems as competition or as an infringement upon the freedom of the profession, and attempts to express this feeling are often viewed, and possibly rightly so, as attempts to maintain the *status quo* in medicine in spite of community needs. The self-study committee of Salem did not concern itself with these problems.

8. That is, if the differentials found between professionals and non-professionals in other studies exist in Salem. For example, compare Mirra Komarovsky, "The Voluntary Association of Urban Dwellers," *American Sociological Review*, 11 (December 1946), pp. 686-98.

CHAPTER 7

General Patterns of Action

IN DESCRIBING the social structures thus far—prestige, agency, and associational groupings—we have given a background of a system that distributes social rights and privileges. A mere description of such groupings is relatively meaningless unless the system operates—does something. A common denominator for action, within and between the groups described, was money. The orderly accumulation and appropriation of funds were of prime concern to all of these groups. Some engage in more, some in less, of this kind of activity. The amount, in either case, aided greatly in status evaluation of the persons or groups involved. The social wealth of the civic agencies was infinitesimal compared with that of the industrial organizations, for example, and one might therefore expect the importance of the former to be socially minimized in comparison with the latter. Such we believe to be the case.

In the materials to follow, we shall describe the actions of three types of groups, in general terms, to set the stage for describing the actions of the specific group in the community that was charged with the responsibility of making a study of health resources and unmet needs. The groupings to be typologically and illustratively described here are, in character: industrial-commercial, political, and civic.

The larger interests in Salem were the industrial and manufacturing enterprises. In order to keep these establishments going, a labor force numbering in the thousands had to be employed. Much of the labor force was drawn from the ethnic groups. The largest payrolls were to be found in the industrial establishments related to leather processing, fuel and power distribution, electrical equipment manufacture, and, until recently, textile manufacture. Because of the size of these industries, the leaders within them exercised considerable influence in decisions related to the distribution of time and money for community physical and social services.

The commercial group of the city was dependent upon the prosperity of the mills and factories, and in turn, the leaders of commercial enterprises looked to the industrial leaders for cues to action. Political, educational, and religious groups were dependent for support on both the industrial and commercial interests of the town, and consequently the latter interests tended to dominate and control policy positions on the boards and bureaucratic apparatus of the former. The pattern of the operative control mechanisms was familiar to anyone who had engaged in community activities to any extent.

"Things that get done" within the groups identified here were done on a large scale. Ralph Douglass and some of the men related to him, for example, had been able to persuade within recent years city councilmen and the state legislature and had run counter to the wishes of scores of organizations and individuals in establishing an electric steam turbine plant and an oil dump on property that was once a playground and a seascape of considerable civic beauty. This set of actions will be more fully described later. Duncan Coker and his brother, Andrew, had ridden the boom of the electronics industry, during and since World War II, and now were major stockholders in a local plant affiliated with one of the largest national combines in the field. Christopher Dowd, through the board of directors of the Naumkeg textile mills, decided to move their plant to the Carolinas and had discharged several thousand employees in the process. Edgar Macon had maintained banking relations with these men and others like them, handling accounts that were large scale.

Other industrialists on the list, such as John C. R. Barden, Donald Arlis, and Jim Foley, represented stable industrial concerns that had participated in the prosperity for the past few years. Lawyers, such as Phillip Reeves and Daniel Hilton, had helped to advise all of these men of their rights and, when the situation demanded it, helped get legislation to legalize actions that might have been illegal otherwise. Samuel Hurst, of the local·press, had recorded some of the actions of these men, newsworthy actions, and had left unpublished some of their actions which had become common gossip. We are not judging any of their actions, but we are convinced, from what we are told, that their operations made them leaders. The control of money was an important element in the action structure.

The writer asked an employee of Jack Brothers, a skilled laborer or "little fellow," what made Chestnut Street so different from the rest of Salem. He immediately replied, "Those people have got all the money there is around here!" The statement was far from accurate, according to our observations, but it accorded with the popular conception of the holders of social prestige and power. In discussing personalities with a host of people in Salem, at one point or another, the subject of money crept into the conversation. The cultural taboo on the subject seemed to be limited, in large measure, to asking a man directly how much he had or made. It seemed permissible to talk freely about the *other* fellows' money. In the process of interviewing, several facts related to money became apparent.

There was a difference between "new" money and "old" money. This was a fact generally known in this community as it is in others. Some of the new money in Salem belonged to men like the Cokers and the Douglasses. Old money belonged to families like the Barrows and the Bentleys, in lesser measure to some of the Pierces, and in greater measure to the Newberrys. Social status between these two groups varied according to the length of time money had been in the possession of the family, and obviously old money took precedence over the new.

It was not a question, in the realm of social status, of how much a man made and spent, but of how much he made and *kept,* and how long he and succeeding generations kept it—the more generations the better. In Salem the kind of ethnic background from which one came also had some bearing on the status accorded one in the possession of wealth. Wealth did raise one's social value regardless of ethnic background. The reverse was also true of the latter situation.

In spite of statements previously made about "Yankee dominance" in the community, there were hundreds of Yankee families living in north Salem who were in inferior social positions to many of the individual members of other ethnic groups. The apparent poverty of this Yankee group punctures the myth of inherent Yankee superiority. Another myth that outlived its usefulness for us during the Salem study was the one related to a proud but poor aristocracy—impecunious old families.

The old families that lost their money lost social position—perhaps not immediately—but unless old fortunes were recouped social prestige declined. As one person put it in speaking of a poverty-stricken lady of a fading family line, "She is socially correct and acceptable in all circles, but she does not attend many functions. She cannot afford to entertain as others do. Her teas are limited to cakes she bakes herself, and she does not feel that she should be obligated to people who can entertain more elaborately."

The recouping of fortunes was sometimes at the mercy of men of power and new wealth. Marriages between the younger members of families of new wealth and old prestige were not uncommon. The "trade off" of prestige and money was quite acceptable. Some of these marriages were preceded by courtships that took place in private schools. Placing a youngster in a fashionable private school was a first step for sons and daughters of the newly wealthy to gain social acceptance. Harvard attendance helped considerably. Some of the men of new wealth, however, had refused to bow to social pressures to marry their sons and daughters to "right" partners, and these men were considered perverse and their wives vulgar. One such family was described as consisting of "fur bearing females and Cadillac driving males," and their offspring, in spite of good educational advantages, had married beneath the social level available to them.

Talk of money, how much or how little a man has, helped to place him in the social structure. We do not wish to overemphasize the point, and we should like to make explicit that the possession of money was not synonymous with social power. Persons in power ascendancy were usually interested in making money, along with a lot of other interests, but not all moneyed people were interested in exercising power.

Once a man had made money, he was liable to become interested in keeping it and in raising his social prestige through engaging in activities that did not involve the risks of power wielding. Men in power ascendancy were usually willing to relieve men of wealth of the responsibilities of the market place and political forum and to help preserve the fortunes of men so relieved, for they, too, might find themselves, in due time, in similar need of aid and protection. Men within the power structure who were in professional positions helped in the maintenance of protective social devices. They did so for proper considerations financially, for a modicum of prestige that attached to their offices, and with the hope that they might participate more fully one day in the fruits of the larger enterprises. The dream of rising above the fears and anxieties of financial limitation helped to make the community system of Salem function, as it does elsewhere, and a news account of Mr. Douglass' rise from coal-truck driver to the presidency of his company helped to keep the dream alive. Mr. Douglass, however, was an exceptional man in Salem, and his rise was an exception, perhaps, that proved the rule. It was said, in some quarters, that Mr. Douglass came from "good" stock albeit not from Salem.

Mr. Douglass was just under fifty years of age and had very

successfully managed the affairs of the Wheeling Coal and Fuel Corporation of Salem for the past seven years. He showed confidence in himself, smiled easily, met strangers with quick friendliness and called them by their first names on brief acquaintance. He, with extroverted behavior, had made an almost storybook public relations man for the company with whom he was employed.

When Ralph Douglass took over the management of the Wheeling Company it was in financial difficulties. In a rather short time the company was making money, and Mr. Douglass accumulated stock in the concern through taking a part of his salary in shares that have steadily increased in value under his aggressive management. About the time of the study, the company had, through a series of stock swaps, become affiliated with one of the larger eastern coal producers and distributors, the Pocahontas Company. In this shift of company fortunes, Mr. Douglass had become one of the board members of the larger company. He was known in the community, particularly by those engaged in business, as a successful and resourceful businessman. To many people he was unknown, or at best known as "that man who runs Wheeling's."

To the businessmen who knew him, however, one of his more resourceful business maneuvers was to locate an oil dump on the property of the new electrical plant. The process of getting the right to locate the oil dumps on harbor property showed the resourcefulness with which Mr. Douglass operated.

A few leaders were eager for the electric company to locate a new plant—one which they were contemplating building in the Boston vicinity—in Salem. The plant would do two things for Mr. Douglass' business. It would give a very large customer, since the plant was to use large quantities of coal for the development of steam, and it would provide him with additional storage dumps for coal and oil.

One thing stood in the way of this otherwise sound economical plan. The property upon which the plant might be located belonged partly to the city, that is, the portion of property adjacent to a piece of land already owned by the power company was a public playground and beach area. This property needed to be acquired before Mr. Douglass and his company could place a fuel dump there. The process of working through this problem was placed in the hands of a very capable Salem attorney, i.e., the task of working the problem through was "delegated" to the attorney.

"It is practically impossible to convert public land to private use in the state of Massachusetts," said the Salem attorney to the interviewer. "Mayor Harrigan [the incumbent mayor] and I had to go down to Boston to the legislature and get an act through which would transfer title of the public playground from the city to the power company. We worked pretty hard on that. The public playground did not amount to very much and it was not used very much, but it was still public property, and the neighborhood kicked up a fuss. The residents of the area were promised a new playground, not along the shore line to be sure, but on a recently filled-over trash dump that was not being used for housing. To complicate matters, the residents of the area were veterans who had built homes facing the sea, and the building of the plant would spoil their view. They protested to the legislature when our bill was introduced, but we overrode their protests and got the bill through."

I asked how they got the city council to go along with their plan. The attorney said, "Most of the time we approach these fellows on the city council informally. We will take them on a boat ride or out to dinner and put whatever proposition we have before them. Most of the time we would not approach the city council directly while they are in session, but if it were necessary we would.

"In the electric plant situation the city council was on the spot because they had to stand up and be counted before a large group of citizens. To many of them it seemed like political suicide to vote for the land transfer, but the big brass in the community had been working on the city councilmen individually, 'reasoning' with them, and they voted for the measure in spite of the fact that most of the civic associations, the veterans organizations, and a good many individual and substantial citizens were against it.

One by one they voted as they were told to vote. It isn't very often that we have to have such a test of strength as this, but when the chips are down the interests that I am talking about will throw their weight around!"

Mr. Douglass did not hold some of the civic associations in very high regard. He had dropped his membership in Rotary, a club that he described as a "dead bunch," but one of his men represented him in the club. Although Mr. Douglass did not hold the civic associations in prime regard, they recognized him as a real leader. "He is one of the men," they said, "who can get things done," and he was looked to for support and advice on innumerable civic ventures. Persons repeatedly told of how Mr. Douglass had "put across" the drive for funds for Salem Hospital following the latter-day expansion of his business.

Mr. Douglass' success in putting over the hospital drive cannot be described as too different from the experience of hundreds, if not thousands, of men in a similar capacity as civic leaders in hundreds of other communities. One informant described his activities in this way:

There are about ten men who run this town. Douglass is a top man among them. He has been a real leader here and now he's reaching out and will be a potent man in this region.

Over the years he has accumulated a list of names of people he can call on to get civic jobs done. He always calls on the same people to work with him. He's a restless fellow and ambitious and is never happy unless he is doing something like buying a company or heading some community venture.

When the Salem hospital needed to raise $150,000, Douglass was the logical choice to head up the drive. He had personnel within his own organization who could carry a lot of the clerical work. As a matter of fact, the overhead of the hospital campaign was carried by Douglass' outfit and four or five other corporations and the exact figure was never tallied.

Besides the help within his own office, Douglass could command support of many others, on a give-and-take basis, and the campaign was a cinch. It was a real feather in Doug's cap!

Only one discordant note was sounded in the general praise of Mr. Douglass and in relation to men like him. It was summed up in a phrase, "There is too much absentee control in Salem."

Many of the men engaged in industrial management, the top power status occupation, lived outside the community. It was claimed that, consequently, they had less interest in what happened to the community than those who were residents. It was felt that the situation created some paralysis in community action programs generally, because the men with large industrial establishments outside Salem, but who ran Salem affairs, were not really dependent upon the community for civic services. And the same applied to many who had establishments in the community and who lived outside. Both groups seemed interested in "keeping taxes down to the detriment of additional and needed community services." The men upon whom pressure was put to keep the taxes down were the ranking local politicians.

It must be said, parenthetically, and in fairness to the interests involved in getting the electric plant placed in Salem, that the project had both lowered the tax rate for the community and had helped to provide additional community services—in the field of health as well as otherwise.

Within the last twenty years Salemites have divided and distinguished between the various segments of their population in several ways. Basically there has been a religious division: Catholic and Protestant. Within each of these two there were further breakdowns. The differences among Salem Protestants may be defined as class-bound. Those most pronounced among Catholics were ethnic: Irish, French-Canadian, Polish, and Italian. The majority of people within the community held certain beliefs concerning the structure of the community. It was generally believed that the Yankee community dominated all of the economic interests in the town, while the Irish and French came into political dominance. This was supported by the fact that there was not a single corporation that did not have its board of directors "packed" with Yankees, and most of the corporation lawyers were Yankees.

Politically the main divisions of the town were along nationality lines. In any election a candidate must be cognizant of the nationality groupings. Traditionally, the Irish had allied themselves with the Yankee group. When the Yankees became numerically impotent they were forced to unite with another group in order to maintain some avenues of political control. The Irish were the oldest ethnic group and informal lines of contact were organized. On several occasions during the period of investigation we were told that Mr. Thomas Bentley, a resident of Chestnut Street and an active member of Grace Episcopal Church, an upper-class institution, was the bridge between the Irish political machine and the remaining Yankee stock.

The two groups, acting through men like Bentley on one side and Mr. Coggins, an Irish politician, on the other, had controlled the political scene for over twenty years. They agreed on a candidate with a minimum of social intercourse, e.g., conferences and telephone conversations. This group "twosome" seldom made a mistake in its selections. In recent years, the one oversight which they seemed to have made was in their support of Mr. Harrigan, a candidate who was beaten by a coalition of ethnic voters who put an Irish mayor in power—a man not backed by Bentley, at least.

A former mayor of Salem, 1948-1949, Mr. William Harrigan, whose administration will be discussed, once said in an address, "Politics is nothing but a reflection of the racial, religious, and economic strength and desires of the people." This, in part, describes the participants in the political structure of Salem since the adoption of its charter in 1836.

For almost one hundred years, the mayors and councils of the city "reflected" the best of the old Yankee families. Such names as Leverett Saltonstall, Stephen C. Phillips, Joseph S. Cabot, David Pingree, Joseph B. F. Osgood, James H. Turner, and Henry P. Benson graced and brought honor

to political office. With the numerical increase of the Irish
Catholics and their interest in political office, the character
of political candidates changed.

After 1917 all of the six mayors to 1952 had been Irish
Catholics. The wedge made by the Irish substantially increased the successful efforts of other national groups to
secure political representation in the affairs of the city. The
French Canadians, comprising one-third of the total population, had consistently maintained a number of city council
positions—although efforts at gaining mayoralty had failed.
The Poles had been similarly successful. In 1952 the first
Italian councillor won office.

It has been emphasized earlier that most of the people in
Salem at the time of the study were not old American. Almost three-fourths or more were from other national groups.
The English, the old settlers, were fast leaving the area. However, in many ways, the new immigrants were much the same
as their predecessors. In their attempt to be recognized and
accepted they deferred to the old patterns of action. Many of
the Irish became Republicans (Senator Baynes, Mr. Coggins).
Even though most of the older group had left and were no
longer directly involved in politics or in other civic or social
activities, Salem remained a very conservative community.

Politics to Mr. Coggins, mentioned previously, was a science, something to be studied and manipulated. Each group,
religious and national, must be wooed, understood, appreci-
ated, and with this treatment made to produce the desired
end-product—votes! To a skillful compilation of the latter,
Edgar Coggins owed his political success. Although he did
not hold office, a man with his political know-how was likely
to be sought and his *ars est celare artem* utilized.[1]

Holding the mayoralty for 10 years, Mr. Coggins was defeated in 1948 by William Harrigan who held the office for
one term. Mr. Harrigan was a local Irish Catholic attorney
in his early fifties who had previously served in the state

1. During five interviews Mr. Coggins was referred to as the "ex officio
Mayor" and "the man behind the political scene."

legislature. A tall, thin, distinguished man, his gruff, frank manner made him unpopular in many circles. Mr. Harrigan believed and worked for intercommunity cooperation and the permanent solution of problems. Both views were unpopular with local politicians because of the detrimental effect they had on the bestowal of spoils. While it is a matter of record that Mr. Harrigan replaced previous appointments and filled a number of city positions with his own friends, thus practicing a typical "spoils" pattern on one level, his attempts at permanent problem solution and cooperation would tend to eliminate it on another. Mr. Harrigan disclosed that the city councillors and other leaders felt it was unwise politically to solve too many problems at once. Primarily it allots too good a record to one man and does not leave residual problems which might be transformed into a political ball for another man to handle.

Mr. Harrigan's candidacy was supported by the old Yankee group in the community. This support was based on the acceptability of his platform, his success in the state legislature, and his willingness to "play ball" with powerful groups and individuals within that segment of Salem structure. During the campaign he caustically referred to the exclusiveness and snobbery of the "Chestnut Street Crowd" in speeches to that group. These occasions were often referred to boastfully by members of this group and derisively by others in the community. Outsiders wonderingly questioned how Mr. Harrigan secured this support in view of his derision. "Chestnut Streeters" referred to the incidents with humor, undoubtedly even with pride in the criticism of the system whose maintenance was so important to them. Certainly Mr. Harrigan's acceptance of dinner invitations and other indulgences offered him by this group indicated the relative unimportance attached to his verbal censure. His defeat in 1949 was due to a combination of religious, social, and economic factors.

During the course of this investigation, Richard J. Corcoran was the Mayor of Salem. Mr. Corcoran, an Irish Catholic in his early fifties, graduated *magna cum laude* in mathematics from Harvard University and secured a position with American Knitting Company when it was attempting to establish a new type of community for its workers. When the position was abolished before completion of the project, Mr. Corcoran believed he was a failure. For many years he "hung around town with no visible means of support" and was the object of much criticism.

When World War II broke out, Edgar Coggins, long-time friend of the Corcoran family, helped him secure an army commission. Upon his release from service, Mr. Corcoran fell back into his old prewar routine. With the help of Mr. Coggins, Mr. Corcoran successfully ran for the Salem school board. Encouraged and stimulated by the experience, he decided to oppose Mr. Harrigan at the next election, having failed to convince Mr. Coggins to make an effort a seventh time. The odds against Mr. Corcoran were tremendous and yet appeared inappreciable when compared to the unfortunate record the "Yankee-supported" Mr. Harrigan had made during his two years in office. Corcoran was supported financially by twelve friends known as the "Apostles," and some financial aid from Mr. Coggins who kept in the background without openly supporting his candidate until a few days before election. With the gambling odds, which usually accompanied this selection, heavily against him, Richard J. Corcoran won the election. Assuming the office, Mr. Corcoran made no sweeping changes in the city administrative personnel even though a list of those individuals who had opposed him during the campaign had been inadvertently left behind in the mayor's desk by Mr. Harrigan. The mayor was interested in the fact that, at the time he assumed office, the very first visitors he had were men on that list.

Corcoran established an ultra-conservative administration and became the first full-time executive in the city's lengthy history. This enabled him to win over many who opposed him, to bring together several factions, and to smooth over, to a very large extent, the severe conflict situation which existed between the Protestants and the Catholics in the community when he took office.

The official body of the city government involved in public health is the board of public health which was controlled and influenced by the council and the mayor. As we shall see later, the council and the mayor were involved in the health study.

It is apparent, as we have seen, that the city council may, on occasion, be forced to move. The interest and demands of unorganized people were frequently overlooked providing positive aspects and supporters might be found for a reverse decision. Whether one decision is good or right or bad or wrong is not within the system of analysis of the social scientist. His interests lie in the analysis of those observed consequences which make for or lessen the adjustment of a given system.[2] It is often merely a matter of opinion, recurrently controversial: the retention of the scenic beauty of a historical harbor versus tremendous tax reduction, the building of a drive-in shopping center which would alleviate downtown traffic congestion, and further business decentralization versus the change in a quiet residential block with an increase of danger from automobiles. The possession of power and prestige or the ability to buy or pay in kind for services rendered were effective tools with which to deal with the Salem councillors, provided an issue were shown to produce something beneficial to the taxpayer at little expense to the city.

The accumulation of money, through taxation, and the distribution of money, through municipal allocations, was a primary set of duties falling to the lot of political office-holders. These tasks bring recognition to the men involved, and many members of the ethnic groups aspired to become politically recognized. Many saw public office tenure "as a way out" of their subordinate social roles. Others saw it in terms of personal gain. While we picked up considerable

2. Robert K. Merton, *Social Theory and Social Structure* (Glencoe, Illinois: The Free Press, 1949), pp. 50-51.

hearsay and gossip relative to petty graft, we did not trace out this phenomenon. Whatever the motivations and rewards, the political structure of Salem was a potent force in distributing money for public services—a force that had to be recognized particularly by the professional administrative personnel dependent upon its largesse.

It was also clear that the force and power embodied in the political apparatus of the community were guided, as the needs required, by the larger elements of social structures already outlined. Thus, the political structure took its place as a functional part of the over-all power structure of the body politic. It acted in relation to other structures in the ways described.

Within the system of community action, in its broad sense, one other grouping remains to be discussed, namely, the organized civic workers. As we shall see at the close of this chapter, civic work may provide a meeting ground for individuals with diverse interests and backgrounds.

The lines between persons of power and those with no power, in an organized civic sense, were sharply drawn in Salem. Distinctions between persons of social prestige and persons of power were discernible, but the lines were less sharply drawn. Persons of power represented a highly active class. They had position by achievement or *doing*. Prestige people had position by assumption or ascription and were less active.

Prestige generally *may* be achieved, but the process, for some, is long and complicated. Power achievement is a good beginning at getting social prestige, in a society sense, but it does not presage an automatic induction into the most exclusive circles of society. Men of power work toward getting prestige through *gaining* recognition. Prestige persons have social recognition.

Some persons who had recognition as a quasi-leisure class in Salem were: (1) women, and in some situations men, dependent upon men of power or who had familiar connections with preeminent living personages; (2) persons who had ascribed status through the inheritance of wealth and social position; (3) certain religious and professional leaders who were granted by society a wide range of freedom and action but whose productive capacity could not be measured tangibly; and (4) retired business and professional persons. Such persons as these were recognized as having a social right to a good measure of leisure. Other persons of leisure might be those who would not work but who the community by and large felt *should* work. Most able-bodied persons in Salem engaged in some work, even the quasi-leisure class. But in the latter case, the "work" consisted of civic endeavors which, in the main, were not economically remunerative and productive.

Those who used a good proportion of their free time in the manipulation of civic boards and civic enterprises of one sort or another were recruited from the quasi-leisure class. They were put forward and they put themselves forward as community leaders—which they were. But the activities in which they engaged were often symbolic and time consuming rather than meaningful in moving goods and services from producer to consumer. They stood in symbolic relation between community decision makers and the large underlying body of persons who actually performed the bulk of tasks that were daily required to keep the community functioning.

A person like Mrs. Thomas Barrow, the wife of one of the industrial leaders, may serve as an example of our meaning. Mrs. Barrow was the daughter of a retired man who had been a successful business executive in the community. The social position of the Bentleys, Mrs. Barrow's family, had been relatively fixed within the upper group for two or more generations. Mrs. Barrow's social position within the confines of the Salem community might have been comparable to society groups in other communities such as the Main Line of Philadelphia, Boston's Back Bay, New York's 400, or San Francisco's Nob Hill. Mr. Barrow was a civic leader who was included in our listing of forty leaders. Because Mrs.

Barrow had some wealth in her own right and would inherit more and because her husband was employed in an executive position in a stable corporation in the community, she had leisure to indulge civic interests. As a matter of fact, she took on civic duties as a responsibility as did other women of her station in life.

Her household duties, which were numerous in caring for a husband and two adolescent children, were performed with help. The relatively free time that she had was devoted mainly to the North Shore Babies' Hospital, where she had been board president for several years. She had also served on the school board in years past as an elected member, and at the time of the study she also held a quasi-political job. She was working with the custodian of the local cemetery collecting names from tombstones and getting burial records classified so that the living might make familial connections with the dead in Salem's historical interment plot. She had from time to time been active as a committee or board member of numerous "volunteer" organizations. She was a member of one of the leading sewing circles. Civic agencies in Salem competed for the services of Mrs. Barrow.

The social functions, satisfied by the performance of a variety of roles on Mrs. Barrow's part, were numerous. Her activities made her an acceptable wife of a successful husband. She helped to maintain the tradition of "service" demanded of her class. She acted as a carrier of information from one activity group to another by the very fact that she was involved in a variety of activities. She lent social prestige to any board she deemed worthy of patronage. She supported certain "worthy" charities by financial contributions as well as through personal service. Important in a civic sense, her name was well known in the community at large, because of her family background and her own gregarious behavior and friendly interest in town affairs, and her presence on a committee or civic board tended to give such a board stability in the eyes of many. "Things cannot go far wrong," people said, "if Ginny Barrow has a hand in their management!" Ginny

Barrow and women of her "breeding and position" just did not go wrong, so they said, and, of course, there was truth in the saying.

There were many factors that kept Mrs. Barrow "in line," and she in turn helped to keep civic boards in line. It is at the point of keeping civic boards in line that elements of power and social prestige meet; at least, it is an important point at which they meet. Money is another important element.

Compared with persons controlling the larger interests, a person like Mrs. Barrow could not be said to hold a critical power position. She had some power. The fact that she held political office and that she had been willing to participate actively in community developments gave her additional claim to power distinction, but the claim was relative to the larger interest. Many of the civic volunteer personnel, upon whom civic agencies and health and welfare bureaucracies depended, were in similar positions.

The power of associational, professional personnel was derived from organizing persons like Mrs. Barrow, as well as men in the larger interest groups, into working teams to get things done. Many of the actions taken by the people who bound themselves into civic associations were extremely beneficial to the community as a whole. What we are about to say should not detract from this fact. The good works of many of the associations might be extolled at length in this writing, but a latent function of some of the associations must be mentioned at this point.

An element in the elevation of a man to a position of ex tended powers was derived from his willingness to be generous with the gifts at his disposal, not prodigal, and to show by public expenditure that he had the welfare of his community at heart. The wisdom of Aristotle, who said, "The virtue of liberality is more conspicuous in bestowing handsomely than in receiving our due," was constantly put to practical use by Salem's leading citizens who could afford the virtue of magnanimity.

The two major sources of revenue of the civic agencies in Salem, including the agencies of government, were those supplied by taxation and private charitable subscription. Since the men who occupied controlling positions in the larger industries and businesses made the largest contributions to various community organizations, their performance of public duty on the one hand, and personal generosity on the other, were widely known. Practicality dictated the terms under which bounty was dispensed by the upper leaders, and consequently, policy matters relating to the final expenditure of funds by associational groups were frugally controlled by the larger donors and tax payers. The frugality and caution of the paid employees and substructure board members of the associations were matched by their devotion to keeping dissident elements of the population mollified. In a very real sense the civic associations performed the function of a rather far-reaching public relations structure for the decision makers in the community control group. Thus, there was an advantageous reciprocity established between donor and primary recipient. Some community associations in Salem were looked upon with more approbation than others by leaders in the top echelons of power and prestige.

Of the 40 leaders, mentioned earlier, who were interviewed during the course of the study, when asked to "name three organizations to which you belong and that you consider important," 14 indicated a choice of the Chamber of Commerce, 12 chose the Community Fund, 11 indicated Red Cross, 9 the Salem Hospital Association, and 6 chose Rotary. Other choices included the Y.M.C.A., the Community Council, the T.B. association, Boy Scouts, Woman's Friend Society, Kiwanis Club, Lion's Club, North Shore Babies Hospital Association, and some 17 other associations in a descending order of preference. The top ten leaders, some in the leadership poll, tended to belong to the Chamber, the Fund, Red Cross, and the Hospital Association.

Qualitative analysis of the memberships of top leaders also revealed that at least three prestige-bearing associations, to which some of them belonged, were not mentioned; e.g., membership on the Hawthorne Hotel board, considered a signal honor in the community, was not named, nor was membership in the 13 Club or the Essex Institute Board. Membership in the latter associations was so restricted in numbers of members that persons who belonged to them did not think of them immediately as civic organizations. They might have been classed as "secret societies," except that they constituted open-secret groups for those who were "in the know." The men who met within these groups got to know one another well, and many things of civic import were discussed at the meetings of the boards of any one of them. The hotel board may be a case in point.

In the normal course of events, a hotel board might not be considered a civic enterprise, but in Salem the hotel had never been a profitable commercial venture. Some of the businessmen wanted a hotel kept in the community to be used for sales meetings of their out-of-town employees and for visiting dignitaries. The hotel was also supposed to encourage tourist trade in the community and provide a meeting place for civic groups. To keep the hotel going, the business leaders had subsidized it to some extent and in the process had taken over its board control. The board had become an exclusive group, and membership on it had become a mark of prestige.

The writer attended a meeting of the hotel board, held on the boat of one of the manufacturers of the community, Duncan Coker. Mr. Coker was acting as chairman of the board for the year. The business meeting of the board lasted only about ten minutes, and the rest of the time the group was together, about three and a half hours, was spent in discussing many other things of business and civic importance in the Salem community. Such informal meetings were a vital part of the action structure of the community. The parking problem, the question of water supply, the movement of the textile mills, and many other problems were discussed, informally, on the cruise in question, and the men in attendance had an opportunity to clarify their own positions in these matters and cue their actions in accord with opinion expressed around the circle. There was no skulduggery in such procedures, it was merely a way of making clearance on vital matters to bring about concerted action. Another more formal method of clearance is found in committee formations.

Committees abound in Salem, as they do elsewhere, and through them much civic work was accomplished. Their functions are paralleled by those described above. The associations mentioned previously were instruments for calling committees together, and the importance attached to a committee's operations was determined in large measure by the general status of the organization calling it together and by the men who attended its meetings. In a series of meetings called by the Community Fund, a high status organization, in connection with an effort to get a united campaign organized in the community, some of the top leaders were in attendance.

One of the more productive meetings, from the point of view of observing the decision-making process in action, may be illustrated by presenting a somewhat detailed account of it. Some of the by-products of an examination of this meeting are revealed in the discussions within it, the formulation of attitudes toward certain groups within the community, the action role of the chest executive, as a mediating person, and a review of some of the larger civic problems that faced Salem made by one of the committee members following the meeting. These were our journal notations:

I was invited by Joseph Colbert to attend a joint meeting of his Community Fund board of directors and some of the officials of the local and Boston Salvation Army. In 1947 the local Salvation Army corps withdrew from the Salem Community Fund. A difference of opinion between the Community Fund and the Salvation Army arose over the fact that the Fund has a rule which states that at the end of the fiscal year if an agency has a surplus such surplus reverts to the Fund. The Danvers Salvation Army unit, which was under the Salem Community Fund jurisdiction, had a small surplus. They wanted to keep this.

When the Salem Community stood on its prerogatives, the Salvation Army group in the Salem area withdrew from the Fund. Since that time they have been raising their own money, but year by year they have been able to raise less. The first year they raised approximately $8,600 in Salem, about $3,000 in Marblehead, and about $2,000 in Danvers. Since that time the amounts they have been able to raise in each of these three communities has declined until last year they were able to raise only a little better than $5,000 in Salem and approximately $2,000 in both of the other two towns.

Recently negotiations have been going on between the executive of the Salem Community Fund and officials of the Salvation Army both in Salem and Boston to reinstate the Salvation Army in the Fund setup in Salem and include them as members of a proposed united campaign. The meeting which I attended was a result of these negotiations and represented an attempt to come to some policy agreement between the two organizations.

Some of the men in attendance at the meeting were persons whose names were gathered as being top leaders in the community. The ones whose names I caught in the introductions were as follows: Winslow Butchart, Duncan Coker, Elliott Epley, Robert Joyner, Edgar Macon, Albert Moise, Lucien Gosset, Jim Foley.

Jim Foley was chairman of the meeting since he is president of the Community Fund. It was interesting to me to note that the "ball of deference" was tossed from Jim Foley to Duncan Coker to Edgar Macon to Albert Moise and finally to Winslow Butchart. Most of the other members of the committee maintained a discreet silence until these men had spoken. The role of the remaining members was that of reinforcing what the leaders had already said. Joseph Colbert was called upon several times to clarify factual points such as the amount of money raised for the Salvation Army in years past.

It was obvious as the meeting progressed that Mr. Colbert would like to see the Salvation Army brought back into the Community Fund, but it was equally obvious that the members of the Community Fund board were not settled in their judgment of the matter. The Salvation Army's present request for funds from the Community Fund amount to $8,500 for Salem, $2,500 for Marblehead, and $1,800 for Danvers. In light of the fact that the Salvation Army has been able to raise only a little better than $5,000 in Salem and $2,000 in the other two communities outside the Fund, it became apparent by the implications of the questions asked that the Fund Board members were not ready to accede immediately to the Salvation Army's request.

The following day, 8/5/52, Mr. Colbert told me that his board is quite unsettled on the question of admitting the Salvation Army and that Jim Foley had called upon James Gilbert to get his opinion on the matter. Mr. Gilbert was definitely opposed to including the Salvation Army for the amount they were requesting. Colbert says the matter is up in the air and will be discussed informally by various members of his board until a decision is reached. He is perfectly willing to abide by the decision. He said, "All I can do is bring these matters to their attention. What they do about it is their business."

During the meeting, Duncan Coker, who had recently been appointed campaign chairman of the Community Fund for this year, raised several objections to adding any amounts, no matter of what size, to the campaign goal for this year. He said that year by year the Community Fund has been increasing its total goal until it is extremely difficult to attain. He feels that the base of the Community Fund has not been broadened enough; in other words, not enough people in the working-class group are contributing to the Fund, and he feels that every effort should be made to broaden the base of giving. Mr. Colbert stated that year after year the base has been broadened. Colbert went on to say that he wanted to invite some of the labor representatives from the National Community Chests and Councils office to Salem early in the fall to hold a labor-management institute around Community Fund giving. Several of the members of his board reacted immediately against this idea stating that if they let these national labor representatives come in they would try to do a little labor organizing on the side. Duncan Coker stated that, even if they didn't do any labor organizing on the side, they would be helping the Community Fund and some of the community leaders to raise the Fund goal, and later on they would probably come back and say that they had been helpful to the local leaders, therefore, the local leaders should help them to organize labor or at least not resist their attempts at organizing labor. It was finally suggested that it would be desirable to get some of the local labor people together with some of the management groups leaving out any national labor representative. Mr. Colbert was directed by his board to proceed with meetings of this sort.

After the meeting Jim Foley stopped to talk with me. Mr. Foley said that he was glad the Board had made the decision to keep the meetings with labor on a local basis. He said that Salem had very little difficulty with labor primarily because a large percentage of the community was French. He said the French people make wonderful workers. They are docile and are not at all like some of the Greeks and some of the newer elements that are beginning to come into the community. He said that the Polish people also make good workers. Mr. Colbert then joined us and there was some discussion about the meeting related to the Salvation Army request. Both men agreed that it was better to have the Salvation Army in than to have them out of the Fund, but they thought they would have to look over the figures submitted by the Salvation Army rather carefully.

We were then joined by Mr. Gosset, a city councillor and French community politician, who was asked by Mr. Foley exactly how many French people there were in the community. Mr. Gosset replied that he thought the French people represented one-third of the community. Mr. Foley jokingly scoffed at this figure and said, "You must count every person that is even distantly related by blood or marriage to a Frenchman. Do you count a girl who is married to a Polish man as a Frenchman?" Mr. Gosset said that he would consider her a French girl and that, if he were seeking votes from her, he would write her a letter and hope that she would persuade her husband to vote for him. Foley then asked if their children would be considered French and how far this would be carried—to one-eighth Frenchman, or one-sixteenth, or just how far? There was laughter at this point and Mr. Foley then evidently wanted to say something pleasant for Mr. Gosset's benefit and he asked me if I had seen the new French church. I said that I had been there, and he said that he was recently surprised when he went there and found that his father's name was listed as one of the patrons of the church in relation to its building fund. He said that he had made a contribution to the building fund in the name of his father, and when they visited the church on Holy Thursday one of his children brought to his attention the fact that John Foley was listed under one of the windows with the long list of French names. He said the name "stuck out like a light" because it was sandwiched in between French names that had prefixes before them of Monsieur and Madame. His own father's name did not have a prefix but was merely listed as John Foley.

I left the meeting with Mr. Gosset. We stood on the sidewalk a few moments before the Community Fund building and talked.

In our conversation he began to talk about Salem and its business community. He said that Salem is divided somewhat between those groups who merely wanted to live on tradition and those who wanted to benefit the community by expanding industry. He feels that there is not enough of a balance of industry here. He says that on two or three occasions Salem has had an opportunity to have a new industry, such as Mr. Coker's electronics plants, but some of the older industries have resisted bringing in new industries because it would break into their labor supply.

He feels that the leather industry in times past has been guilty of dominating the Chamber of Commerce and to a certain extent the banks in an effort to try to keep industry out. He feels that there is some reversal of this trend but it is still difficult to sell some of the older men on an aggressive program for industrial expansion. He says that the City Council is seriously considering employing a person in the Chamber of Commerce who would set up a developmental program for the community on its industrial side. He feels that the threat of industry's moving to the South is a very real problem for the community, and, if they have a professional person who would make a very thorough study of the situation, they might, through working with State developmental bodies and other community developmental bodies, propose a program that would be a good one for Salem.

Traditionally the cooperation between communities outlying the city of Salem has been between the various City Councils of these communities. The process has been cumbersome and has not often been productive of adequate decisions. He feels that now the city is moving in the right direction to get some professional help in the matter.

The next day in talking with Joseph Colbert, we had a brief

discussion of the Salvation Army budget, and Mr. Colbert was anxious to clarify one item of it. During the previous meeting, the Salvation Army men had made a great point of the rock-bottom character of their budget. They had said that they were "able to stretch a dollar further than most any other organization." They said their salaries were low and would compare favorably with any welfare organization that the Community Fund supports. Some of the lay members of Mr. Colbert's Board agreed with this and one of them said, "As I look across the table here and see Captain ———, I don't understand how he is able to eat on the salary he makes. He has a wife and four children to support and on his salary it does not seem possible to me that he can eat adequately." One of the other members of the board responded to this saying, "It's probably true that the Captain does not eat like some of the rest of us may. He may not belong to a bunch of clubs like some of us do, and he may be more right than we are. Maybe we do a lot of things that we don't need to do." Colbert felt that there was some slight dishonesty in the Salvation Army position because the local Captain makes a salary of $2,500 a year but he also gets his house and furniture free as well as an $800 a year allowance for an automobile and an adequate expense account in travel, and other items which normally go with a home budget.

Thus, too, the civic groupings were concerned with fund allocations. Attendance at meetings, such as those described, served to build up and enhance a man's community prestige and broaden his powers. Participation at these meetings was widely publicized. The community was assured that their interests were being jealously guarded and husbanded. The careful weighing of facts, the attention to protocol and ritual, frugality, and the strict observance of status considerations made the meetings carriers, in part, of social order. Finally and as importantly, they were a means by which social solidarity was achieved, particularly between control elements and agreements reached relating to social goals.

CHAPTER 8

Choosing the Self-study Committee

THE PROCESS BY which groups or several individuals in a community have attempted to study problems and initiate remedial programs has recently gained widespread interest among lay and professional groups. Hardly a popular magazine is found on the American newsstand which has not published at least one article on "How Jonestown Got a Doctor," "How Pixton Beat the Bigots," or "Operation Clean-up—a Community Answers Back."

The technique of observing one's own community is popularly referred to as self-study and has, through copious usage, gained the interest of the social scientist.

The definitions of self-study used by its many proponents have been legion. In some conflicting instances these definitions have stipulated that resource aid could not come from outside of the community, or that, in reverse, this aid might be in the form of a study stimulated by outside resource interests, or even that any resources might be utilized provided the initiative for self-study originates within the community.

In order to clarify our own thinking, as well as that of the community leaders we were to observe in action, we defined self-study as a social process in which several individuals or even a large group become aware of the health problems in their community. This awareness must be expressed by overt action in the form of investigation and must tend to lead toward problem solution. It was felt that the stimulation for action should come from within the community rather than from outside agencies or interests. We looked toward

Salem for a test of our definition and for insight into the process we had visualized from the reports of others.

An appointed committee conducted the Salem self-study over a seven-month period from September, 1952, through March, 1953. Utilization of such a body might certainly have been foreseen. The over-all importance of the committee in American organized life can hardly be estimated. It has become a fetish whose mere existence prophesies fulfillment. The self-study committee was an expansion of the health committee of the Salem Community Council, a voluntary association consisting of representatives of the various Salem health and welfare organizations together with interested citizenry whose united function was community betterment.

The story of the growth of the health committee from a small two-man unit in the spring of 1952 to a large 14-man body in the fall represented an interesting development. Several years ago when Dr. Margaret Lassiter, a retired state public health physician, was president of the Salem Community Council, she emphasized health areas to such an extent that finally, in January, 1952, a committee of two was appointed to make recommendations concerning a permanent health committee. This committee consisted of Dr. Henry L. Tracy, health agent of the Salem board of health, and Miss Katherine Schroder, executive secretary of the Salem Tuberculosis Association.

For several years a rather unique working relationship of which they were extremely proud had existed between these two. Once a week they jointly sponsored a local broadcast, "The Health Forum of the Air," as well as a column in the *Salem Evening News*. When the state legislature passed a law which required that cities pay a large sum annually for the upkeep and care of tuberculosis sanitariums, many municipalities fought it. However, Dr. Tracy recognized the necessity of such a law and aided in the appropriation of Salem city funds to the local tuberculosis association. In 1950, by involving the Community Fund and the Community Council, Dr. Tracy and Miss Schroder initiated a city-wide X-ray program. They hoped to use service organizations and several hundred lay people throughout Salem who had shown interest in a possible survey of the health problems of the community.

Just as in a play where stage movement becomes most meaningful when the characters have become real people to the audience, a description of each participant in the Salem self-study will make their activities more meaningful.

The thumbnail sketches which follow do not pretend to shed much light on the personalities of the self-study committee members. They do attempt to highlight pertinent facts which should enable the reader to comprehend more clearly their position in relation to other committee members and to the community as it engaged in health study. The committee might easily be divided into three groups. The first, consisting of Dr. Tracy, Miss Schroder, and Dr. Gage, initiated action, stimulated or made committee appointments, and perpetuated the action during the seven-month period.

Dr. Henry L. Tracy was a distinguished looking white-haired man in his late forties. A graduate of the unrecognized Middlesex Medical School, he earned his living before World War II as a podiatrist. During the war he served as a Navy pharmacist. Upon his return to Salem, Tracy renewed the pattern of his pre-service life. In time it was not unusual that he should run for membership on the Salem school board, a coveted elective office. Tracy's family had been active in politics for years. The parental home had been a haven and a resource for the successful and the hopeful, the fallen and the lost, the boss and the healer. Dr. Tracy's brother was the permanent city clerk of Salem and probably knew more than most people about the intricacies of formal and informal politics in and around Salem. In 1948 Henry Tracy applied for the position of health agent of the Salem board of health.

Dr. Tracy was a conscientious worker and had attempted, as well as his previous education and the several public health courses he took at Massachusetts Institute of Technology would allow, to improve his department by increasing slowly the size of his staff, broadening his interests in the health field, strengthening the relationships between private and public health organizations, and attaining a physical distance from "city hall" while preserving a social distance. It is important to recognize that the permanence of Tracy's job had been threatened by the state department of health which was attempting to help smaller Massachusetts communities provide better services by unification of several health boards under the helm of a qualified public health physician. The Union Health Plan, as this was known, indirectly eliminated the position of health agent. This development did not help to create a spirit of friendliness and *esprit de corps* between health agents and state workers.

An important problem which was seldom expressed verbally was the fact that Henry Tracy was one of the few Catholics in Salem working in an administrative capacity in the social welfare field. The old Yankee Protestants' zealously guarded historical interest in health and welfare organizations has always placed the occasional Catholic worker in a position which is numerically and socially inferior. Dr. Tracy had to contend with this problem when attempting to function effectively with other agencies.

Tracy, an opportunist in relation to the local department of health, saw the University of North Carolina's interest in Salem's health movement as the stimulus necessary to initiate the all-purpose health study necessary to secure some of the improvements he felt were necessary for adequate functioning of health agencies. The Board of Health of which he was agent consisted of three members appointed by the mayor, one of whom served as chairman. During the course of this study, Dr. Max Katzenstein held the chairmanship.

Dr. Tracy's position on the study committee could not help but reflect a composite of the relationships mentioned above—a complex of an Irish, Catholic, Democratic party allegiance, an insecurity of professional status and job, along with a lifelong, close acquaintanceship with the local political structure.

Miss Katherine Schroder was the executive secretary of the Salem Tuberculosis Association, a position she secured by advancing through the ranks from clerk. In her forty years of service dedicated to the care and rehabilitation of the tuberculous, she saw tuberculosis fall from its position as one of the most important causes of death in the United States to a position far down the scale. She had seen the T.B. Association's concern for the infected extend from the doling out of proper clothing to the poor in order to protect them from exposure as they sat out of doors for the winter cure, through establishing the later abolished summer camps as a treatment method, to providing sanatorium care and the rehabilitation programs of today. She had seen the Association change from an organization which once raised its own funds to a Community Fund agency which retained only the right to hold seal sales at Christmas. The shifting in Massachusetts of administrative officers from the community to the county, as well as the setting of higher educational requirements for directive personnel, represented a continuing threat to the permanence of the Salem association and its executive secretary. It had been suggested that the county assume rehabilitative functions and that all other services of the Association be shifted to the local health department. Such actions would dissolve the local office. Miss Schroder, recognizing the importance of such a move for the future of the national organization and without regard for the personal loss, had been instrumental in much of the planning.

Her day usually began at 7 A.M. and continued far into the small hours of the following day. Organizing clinics, making radio broadcasts, scheduling X-ray appointments, doing follow-ups on patients with arrested tuberculosis, paying a friendly, reassuring call on families whose loved ones had become afflicted and were fearful of the future constituted a crowded schedule. She had long since recognized the importance of family support and stability in the continuance of medical treatment in or out of the sanatorium. It was a source of amazement to the writer in journeying through the various levels of Salem society to note that there were few whom Miss Schroder had not touched. The local politician, the banker, the senator, the mill hand—all had seemingly known her touch when the disease was prevalent.

Miss Schroder's contributions to all health and welfare activities in Salem, her success in cooperative endeavors, her service to her church, and her complete unselfishness made her revered by all who knew her. The length of her service period had enabled her to acquire the friendship and loyalty of rich and poor, Yankee, Pole, French, and Irish.

Dr. Carlton Gage personified in person and in personality the prototype of the successful Unitarian minister. Dr. Gage automatically assumed a fairly high status within the community since he was pastor of the old First Church which figured so prominently in the history of Salem as far back as the witchcraft trials. Today membership in this church usually represents undoubted top-prestige status to those in the upper socio-economic classes. Dr. Gage attempted to fulfill his Christian responsibilities by participating in civic service on several levels and had bridged an important breach between the church and other community organizations. An intellectual, he had been instrumental in organizing a Great Books Club in the town. His social services were rewarded in 1952 when he was elected President of the Salem Community Council. As president he automatically became a member of the study committee.

The second group consisted of seven members, Colbert, Grogan, Carletno, Epley, Norwood, Patterson, Sutorius, who were appointed because of the organizations or interests they represented.

Once a year, three North Shore communities—Salem, Danvers, and Marblehead—united under the professional guidance of Joseph Colbert, executive director of the community fund association, to raise money for the support of health and welfare agencies. Mr. Colbert was one of the few individuals within the community who assumed a bird's-eye view of leadership and leadership potential as well as of welfare and economic programs. His metier made a working knowledge of community organization mandatory. In the everyday administration of the community fund, Joseph Colbert had to gather about him and shape recognized, influential leaders into board and chair members and fit young, potential aspirants to community leadership into various committee memberships. While membership in these associations did not improve his social prestige to any appreciable extent, they did enable him to work on familiar terms with the most important echelon of community leaders. His enthusiasm and drive gave him certain recognition in several local service organizations, one of them the Rotary Club. Colbert had remained in Salem longer than both his ability and the precedent established by fund directors indicated. Observation and rumor attested the director's interest in bettering both his economic and social status. On several occasions local industry beckoned and at least one vied for his services. A domineering, aggressive man and acknowledged leader, he encouraged the University of North Carolina staff to use Salem as a research center. Colbert was appointed to the committee because of his participation at the early meeting and because of the possibility that the Community Fund might be a source of future financial aid for some segments of the study.

Peter Grogan, executive secretary of the Chamber of Commerce, was asked to participate in the self-study as a result of the interest he showed in the study at community council meetings. Grogan was a relative newcomer to the community and had previously participated in a health study in a small town south of Boston. His activities in the two years spent in Salem before the self-study had been confined to the Chamber of Commerce and to the Knights of Columbus in his local parish. Grogan had made neither a particularly favorable nor particularly unfavorable impression upon community council members. His work, which in essence was public relations, had nurtured a spirit of competition between himself and the director of the Community Fund, Mr. Colbert, whose job was similar.

Paul Carletno was superintendent of education in Salem. An Italian Catholic with an educational background in business law, he represented a compromise candidate for the superintendent's position after the Protestant and Catholic segments of the community split over the appointment of a Protestant superintendent. When the position became open, there was a general feeling that a Catholic should be appointed since 80 percent of the population was Catholic. Despite this, a Protestant from outside the community was brought in to fill the vacancy. Carletno was assistant to the controversial candidate for the short time he held the office, and after Carletno became school superintendent he continued the superior educational plan which his predecessor instituted. He was known as an ardent, sincere worker who, attempting to overcome the almost unsurmountable odds of his having obtained the position during a tense religious conflict, had to deal through a popularly elected school board and with a city council which firmly grasped the purse strings. Carletno was placed on the study committee because of his interest in school health and because a representative of the school department might prove to be valuable during the course of the proposed investigation.

Elliott Epley was treasurer of the *North Shore Evening News,* a daily paper which was distributed along the North Shore area above Boston. Mr. Epley, who had spent a lengthy period in the U.S. Army, wrote a column, often from the white sunny sands of a Miami beach, on national political outlook. The *News* stayed shy of controversial material on local issues and was known as the only paper of its size in Massachusetts without an openly stated editorial policy. Mr. Epley was invited to participate in the self-study in order to assure adequate favorable publicity on the study procedure and findings.

Marvin Norwood might boast of birth within the Commonwealth but not within the confines of the Salem community. Brought to Salem in 1950 to assume the lay administrative duties of the Salem Hospital, Norwood quietly assumed his duties and carefully refrained from forming hasty associations with the multitudinous agencies and organizations within the city which begged his attention. Although, because of his position, he was an automatic member of the Salem Community Council, he had never participated before his appointment to the self-study committee beyond the token gesture of paying annual dues. His position at so important an institution in the organized health structure of Salem as the hospital made his membership on the committee desirable although his ability to contribute was untried.

Mrs. Patterson was the wife of Dr. Donald R. Patterson, chief of the urological service at Salem Hospital. A young civic leader, her interest in social services, other than those connected with the hospital, had been directed toward aid to children. She was president of the North Shore Children's Friend Society and an active member of the North Shore Society for the Prevention of Cruelty to Children and the Salem Community Council. Her value as an active participant in the above programs was augmented by her position as a society leader. This fact made it possible for the upper socioeconomic levels of Salem society to be drawn into community service as well as for an avenue to be established by which information might be disseminated to that group. For these reasons it was felt that Mrs. Patterson would be a valuable member of the study team.

James Sutorius was a young Salem attorney of Italian descent. Representing one of the lowest ranking ethnic groups in the community, Mr. Sutorius ran for political office in the Salem City Council and was the first Italian to be elected to that position. In order to limit the possibilities of failure encountered by other communities which had engaged in self-study and neglected to defer to the local political unit, it was felt important to appoint a representative of the

Salem city government to the committee. James Sutorius' connection with one of the best law firms in the community and his suave, intelligent attitude toward city council activities in the past automatically assured his appointment.

The third group consisted of the four physicians who completed the professional representation. Each, however, differed from the other in training, understanding, and temper.

Dr. Max Katzenstein was on the staff of Salem Hospital, a practicing physician in the community, and chairman of the Salem board of health. He grew up in Salem, attended Salem High School and chalked up an imposing record on the football field. After receiving his medical training, he returned to Salem about the same time his employee, Dr. Henry Tracy, the health agent, returned from Middlesex.

Dr. Katzenstein had participated in sufficient community activities in which he was interested to be selected, on occasion, by social welfare organizations to act as liaison agent between a new program and the medical profession. While he had served willingly he had not served effectively. After participating in organizational meetings, he seldom, if ever, would even attempt to approach his professional colleagues for support. His position as a Jew might have been responsible, since it was a matter of record that careful consideration had been given to all minority appointments into the closed and sacrosanct confederacy of the staff or administration at the Salem Hospital. Each appointment, physician or trustee, had been made purposefully. It was likely that such deliberation did not encourage unrestricted intercourse between the elite and those below them on matters which might not have reached a state of complete professional acceptability. Although Dr. Katzenstein was often reluctant to demonstrate it, his interest in public health and his position as a member of a minority group gave him a more temperate attitude toward social programs and community activities than that of most of his professional colleagues.

When Drs. Carlton Gage and Henry Tracy, as president of the community council and chairman of the council's health committee, were selecting members for the self-survey committee they thought that by selecting a physician who would represent the medical profession, professional approval might be won. After they had mentioned the candidates, they decided that they could not make a final decision without first approaching the gentleman who was the recognized leader of the Salem medical profession, Dr. Stewart Phills, then president of the staff at Salem Hospital. Dr. Tracy was commissioned to ask Dr. Phills's advice, and the appointment of Dr. Joseph Bradshaw resulted. This action represented a clear-cut example of clearance with a recognized top-level leader.

Dr. Bradshaw, a tall man in his late fifties, who was a leading Catholic layman, was general spokesman for the profession in the fight against "socialized medicine." He was the proud father of nine children. He was a surgeon with a general office practice and was head of the Cancer Clinic at Salem Hospital. Throughout the year in which the community was under close scrutiny, Dr. Bradshaw's name appeared frequently in the local newspapers as a result of his work on the State Medical Society's "protective" legislative committee in Boston or an address to a local organization against the evils of an amoebic, grasping "Leviathan," free medicine, which reached out to clutch and bind a "holy" service. He was, in truth, the protagonist, par excellence, of the self-study committee. His interest in safeguarding the profession against "unauthorized" encroachment predicted from the beginning a few interesting moments at committee meetings.

Dr. Margaret Lassiter was an 84-year old retired public health physician. After several years of practice as one of the first women physicians in Salem, Dr. Lassiter was invited to participate in the venereal disease program for World War I servicemen. With this entree into public health she developed an interest in cancer control and worked for the Massachusetts State Department of Health in that field for many years. The New York State Chapter of the American Cancer

Society requested Dr. Lassiter's services when it set up a similar program. Returning to Salem in retirement, she actively participated in the community council and became its president in 1949. Dr. Lassiter was known as an outstanding Unitarian laywoman and a zealous worker in the League of Women Voters. Her approach to the solution of community health problems differed from those of her professional colleagues and undoubtedly had been tempered and broadened by her years of experience in public health. Dr. Lassiter's advanced age and previous state and community contributions tended to protect her from open censure by conservative groups within the community.

Dr. Pauline Sims had been a psychiatrist for the State Department of Mental Health for some twenty years in charge of the outpatient department of Danvers State Hospital located in Danvers, Massachusetts. During that time she devoted one morning a week for nine months of the year to conducting an area child guidance clinic for disturbed children in Salem, the only service of its kind offered in the community. Dr. Sims, a member of the Salem Community Council, took no other active part in Salem activities since she maintained a home in Danvers. The clinic, staffed by Dr. Sims, a psychologist, and a social worker, could not minister to all in need nor do any intensive work in Salem because of the limited time they spent there. Since there was a continuous need in this area, Dr. Gage and Dr. Tracy placed on the committee a person qualified to study that need.

The study committee of 14 described above consisted, therefore, of four physicians (one of whom was a psychiatrist and one of whom was retired), a minister, an educator, a hospital administrator, a politician, a health educator or worker, a society woman, a newspaper man, a public health agent, and two public relations men or community organizers (one the executive secretary of the Chamber of Commerce and the other the director of the Community Fund). Ten were members of the Community Council; two of them had been president and four others had held some office in that organization. Seven committee members were connected with organizations or programs which received community fund support, and five more had actively participated in the fund campaign. Three members were on the payroll of the Salem city government. Out of 14, seven members could have been considered workers in the field of health on several levels—government, private health agency, general medical practice, and hospital care.

In Salem, as in every community, a variety of factors separately or in combination, gave some persons more prestige than others. We have mentioned identification with a specific church, marriage into an established family, membership in a racial or national group as measures of social status. Five committee members, Tracy, Bradshaw, Carletno, Grogan, and Sutorius were Roman Catholics. Dr. Katzenstein was the one Jew on the committee. The rest were Protestants. Representing the national groups in Salem, three members were Irish and one Italian; there were no Poles or French Canadians. While the study was limited specifically to Salem, four members, though working there, lived outside the political boundaries. Mr. Epley lived in Swampscott, Mr. Colbert and Dr. Sims resided in Danvers, and Mr. Norwood commuted from Malden. The variations in status and rank in Salem society, as affected by ethnic divisions and other accompaniments of community life such as residency and associational affiliation briefly mentioned above, could not help but reflect on committee interaction. A digression at this point in our discussion to consider briefly the ranking system in Salem at the time of the study will facilitate the analysis which will be made of committee activities.

Along the rugged New England coastline, hovering close to the shore, may be seen the brilliantly colored lobster markers floating and bobbing with the tides. Each is painted a specific design and color to represent family ownership. Every marker helps to form a varicolored mosaic of differentiation across the water. So, too, the life of each member of the self-study committee was a small marker of differentiation with that difference fitting into the larger status configuration that is Salem. The full attention which this study of necessity tends to give to the individuals of the study committee is not, of course, commensurate with the importance of their position in the total community structure. The antiquity of social inequality in Salem is a matter of written record, and recognition of its ubiquity must be effected by placing committee members in their appropriate positions.

The problems posed by the contemporary question of whether American society consists of relatively distinctive social classes or of a legion of overlapping social positions were not investigated. It seemed sufficient to recognize that all known societies have some system of ranking their members and groups along some kind of superiority-inferiority scale. The depth of analysis of many of the social class studies in which respondents have been requested to identify themselves or others with one of a number of classes and in which data have been gathered on personal income, family background, occupational prestige, dwelling unit and residential area, in an effort to reveal the pattern of social class structure, would have been far too time consuming and costly for this research. Throughout the field work period informants from the various income and occupational groups were questioned concerning the general class structure of Salem and the position of those men and women whose activities had become our major interest. We acknowledge the limitations of this procedure but likewise assert that the picture of Salem's class structure derived through careful observation, the subjective determination of classes, and the ultimate placement of community members within this framework seemed to produce an adequate backdrop for our analysis. We believe that power structure makes the class structure backdrop operative.

There were visibly three social classes, all dependent and interdependent. To determine which was the most important was impossible, for time had proved the ability of each to function successfully. The length and importance of Salem history had divided the smallest of the three classes, the upper, into "old" families who had had and retained social position for several generations with or without the comforting assurance of wealth and "new" families who had recently climbed into the upper stratum, usually by means of their financial position. "Old" families in Salem, similarly observed by Warner in the Yankee City study which provided scores of helpful suggestions to us,[1] had a relatively secure, judiciously guarded place in the social structure above the "new" families. Mobility between the two segments of the upper class was fairly rigid and had depended upon a well-developed system of deference. With the decline and death of many distinguished families, friendships and even marriage with some select "new" comers had become a necessity if the top stratum was to maintain a degree of stability.

Next in size came the middle class, less wealthy, prominent but prestigeless, active civic servers whom we might characterize as the workers, ever alert for opportunities of association with or service to the upper class. Here one might find a continuum of acceptance. Individuals of ethnic or religious groups who had recently acquired professional prestige or wealth ranked lower on the ladder or continuum. The upper limits consisted of the professional man, the businessman, the civic leader who owed deference to those above. Below, and largest of all the units, were the skilled workers, small shopkeepers, and clerks. These were reported to belong to "nice families" but were not ranked high socially. Recognition, which on the upper stratum came from wider and ever wider circles, emanated on this level from those close to the individual in organizations such as the church.

Below this large and numerically imposing group came the lower class, consisting first of unskilled laborers, closely knit in time-worn housing units about the mill, in "Blubber Hollow" around the tanneries, or near the harbor about Derby Wharf; and second, ranking below them, the least

1. W. Lloyd Warner and Paul S. Lunt, *The Social Life of a Modern Community* (New Haven: Yale University Press, 1941), pp. 86-87, 93.

fortunate members of the community, a high percentage of them on relief, all poorly housed, over-crowded, often the scapegoat of those immediately above them.

Each of the classes as a functioning unit was supported and maintained by social organizations which aid it. Some had latent functions which far outweighed those that were manifest. For example, the Woman's Friend Society, a formal organization paralleling the less formal sewing circles already described, was organized over one hundred years ago to provide a comfortable, respectable home for working women. The society which ran it had been recognized as a socially elite group. For many years a woman who became its president was assumed to have reached the ultimate in social position. Many years ago the Society assumed the support of the Visiting Nurses Association.

Because much nursing time is spent in French Canadian and Polish homes, the nursing supervisor requested that representatives of these groups be invited to society membership. In retelling the incident one of the members added: "Naturally we refused. It is true that the French and Poles are becoming educated and probably will some day secure membership. However, we told Miss Cutler (the nursing supervisor) that we would not hear of such action at this time. It will just have to wait until we die."

As stated earlier, the House of Seven Gables was operated as a tearoom for the benefit of a settlement house for Polish children. The tearoom, in turn, provided a charming afternoon meeting place for society and club women in Salem. Catering to middle and lower classes were some of the service clubs, veterans' organizations, and national fraternities (French-Canadian, Italian, and Polish). Often their reasons for exclusion were just as decisive as those of the upper class. The French Catholic Church bound its members into an exclusive whole to the very pointed and almost absolute exclusion of outsiders through the preservation of the French-Canadian dialect in church, school, and other organizations.

All of the 16 Protestant churches or sects in Salem are class stratified. Class differentiation enables the Protestant community of approximately six thousand to maintain two Baptist, two Methodist, two Congregational, two Episcopal, and two Unitarian churches. The First Church Unitarian, Dr. Gage's ministry, is recognized as the church of the elite. One of the Episcopal churches was considered a "climbers'" and "new" families' church. There was much evidence of membership transfer between churches as an individual's or family's position and prestige increased.

Each of the three classes overlapped. Mobility between upper and middle was much more limited than between middle and lower classes. The self-study which we were observing was affected by the system outlined above. Where then did each of the participants fit?

Indications of the class in which these men and women were located may be determined by noting their background, organizational membership, and recognized indexes such as occupation, source of income, and dwelling area.

Not one of the 14 committee members could claim kinship with the "old" families of shippers and bankers. Mr. Epley was the nephew of a man who accumulated a considerable fortune and owned the *North Shore Evening News*. The gentleman's death had placed him and other relatives in competition but had bestowed upon each a fair degree of wealth. Epley had not attempted, to any serious degree, to break into Salem society but had adopted a neighboring community, Swampscott, as his residence and area of social participation.

All but two of the committee members were professionals if we use the term loosely—four were physicians, one was a lawyer, one a minister, one an educator, and five were secretaries or directors of social agencies. Although Mr. Epley wrote editorials for the *North Shore Evening News,* his primary concern was with the management of the paper as its treasurer. We, therefore, classify him as a businessman.

Mrs. Donald Patterson, as the wife of a staff member of Salem Hospital, was known as a society matron in the lower upper stratum who participated freely but selectively in many civic endeavors.

Two of the physicians, Drs. Bradshaw and Katzenstein, apparently had lucrative practices and were considered self-employed. Mr. Epley's source of income was both inherited (but "new," nevertheless) and earned. His earnings were known to be considerable. With the exception of Dr. Lassiter, who had a state retirement pension, and Mrs. Patterson, the other committee members were all salaried and found it necessary to work full eight hour schedules without interludes of golf or yachting—recreational activities reserved by custom for those above them in social rank.

Dwelling area is often indicative of social status and class. Ecologically Salem may be divided into the French-Canadian, Polish, Irish, and Italian areas with several heterogeneous fringe sections. These areas were recognized by Salemites and, over the years, had been stigmatized, as suggested earlier, by such identification as "Derby-Town," "Polack-Town," and "Blubber Hollow."

Near the center of the town, edged by the Italian section and pressed by the business district, lay a residential area of extreme social value, as indicated earlier, known as Chestnut Street. Because of its strategic position in Salem affairs, we shall here reemphasize its importance. Chestnut Street consisted of several small blocks, lined with beautiful old Federal style houses stretched along tree-rich, brick walks. Built by the old sea captains and their financiers as a monument to their ingenuity, the elite have continued to live there for over a century and a half. With the pressure of land, many "new" families have built in desirable suburbs in neighboring communities. There is little doubt that the attitudes implied in the term "Chestnut Street" extend beyond its physical bounds to the shores of Marblehead and Swampscott.

Only one member of the committee resided on Chestnut Street—Dr. Carlton Gage. The First Church Unitarian long ago was "willed" a fine Chestnut Street residence as its parsonage. Automatically, each pastor of the Church assumed with the dwelling a position in relation to, but certainly not on a par with, the upper class to which he ministers.

Dr. Bradshaw and Mrs. Patterson lived one block north of Chestnut Street in houses which were considered large and in keeping with the architectural standards of the community. Many of the large homes on this Street (Essex Street) had been purchased by physicians as old families died or found the large houses impossible to maintain. The street had evidenced a change, as the doctors' shingles boldly evidenced, of being converted to "physicians' row." Dr. Lassiter lived nearby on Federal Street, one time rival of Chestnut, in an apartment. At least three of the participants rented homes. Epley lived in a large, beautiful, modern home on what one might casually refer to as "Chestnut Street Annex" in Swampscott. Norwood, Colbert, and Sims lived out-of-town in respectable middle-class units.

The importance of ethnic group differences as well as religious differences could not be minimized in the light of their significance in historical development. By maximizing group differences, community leaders—business and political—have been able to exert a powerful control. Four of the committee were of Anglo-Saxon background: Lassiter, Epley, Patterson, and Norwood; two members were of Italian extraction—Sutorius and Carletno; three were of Irish descent—Grogan, Bradshaw, and Tracy; one was of German extraction—Schroder; one was of English-German extraction—Gage; and the other three were of heterogeneous stock. Five committee members, as previously stated, embraced the Roman Catholic faith. Two were members of the famed and socially elite First Church Unitarian: Lassiter and Gage (although Dr. Lassiter frequently visited and served a Unitarian Church in Boston). Miss Schroder was an ardent worker in the Wesley Methodist Church which is an upper-lower- and lower-middle-class church. Dr. and Mrs. Patterson held membership in the lower-upper Episcopal Church. Dr. Katzenstein was a member of the Jewish Congregation of Temple Schalom. Mr. Norwood, Mr. Colbert, Mr. Epley, and Dr. Sims were members of Protestant churches in neighboring communities. It was interesting to note that a Congregational minister in Salem once remarked that over half of his congregation passed the doors of at least two other Congregational churches between their homes and his church!

The educational backgrounds of the committee were also revealing. Only one member, Miss Schroder, had not attended college. Nine members had done postgraduate work in either medicine, law, education, or administration. The facts attested the professional character of the group.

With the exception of Dr. Lassiter, Mrs. Patterson, Mr. Epley, and Dr. Gage, none of the members of the committee belonged to social prestige organizations. However, almost everyone except Dr. Sims, who could not be considered a member of the community, had very real contact in the form of their executive board members, patients, or through service or civic organizations with the upper stratum of Salem society and the top policy makers.

The facts indicated that the committee was a working committee consisting of middle-class professionals who both helped to formulate policy and carry it out. Always, contact existed between top leaders, society matrons, and the committee. We do not assume here an interest by the top levels of community leadership in the self-study—merely the existence of structural connections which could act as functional avenues if movement on a broad front became important.

The self-study committee appointments and activities which took place in the fall and spring of 1952-1953 were preceded by two meetings in April and May, 1952, between selected Community Council members and staff from the Institute for Research in Social Science at the University of North Carolina. In March, 1952, after the receipt of the letter of inquiry from the University, Joseph Colbert of the Community Fund, aware of the interest of the temporary health committee through his membership in the Community

Council, responded positively to the question as to whether or not there was a health movement in Salem.

On April 18 and May 20, persons representing the Board of Health, the Tuberculosis Association, local courts, State Department of Mental Health, Salem Hospital, Visiting Nurse Association, Chamber of Commerce, Woman's Friend Society, federal and local government, Society for the Prevention of Cruelty to Children, and the Boy Scouts met with the University staff members. Representation from the school department or board was noticeably lacking. Several participants at these early meetings were later to become members of the self-study committee: Dr. Carlton Gage, Dr. Henry L. Tracy, Dr. Max Katzenstein, Peter Grogan, Dr. Pauline Sims, and Miss Katherine Schroder.

At the two meetings discussions took place concerning the mutual expectations of Salem and the research team if the project located in the community; the meaning of the term, "self-study"; the role of the University of North Carolina staff; and the health problems recognized at that time. Interpretation of the University's role was difficult, and there was constant need for interpretation terminating only at the time of final withdrawal from the community in June, 1953.

Essentially, in an effort to observe and record decision making, plan formulation, and the initiation of action programs carried out to meet health problems, our staff determined to maintain a passive role. While we committed ourselves at the two meetings to answer any question directed specifically to us, we did not wish to assume a directional or resource role. Paramount was the desire to observe deliberately the process itself, by itself, without the directional or activational effect which our staff might nurture and which might distort what would have otherwise occurred within the community. On May 26, 1952, after extending an invitation to the University staff to use Salem as the locus of its study, the Salem Community Council, at its monthly luncheon meeting, went on record as the sponsoring agency of the self-study.

The commitment of the Community Council in the self-study process was followed by almost three and a half months of dormancy. During the summer an exodus to the rock-bound shores of famed Marblehead, the sands of Ipswich, or the inland hills and mountains of northern states impeded much community activity. Civic intercourse had to wait until after the Labor Day holidays. Quiescence in the self-study process finally ended early in September when a series of informal meetings took place, committee members were appointed, and committee activities began. A running account of the high lights of the events are pertinent.

Early in the week of September first, Dr. Henry Tracy called Miss Katherine Schroder to discuss the steps necessary to launch the enterprise. A contemplated use of the lists of names of participants in the successful tuberculosis survey and the organization of a central steering committee were considered. Several new members were suggested, such as Dr. Joseph Bradshaw, associate visiting surgeon at Salem Hospital, who was discussed above; Dr. William A. Stribling, who had once been associated with the Marblehead Board of Health; Dr. Frank Duffy, a socialite osteopath who was on the State Board of Registration for the medical society and an active Rotarian who had stimulated that organization to an interest in health programs; Thomas Barrow, treasurer of Jack Brothers, manufacturers of games, and president of the Salem Tuberculosis Association; Joseph Colbert of the Community Fund Association who had been active in the initial contacts with the University of North Carolina; Peter Grogan, secretary of the Chamber of Commerce; and Miss Jean Cutler, of the Visiting Nurse Association which was co-sponsored by the Woman's Friend Society and the Community Fund.

In an effort to gain a full perspective and to provoke as many questions on "proper" procedure as possible, the health agent and tuberculosis worker went to Quincy, Massachusetts, for a visit with a health educator. The latter had participated in a self-study program which had been written up by the

Health Information Foundation of New York and widely distributed in bulletin form. Dr. Tracy and Miss Schroder questioned the worker and found that in many respects people in Salem worked together much better than those in Quincy, regardless of the information that had been published in respect to the latter community. It was also the opinion of the Salem visitors that the whole program which had developed in Quincy was being held together by one person, the health educator, and if or when that person stepped out of the picture everything which had been accomplished would collapse.

Judging from the results of Quincy's experiment, it was felt important to have as many individuals as possible participate in the Salem Study. On Tuesday, September 9, 1952, Dr. Tracy and Miss Schroder met to consider organizational procedure. They decided to call a meeting of a central committee consisting of Dr. Carlton Gage, president of the Salem Community Council, Dr. Joseph Bradshaw, and Dr. Max Katzenstein, and to aim at "grass-roots" participation. Dr. Tracy was undecided about extending an invitation to Dr. Katzenstein and expressed apprehension concerning the contribution his superior might make as well as some resentment toward the latter for his criticism, at a previous meeting, of the accomplishments of the health department.

In an attempt to involve the grass-roots level, Miss Schroder suggested that it might be possible to utilize the health and/or welfare committees of the men's and women's service organizations, e.g., Rotary, Lions, Chamber of Commerce, Zonta, and perhaps the adult playground groups which operate in the summer. Since these committees had done little more than call in speakers or give medical supplies to the needy, it was felt that they might welcome a more active program.

Much emphasis was placed in the discussion on the ways and means of securing a working group which would be representative of every religious and ethnic unit in the community. Miss Schroder questioned the representativeness of the health committees of the Rotary, Lions, and Chamber, and wondered if perhaps, by using these organizations, the committee might tend to tap the upper socio-economic levels—people whom she felt did not represent different religious or national groups. This was discussed at length, and it was decided that most of these groups were quite consciously representative in order to appeal to and secure support from the various groupings within the community.

Dr. Tracy was instructed to contact and to find out how the presidents of the various service organizations felt about active participation in the health study. It was hoped that the presidents, as well as the chairmen of the various health and welfare committees of these organizations, would attend the proposed central committee meeting on September 23.

The intended meeting did not take place. During the week of September 14 the health agent visited and secured the cooperation of the secretary of the Chamber of Commerce. He then contacted Joseph Colbert of the Community Fund who volunteered to send a letter calling a committee meeting of those designated and to sign the name of Carlton Gage, president of the Community Council.

That evening, upon his arrival home, Dr. Tracy found a message to call Colbert. When reached, Colbert firmly suggested that it would not be advantageous at that time to call a meeting such as Dr. Tracy had planned. The director of the Community Fund felt that nothing ought to be done until Mr. Hunter of the University staff came to the community and expressed his feelings concerning the best method of procedure. This lack of understanding of the role assumed by the University of North Carolina and the possible delay in the study process disturbed Dr. Tracy.

Because the role played by the University staff had been interpreted to Mr. Colbert several times, it seemed improbable that he had misunderstood. It seemed much more likely that the annual community fund drive, which was about to begin, might have been of greater significance. Not only did the drive involve Mr. Colbert's time but, of necessity, required the services of representatives of the various service organizations. It is not unlikely that Colbert might have attempted judiciously to withhold groups that he was so dependent upon from additional commitment to the self-study activity.

Mr. Hunter's visit to the community on September 22 clarified again for Colbert the role of the staff. In defending the delay, Colbert said he felt that Dr. Tracy and Miss Schroder were attempting to run the study when actually the Community Council had selected a committee to undertake that job. When he was told that the two people in question were the committee, he rescinded his statement and spoke at length on the fallaciousness of involving people from various organizations who had little or no understanding of the health situation. Utilizing a technique of good community organization, he emphasized the importance of not by-passing the Community Council in the plan-making process. Colbert discussed procedure with the health agent by phone and asked the latter to prepare a report on self-study proposals for the next Community Council meeting—a request which seemed to be without authority.

On September 23, 1952, Mr. Hunter and Mrs. Schaffer went to see Dr. Carlton Gage at the First Church office to reinterpret to him, as president of the Community Council, the position of the staff in the community. At that time Dr. Gage inquired whether we knew why the meeting which was scheduled to be held on the twenty-second was postponed. When told that Mr. Colbert felt the delay advisable, Dr. Gage questioned Mr. Colbert's authority. The lack of understanding and the conflict which resulted seemed to stem from an attempt of the participants to define their roles in the study.

At the monthly Community Council luncheon meeting on September 29 the process progressed further. Dr. Tracy redefined the University staff's role and steps were taken to enlarge the study committee. Dr. Tracy described the staff's role to the group in part by saying: "They are here to see how a democratic city solves its problems in a *democratic* way." In response Peter Grogan, secretary of the Chamber of Commerce quipped: "You mean non-politically?" and then, amid laughter, he proceeded to assert that the Community Council ought to emphasize specifically the self-study as its one big important project. Officiating in his capacity as president, Dr. Gage promised he would get together with Dr. Tracy to select additional supplementary committee members. Meanwhile the following were temporarily named to the roster: Dr. Margaret Lassiter, Peter Grogan, Father Doolan, and Mrs. Donald R. Patterson.

Several days later Drs. Gage and Tracy met to expand the membership of the Health Committee to a size and composition which would make a self-study possible and effective. Utilizing their knowledge of the functioning of those segments of the community usually involved in the type of action anticipated, they expanded the committee from 6 members to 15. The aims of the latter expansion were threefold: (1) to include representatives of the community's health professions and organizations; (2) to secure individuals who would not only represent certain segments of the population but who would shoulder the work involved in a comprehensive study; and (3) to secure representatives of organizations whose cooperation would ultimately be necessary for the successful implementation of any recommendations that might be forthcoming.

The committee finally consisted of the persons previously identified in the biographical sketches. In addition Father Doolan, director of the North Shore Catholic Charities, was included. Father Doolan found it impossible to attend meetings of the committee and was dropped from membership, reducing the committee to 14 members.

The skills and techniques utilized to reach a level of accomplishment may differ from city to city and from organization to organization. The complexity of selecting a committee was transcended by the process of molding the usually heterogeneous group into a functioning unit. From this point, utilizing the wealth of information we had gathered on leadership, power, decision making, etc., as an analytical guide, our focus was directed to the dynamics of committee interaction.

CHAPTER 9

The Self-study Committee Goes to Work

BETWEEN October 8, 1952, and March 27, 1953, the self-study committee met 13 times to deliberate, study, and act. At no time was every member present at a meeting. Attendance for three meetings was as low as five, but nine meetings had an attendance of seven or better. Of the 14 people who attended the committee meetings eight were present at more than half. Four members were conspicuous by their numerous absences.

From early fall through December, Joseph Colbert was involved in the arduous task of supervising the community fund drive. During that time he attended only one meeting out of seven. After the new year began, he missed two out of six. Paul Carletno attended regularly until the Christmas holidays. Pressure of the preparation of the school budget and the political problems involved in a public school health program run by the school department versus a parochial school health program maintained by the health department —a program which was studied by the committee—may have made his attendance difficult.

James Sutorius, appointed on October 23, attended only three of the ten meetings which followed the October date. After assuring the committee that he would support any recommendations which might reach the city council's ear, he considered his job completed and attended only enough meetings to reassure the committee of his continued support.

Elliott Epley attended four meetings out of 13. During the fall months preceding the presidential election of 1952 Mr. Epley felt the pressure of Republican duty. Because he was "pushing the elephant" at meeting after meeting, he was unable to attend many of the fall sessions of the committee. In December he migrated, as was his custom during the winter months, to the shores of Florida. Attendance was then impossible.

During the period under examination three sub-committees evolved. Two were appointed to process some of the work of the larger committee, and the third grew informally to satisfy special needs. The first of the three committees was appointed on October 23 to determine what techniques in the form of questionnaires or schedules would be used. This committee, consisting of Miss Schroder, Dr. Gage, and Dr. Tracy met once for an hour and a half.

The second committee appointed by the surveyors was asked to write a report on the findings and recommendations of the study. The complexity of the work necessitated four meetings of the committee consisting of Dr. Tracy, Miss Schroder, Mr. Grogan, Mr. Norwood, and Mr. Sutorius. The first three attended every meeting, Mr. Norwood attended three, and Mr. Sutorius, one.

We have discussed in some detail the 40 men and women in Salem who were found to rank high as a group in the decision-making processes involved in community living. Recognizing that these leaders represent many areas—civic, business, church, political, etc.—we see that this range of interests automatically placed the 40 on different levels or ranks in the power system. Some were not top decision makers, but because of their professional esteem or their close association with the venerated, they assisted in the planning and aided in forging decision. Four, representing the latter group, on the list of 40 were members of the self-study committee. These were Paul Carletno, Dr. Margaret Lassiter, Dr. Carlton Gage, and Joseph Colbert. All could have been considered professionals in the loose sense of the word, and all were in a position to indicate discrepancies between levels and standards in social welfare programs. As superintendent of education, physician, clergyman, and professional community organizer they filled certain fixed positions in community life. The major expectation of these positions was program planning. Two out of the four made the list of top ten leaders in the community—Dr. Carlton Gage and Joseph Colbert. The relatively high social position which has traditionally been awarded the minister of First Church for generations, as well as his participation in civic betterment which is expected of a Unitarian churchman, would result in a high-level prestige rank although actual high-level decision making might have been limited. Mr. Colbert, as director of the Community Fund, might have been expected to exert considerable influence on decision making. All of the top leaders had worked closely with him in fund campaigns and recognized his ability as a policy decision maker in his own specific area. The inclusion of the four leaders on the self-study committee represented an observable link with the top level of power in the community.

When the University staff entered Salem in June, 1952, a health committee of two, with Dr. Henry Tracy as recognized chairman, existed. This committee represented the base from which supplementary action would emanate. It might be inferred, therefore, that Tracy would assume the same position in the expanded Community Council committee. From early summer to fall he emphasized to members of the University staff that he did not wish to assume the role of chairman. After things began to happen, he wished to "take a back seat."

Tracy explained his attitude in terms of his position as health agent of the board of health. Much that he visualized as problem areas centered in and around health areas which were the city government's responsibility. As its agent, he felt he would not be as free to criticize and make recommendations as someone working from outside the political structure. In the informal meetings which took place between the health agent and Miss Schroder or Dr. Gage, he again and again reiterated his feelings. When he met with Dr. Gage on October first to expand committee membership, he suggested that Robert Purcell, a retired Boston banker, who previously had been lay chairman of the tuberculosis survey and had directed Red Cross campaigns, be made chairman.

Dr. Gage was unreceptive to the suggestions since he knew Mr. Purcell intimately as a member of the First Church and believed that Purcell's health would be impaired by undertaking such strenuous work. Mr. Purcell was along in years and Dr. Gage felt that the chairman ought to be a member of the Community Council and should be someone who could not only direct the study but implement recommendations over a period of years. It might not be possible for Mr. Purcell to fulfill the latter requirement. Likewise, Mr. Purcell did not always have initiative, although he was able to perform aptly and intelligently an assigned task.

Thwarted in his attempt to suggest an alternative, Tracy assumed the chairmanship urged on him by Dr. Gage "only until one could be elected from the study committee."

The initial meetings of the committee were chaired by the health agent. On November 17, 1952, after five meetings of the study group and after numerous informal comments from time to time concerning his reticence to remain at the helm, Tracy finally acknowledged the permanence of his position as chairman. Questioned by the field worker as to whether he intended to remain as chairman of the group he said, "Well, it looks as if I'm going to have to. I wanted to stay in the background and that's why I haven't made a move concerning agenda, but I guess if I'm going to be chairman I'll have to work that out."

The decision had at last been made. Probably psychological reasons, related to the insecurity of his position, made it difficult for the health agent to release the reins. More pronounced was the fact that the initiative and push in getting the study started and enlisting the interest of the participants must be attributed to Tracy. It is improbable that study activities would have begun or continued without his and Miss Schroder's continuous efforts. While on occasion dominant leadership was noted among the group, none was persistent enough to indicate an interest in the permanent chairmanship with its multiplicity of administrative duties.

Einstein and Infeld once said: "The formulation of a problem is often more essential than its solution." They might have added, "and often more *difficult*," as the early meetings of the study committee indicated.

Basically there was little understanding of the job which was to be done. Not even the health agent knew what a self-study was. He did, however, know what he wished it to accomplish and tended to direct interest and activities in that direction. It may be remembered that even before the staff of the University of North Carolina entered the community Tracy stated that he desired a community health center, an incinerator, and additional staff in his department.

The level of discussion in the meetings which followed was professionally unsophisticated but revealing because of the problems considered. The interest of the group fluctuated. It would be satisfying and very "American" in the popular sense to describe the complete dedication of the group to the task at hand. It would be equally hypocritical.

With vested interests and the hope of being able to secure financial and psychological help in doing a better job, both Dr. Tracy and Miss Schroder were perhaps the most devoted members and sacrificed the most in time, effort, push, and enthusiasm. Dr. Lassiter's interest was a rational and continued one supported by her many efforts both in an administrative capacity and as an arbitrator between the physicians and the committee as a whole. Mrs. Patterson and Mr. Norwood, in part, contributed out of their basic interest in the effect the study might have on particular social agencies of paramount importance to them. Carletno's interest throughout the fall was reflected by his continuous referral to school programs.

Grogan and Colbert participated, one more liberally than the other, because their positions as community organizers dictated a certain amount of such participation. Colbert's name, particularly, may be found on most community-wide committees and civic activities. Men like Sutorius and Epley were continuously being invited to committee membership because of the services they could bestow as a result of their singularly influential positions.

With the exception of the physicians, who represented a specific type of member selection due to the nature of the study, most of the committee did not aspire to make a vast exploration of health problems nor did they feel a burning interest in the subject. In truth, they probably would have shown just as much or just as little enthusiasm if they had been considering a drive to increase the number of foreign films being shown in the local cinema houses or the need for additional modern school plants.

Although the degree of group "we-ness" increased as the study proceeded, the temporary nature of the work deterred much individual interest. The importance of the group aim never truly overcame this lack of individual interest.

The atmosphere of the group process was informal and both permissive and inhibitive, cooperative and competitive, friendly and hostile. Most of the members knew each other from previous association. With the exception of Dr. Sims and Dr. Lassiter (in deference to their position and age), all of the participants called each other by their first names. This increased the informality of the discussion.

There appeared to be a definite pattern of deference in the group. The women, as a group, deferred to the men. The physicians, Katzenstein and Bradshaw, were more or less forced on occasion to defer to the lay members of the committee. Although Mr. Epley said very little at the few meetings he attended and although these few statements appeared to be only "for the record," the group listened carefully to every word and tended to heed them. Less apparent, yet ever present in the general meeting procedure, was the careful deference of Catholics to Protestants. Particularly was this noted in the relationship of Catholics to Dr. Carlton Gage. One ranking committee member once said, "Carlton likes me, but you must always remember that he represents 'Chestnut Street Protestants' and I'm still a Catholic."

It was also interesting to note that during the early meetings when Grogan, who was a relative newcomer to the community, was not fully accepted, he remained quiet in Colbert's presence. The competitiveness and the similarity of their work and the people with whom they had to deal would tend to create some problems between them. After having done an enormous amount of work and having received expressions of group friendship, Grogan took a higher position within the committee than Colbert.

The first meeting of the self-study committee took place in Dr. Henry Tracy's office on October 8, 1952, four months after the University staff had entered the community. Letters informing the committee appointees of their selection were written early in October by Dr. Carlton Gage. The responsibility of calling the committee together fell to its chairman, Dr. Tracy. Giving less than three days' notice, Tracy informed all who could be reached by phone of the time and place of the first meeting. Since all but two of the committee meetings were held in the offices of the board of health, its facilities were worthy of physical description. The board of health offices were centrally located on a side street between two of the city's main streets. Around the corner and down a few doors, surrounded by buildings typical of those one expects to find in a central business zone, stood the city hall. The few wooden buildings on Church Street, old and dilapidated, were huddled about the central fire station. Next door to the fire station, above the veterans' office, and up a long, steep flight of wooden stairs was housed the board of health in three large, square rooms.

Paneled in knotty pine, furnished with the usual desk, conference table, bookcases, and chairs, Dr. Tracy's office overlooked the firehouse. Here the committee began its job. On one wall hung a large calendar whose pictures hinted at some of the beauty which is New England's in successive months of the year. A chart indicating an ideal health department organization adorned another wall. The view from the two windows facing the river attracted the eye of many of the occupants during periods of waiting or boredom. Here one might watch the agile sea gulls on a roof which jutted out below the window pick and choose from the food thrown on the tar for their pleasure, or listen to their rasping cry as they floated in graceful symmetry about the old buildings.

The self-study process took place in thirteen meetings and may be divided into four stages: (1) the initial kickoff meetings, (2) the research sessions, (3) the report writing and report period, and (4) the sub-committee and advisory stage. Each was important in the developmental process.

In this chapter we shall discuss the first two stages of the process which relate to work within the committee.

The stage of initial action, the kickoff meetings, consisted of three meetings on October 8, 17, and 23, 1952. These were the meetings at which the committee attempted to get started and to reach a common denominator, individual to individual, from which to work. There was little question on the part of the participants concerning why each had been selected to serve. There appeared to be considerable anxiety about what was to be accomplished, how to fulfill the assignment, and, on occasion, what the assignment actually was. They had accepted the call: because it had come from people they knew, individuals who, like themselves, often served on civic committees; because the call had come emphatically in the guise of community betterment or improvement; and because either sometime in the past they had issued or in the future they would be issuing a similar bid for cooperation.

To Dr. Tracy fell the task of launching the quest. The first three meetings were glutted with difficulties. The committee met, matched idea for idea, personality with personality, and finally reached a working basis. Problems predominated: Will people cooperate? Should only Salemites participate in the making of the study? Is public health a concern worth focusing attention on? Will this study invoke socialized medicine? What is health? How do we go about making a study? Such questions tore, split, educated, and angered the committee members and yet drew them closer together until they finally decided upon a course of action.

Attendance at the first meeting on October 8 was poor because of the failure to contact all involved. The last two meetings of the initial stage were well attended. Dr. Tracy opened the first session with a brief explanation of the study. However, the appearance of new members at each of the three meetings necessitated several periods of orientation. He told the group that it was the feeling of a number of people in the Community Council that a health study should be made and that the group had been drawn together to work out a self-study of Salem. Often somewhat unsure of what properly should be said, the health agent attempted to draw out the attitudes of those present concerning the project. Discussion followed no prescribed channel but ebbed and flowed and drifted. Much of the material prescribed here has been grouped to facilitate comprehension.

During the first meeting, in an attempt to answer the many pertinent questions of what, how, who, and why, Mr. Carletno, superintendent of schools, commented that there would be many difficulties involved in any work that attempted to secure the services of people. "You know," he said, "people in Salem just do not cooperate." During the third meeting he created a problem by initiating a discussion in which he emphasized the importance of enlisting the aid of Salemites only in the study investigations. Carletno said that too many of the professional people and important people in the community lived outside of town and really could not have any great interest in the community. Four members of the study team lived outside of Salem. Consequently, feeling was strong against Mr. Carletno's suggestion. The lack of additional residential land within Salem had forced many families to seek dwelling units in neighboring communities. Employment and aften social ties still bound these families to the city. The definition of community has unfortunately not reached beyond its political confines, and the allegiance of the outsider is often questioned. A definite decision of exclusion-inclusion was never formally reached.

Throughout the discussion on the necessity of involving people in a health study, Dr. Tracy and Miss Schroder emphasized the positive aspects of self-study and the importance of moving on problems with the assumption that movement would be synonymous with progress. Dr. Bradshaw assumed a diametrically opposite position and questioned the importance of a self-study, pointing out for the edification of the group that the most outstanding problems were already realized and that study or investigation would shed little or no additional knowledge.

To elucidate, he proceeded at the first meeting to describe a paper given in New York City on cancer detection, one of Dr. Bradshaw's fields of interest. The paper cited the foolishness of surveying thousands of men and women over the age of 35 to determine whether or not cancer was present. This conclusion was based on a study in which very few cancer cases were uncovered. Unrealistically he identified the anticipated self-study with his acceptance of the conclusions concerning a cancer detection population.

It was not until the second meeting that the committee, as a group, recognized officially that public health was a matter of concern to them all, a matter upon which it was worth focusing their attention. Though dedicated to the study, doubts and fears continued. Immediately after the committee took a positive stand for action, Dr. Bradshaw asked whether the time required for study would be valuably spent. At times like this, when a member of the committee was attempting to fill his role, moments of conflict and derision arose. During the discussion of Dr. Bradshaw's question a few statements were made which indicated that tension existed and that several committee members were slow to realize the potential importance of their investigation. Each meeting held resembled a boxing match in which the participants must win, lose, or draw. The following appears in the journal of the second meeting.

In reply to Dr. Bradshaw's half question–half statement, Mrs. Patterson said, "Well, Dr. Bradshaw, it is our time." Miss Schroder continued to follow up Bradshaw's innuendo by saying, "Perhaps we have no problems. Perhaps we are just a conservative New England community that will say: 'We have these problems but we're always going to have them and so let's forget about evaluating where we are and where we ought to go.'" Dr. Lassiter continued, "Well, then, are we going on record as saying that there are no problems in Salem?" These statements were disturbing to the group.

Almost immediately after the three women threw their united strength against Bradshaw, the negativistic approach was dropped and procedural plans were formulated.

A summary of the initial self-study committee meetings would be incomplete without reference to the discussions which took place concerning the role of the University of North Carolina staff. We have previously described the role as that of passive observer unless questions were asked us. Although attempts had been made to reiterate and interpret that role at formal and informal meetings throughout our four months' stay before the committee meetings, several of the newly appointed committee members had not been successfully reached.

Dr. Tracy introduced the field worker at the first meeting without clarifying her role. During the proceedings, in the midst of a discussion of health problem areas in Salem, Mr. Carletno, superintendent of schools, said that he was rather confused about what the study was to do. He remarked that in the spring he had read in the newspaper that the University of North Carolina was going to make a study in Salem, and he felt at the time that was just fine. As he understood it, the University of North Carolina was coming in, was going to make a survey of the health problems, and was then going to give a report to the community so that it might work on them. He said that he had not realized that the community was to make a study of itself.

Several moments later, Dr. Bradshaw likewise indicated an interest in the role and position of the University staff in Salem. He asked, "Who had decided that a study was important to the community before the University of North Carolina began to interrogate Salem?" Turning to the field worker, he asked whether the staff could not tell them what the findings of four months' field work indicated as their major problems. Mr. Epley, in his turn, said that he felt it was extremely important that "Mrs. Schaffer tell us what our health problems are and what she has found out this summer."

Mr. Epley spoke infrequently at meetings. When he did, people usually hung on each and every syllable. While the field worker had not been given an opportunity to answer Mr. Carletno and Dr. Bradshaw's questions, the chairman called on her to answer Mr. Epley. In reply she re-emphasized the role of passive observer and established the impossibility of letting the committee in on staff findings at that time. She explained that there were several agencies who would be glad to enter the community and make a study of Salem's health needs. The University was not interested in that type of research but rather in determining how Salem solved its own problems. The staff had selected the community as a research center because there were indications of movement. However, if the Community Council's committee were to abandon the idea of making a study, our staff would be just as interested.

This remark was repeated later on several occasions. Once, when a member of our staff was questioned in regard to the functioning of a committee by a member and was referred back to Mrs. Schaffer for an answer, the member replied, "I asked *you!* It won't do any good to ask Ruth how to make our efforts successful, because she doesn't care whether we fall flat on our faces or not."

Mr. Epley was annoyed that the staff was unwilling to

present the community health problems to them and expressed concern over the field worker's "attitude." Mr. Carletno and Dr. Bradshaw expressed a greater understanding of the field worker's position.

During the second meeting, on October 17, 1952, the University's position was again reviewed for the benefit of Mrs. Patterson who had not attended the first meeting. With the exception of the normal flow of questions which might be expected, the role of the University staff remained relatively unquestioned after the initial meetings. There were, however, several problems which arose from which the staff's presence in Salem was not completely divorced.

Without question one might assume that any action which involved representative leaders would not only arouse interest but even some suspicion. It is difficult for men generally to refrain from attempting to determine the motivation connected with activity—particularly other people's activity. When a community organization opens its membership to a group which had previously been excluded, rumors of explanations are legion and help the public adjust to and accept the structural change as a result of their having rationalized it.

During the second meeting evidence of uncertainty and distrust manifested itself. Dr. Bradshaw suggested that a community attempting to study its health problems might be laying the groundwork for "socialized medicine." Mr. Grogan, who had been discussing the avenues open in problem solution, contradicted Bradshaw by saying that the group from the University of North Carolina was making this study to fight socialized medicine. He said he had discussed this with Dr. Sheps and had come to the conclusion that that was one of the primary reasons for making the study.

Dr. Bradshaw continued to assert vehemently that "socialized medicine, of course, is behind the study." Grogan proceeded stubbornly to defend the University's intent but finally questioned the field worker with: "I'm going to put you on the spot to answer this." The field worker told the committee that the University was only interested in learning how communities solve their own health problems.

Dr. Bradshaw then said, "I'm against the U.S. Public Health Service and against governmental sponsored medicine and against government anything and, if that's your approach, it sounds very fresh and most reassuring." The discussion continued more placidly.

Again, while thumbing through a publication on a self-study made in Waltham, Massachusetts, Dr. Bradshaw said, "Aha! You see, they advocate the Union Health Plan!" The latter program had been unpopular with some segments of the state medical society as well as many local public health workers. A brief explanatory discussion of this program to draw communities into health service areas was presented in Chapter 5.

Dr. Bradshaw's comment was anticlimactic and the other committee members appeared restless and impatient. Dr. Margaret Lassiter replied, "Don't you think, Dr. Bradshaw, that we ought to approach socialized medicine or union health plan or anything else with an open mind?" Obviously the question was not to Bradshaw's liking, and he launched into praises of the legislative committee of the Massachusetts Medical Society, in which he had participated, in "protecting" the citizens of the Commonwealth from miasmatic programs.

Finally during the third meeting several statements were made which ended open discussion of suspect intentions. Dr. Katzenstein, attending a meeting for the first time and attempting to orient himself to the work of the committee, said he had got the idea from Joseph Bradshaw that the study was going to boost the Union Health Plan in Massachusetts. Dr. Bradshaw denied he was spreading these rumors and hastened for the remainder of the meeting to cooperate fully. The presence of another physician more closely associated with the formal medical structure of the community than Dr. Sims or Dr. Lassiter tempered Bradshaw's attitude toward the study activities.

A man's position and the roles ascribed to it affect and qualify his social participation. Observation provided illustration after illustration. Dr. Tracy's position as health agent frequently guided discussions of health into the areas in which his department had jurisdiction. Miss Schroder seldom failed to take advantage of an opportunity to expound on the activities of the Salem Tuberculosis Association. Each member interpreted discussions of health problems or procedures in terms of his own work and his own accomplishments. Child health to Mr. Carletno was synonymous with the school health program; to Miss Schroder it entailed chest X-rays; to Dr. Sims it suggested the inadequate mental health facilities for children; and to Mrs. Patterson it recalled deficiencies in both mental and physical health services available to the social agencies she served. Definitions and procedural techniques which evolve from so heterogeneous a group must of necessity be a reflection of a compromise, synthesis, or dominance of opinion.

In every organized effort, large or small, national or local, there are four important phases—organization, procedure, finance, and propaganda or publicity. The organization or structure of the self-study committee remained fairly constant after the first three initial meetings. The problem of "how," of procedure, was of primary importance. While only a few of the numerous suggestions offered were undertaken, a brief survey of the various approaches suggested is deemed necessary.

Although the committee had been assembled to study community health, little or no attempt was made to define health. Several committee members on different occasions had asked the field worker to define health and she had quoted the World Health Organization definition.[1] There was an attempt made to differentiate between public and private health, but further definition was limited. The complexity of reaching a satisfying definition might have tended

1. Health is a state of complete mental, social, and physical well-being—not merely the absence of infirmity or disease.

to hamper exhaustive study. With the exception of a few volumes at Salem Hospital which might be useful, the public library facilities in the field of health and medical care in Salem left much to be desired.

Conceptually it was logical that the committee would assume an understanding of the term and involve itself in the study of commonly recognized health areas, which would tend to contain the investigation within a narrow frame of reference. Several members did attempt a theoretical approach. Mr. Carletno concluded a brief discussion of school health at the first meeting by saying, "People are beginning to realize that health is a purchasable commodity; it is not just a gift from heaven." At a later meeting he added: "It is a very important part of our role as citizens to be interested in community health and community improvement. Community health is never as bad as it could be or never as good as it should be. Citizens must evaluate their community and must study where they are in relation to other communities."

Dr. Lassiter, commenting on "next steps" of the study committee read at the third meeting, wrote: "Public health is a concern of all; public health is purchasable; and its pursuit is a business."

At first, procedure followed no logical order. While it might be advantageous to read some order into the various suggestions, chronological presentation of these suggestions, by meetings, shows clearly the difficulty, the fumbling, the hesitation involved in group action.

Almost as soon as the health agent had dispensed with the necessary introductions of persons and sundry introductory matters at the first meeting, he turned the group's attention to Miss Schroder. Without hesitation or consideration of the "what" and the "how" of the exploration, she suggested that the health and welfare committees of the various service organizations be requested to make the detailed study under the guidance of the Community Council Committee. Each would select a particular topic of interest to them. Miss Schroder also suggested that perhaps one or two sections of the city would be interested in studying the individual problems. This latter suggestion was not elucidated further, and it is uncertain whether formal or informal organization was to be involved in studying a section.

A suggestion made by Dr. Bradshaw was utilized in a somewhat limited fashion. Bradshaw asked whether any other communities had been involved in self-study, how they had organized, and what benefits the participants felt the community had received. Dr. Tracy and Miss Schroder reviewed their visit to Quincy, Massachusetts, and distributed several publications which enumerated the prognosis of several action groups.

In summary, most of the programs seemed to indicate that the apex of gain was in the area of education. Dr. Bradshaw's response to these findings was: "We know what the value of health education is without making a study, and we know all the problems in our community." However, the doctor did feel that an investigation of what some of the communities comparable to Salem actually did would be of interest. After thumbing casually through the Waltham, Massachusetts, report, Dr. Bradshaw announced his intention of visiting several physicians he knew in that city. Mr. Carletno told him that a visit might prove little as he might possibly meet two or three persons who had not agreed with the study philosophy and had not foreseen a need for it while the rest of the community might be excited about it. Bradshaw promised to see as many people as he could.

At the third meeting Dr. Bradshaw reported his findings. Instead of visiting Waltham, he had gone to Quincy. Without making even a casual attempt at detail, he summed up his experiences by saying he had discussed the self-study with several physicians who said, "Blessings on you, Joseph, but nothing will come of your study either."

Dr. Gage remarked that if nothing had come of the Quincy study, as the physician's remark seemed to indicate, there must have been a reason. He suggested that the committee investigate the shortcomings of the other communities in order to prevent duplication of their errors. Taking exception to this suggestion, Dr. Tracy terminated further discussion on reviews of other self-study situations by stating that he felt the Salem group should not worry about what other communities had done. He continued, "We have the leadership here, and the intelligence, to make our own study and determine what Salem needs without regard to other communities except as a standard by which to measure problems. Communities differ and it would be impossible," he added, "to really evaluate what has happened in other communities."

During the second meeting Mr. Carletno, who had shown great interest and concern in the technical design of study making, suggested, "Perhaps one device by which we may approach our dilemma is to write a questionnaire and find out what the public's reaction is toward public health and toward the facilities that are offered." Mrs. Patterson suggested that the committee list all possible problems and then decide on ways of studying them. Neither was utilized nor evaluated.

In the course of the third meeting Dr. Katzenstein, making a first appearance, added to the complex of ideas by stating that he thought the committee had been set up to screen health problems that individuals or agencies felt existed in the community. Dr. Katzenstein thought that, should he bring his problems to the committee, it would discuss them, decide what could be done about them, and give him some advice as to how he ought to handle them. This would assume a perpetuating committee. In discussing this suggestion, Dr. Katzenstein felt that a specialist in each health area might present the situation to the committee, i.e., Katzenstein and Bradshaw on the hospital program; Will Carroll, court probation officer and active worker in Alcoholics Anonymous, on the alcoholics problem; a local psychiatrist on general psychiatric services. Dr. Katzenstein, after a few minutes' thought, reiterated his idea and narrowed the suggestion. He said that if the committee could solve one problem and do a good job a great deal might be accomplished.

It is interesting to note that most of the suggestions showed little perceptive thought as to continuity of study from conception to termination. Mr. Grogan of the Chamber of Commerce did attempt an analysis of the complete job when the health agent asked for his comments during the second study meeting. From the very beginning, he said, he had definite ideas concerning the self-study. He felt that first of all the self-study should be sponsored by an agency, and it was. Second, he thought that a citizens' committee should be appointed from the very best volunteer group that could be found in the community. Third, he suggested that there should be a steering committee, and this had been selected.

Continuing, he stated that in his opinion there were two ways to go after health problems in Salem. The first way was to have someone present a problem to the Community Council, to have the Council set up a committee to discuss or investigate the problem, and then to have the Council make recommendations. This had been the usual procedure of the Council. The second way was to make a total study of the facilities and determine what the problems were and what facilities were available. Problems ought then to be ranked on a priority list. When an agency desired to change programs it would initiate change in relation to the problems on the list. "Therefore," Mr. Grogan concluded, "as we continue to grow and as we change, we change in a direction which pacifies and solves community problems."

Climactically, during the third meeting, Mr. Epley insisted that the time had come for action. The committee recognized the importance of self-study, and he stated that it did not matter what was done as long as the committee began to act. "If we go up the wrong street, we can always come back and start again," he commented.

Mention of the American Public Health Association Community Health Evaluation Schedule was introduced during the third meeting. A committee, consisting of Dr. Henry Tracy, Dr. Margaret Lassiter, and Miss Katherine Schroder, was appointed to report on the possibility of profitable utilization of the schedule. It was hardly thinkable that Dr. Bradshaw might permit this action without making some comment. Speaking in a determined manner, he questioned the form's value. Dr. Lassiter, who seemed always willing to contend with the doctor, spoke to the point by saying that the A.P.H.A. schedule had been devised by experts in the field of public health, had been tested many times, was under constant revision, and was above suspicion. Dr. Bradshaw's response was a surprising "Well, then, let's get started."

As a result of the emphasis which Dr. Katzenstein placed on his failure to secure better service by the Salem Board of Health due to reticence of the local politicians to promote such programs together with the remarks contained in other community self-study reports of the catastrophic effect of neglecting to include representatives from the political structure in initial health planning, remedial steps were taken by the Salem committee. Several names were suggested, including that of the mayor. Dr. Gage suggested Mr. MacNamara or Mr. Gosset. Dr. Katzenstein vetoed MacNamara on the grounds that past experience had proven him ineffective. Mr. Epley commented that since there was no insurance involved he was certain Mr. Gosset, who was a local realtor and insurance broker, would not be interested in serving. Dr. Tracy suggested James Sutorius' name and was immediately complimented by complete agreement on Sutorius' appointment.

The record of committee meetings does not indicate smooth, pleasant interaction nor dedication to task. However, these meetings accomplished much that was important for future action. The mere gathering and meeting of the 14 members lent to the study certain necessary community sanction. Discussion channeled committee and individual interest into a pattern of health areas which could be followed in the actual investigation. Most important of all was the opportunity it gave members to get to know one another and to gain insight into the understanding, conjectures, speculations, desires, prejudices, and opinions each had concerning the area of deliberation. By placing themselves in relation with their fellow members and with the problem, they helped to define the roles which each might take. With this understanding it would be possible to know those with whom one might join forces during conflicts which might arise.

CHAPTER 10

The Self-study Committee
Completes Its Job

WITH THE APPOINTMENT of a special committee to investigate the possibility of using the American Public Health Association schedule a new stage of the committee's work began. The committee recommended the adoption of the Public Health form and ordered copies for distribution to committee members. Sections of the schedule were assigned for investigation, studies were made between November 6, 1952, and January 22, 1953. Individual section reports were then presented to the group and the various health problems were rated. At that point the group again began to cry, "Oh, where do we go from here?" The manipulation and work involved in the study, step by step, the aspects of health selected, and the general procedure used by the committee follow. The deliberations of the special committee were not deep-searching, but certain aspects of their discussion were enlightening.

Although Dr. Margaret Lassiter was appointed to a special committee which was to present a report on the use of the A.P.H.A. schedule, she was not present at the one meeting held by that group on November 3. Dr. Gage, who had not been appointed to the committee but whose ex officio right as Community Council president could not be disputed, met for an hour and a half in the tuberculosis dispensary with Dr. Tracy and Miss Schroder. A large portion of the meeting was spent in reviewing the events of the first three meetings. Although no reference to the speakers will be made, several comments were of interest. There appeared to be some concern about the tediously slow progress that had been made during the first two months, the failure of several committee members to attend meetings, and the possibilities open in the detection of health problems.

Discussion eventually focused on the order of business. Although the A.P.H.A. schedule was not discussed in great detail, the 16 categories of health which it considers were mentioned. Eventually any misunderstanding concerning the use to which the schedule might be put was clarified, particularly after it was made clear that the schedule is not agency-specific but problem-specific and that it would be impossible for any one organization to complete the filling out of the schedule or of any particular section. Dr. Gage suggested that the schedule be adopted for use and that, for example, Mrs. Patterson work with Miss Schroder on the T.B. section and that Salem Hospital fill out the portions upon which they had available data. It was the conclusion of the committee that the schedule would fill their needs since it excluded long, drawn out historical discourses on which many agencies are prone to dwell. Dr. Gage remarked that in many ways the study would be a job analysis. The Community Council, he said, had been continually involved with one problem. It had studied one problem, solved one problem, but never solved it in relation to all other problems of a similar nature.

The recommendation of the committee was that the American Public Health Association schedule be used. Even before presentation to the committee of the whole for confirmation, 20 copies of the schedule were ordered for the next meeting.

In six meetings between November, 1952, and January, 1953, the self-study committee concerned itself with the difficult task of assembling meaningful data. While Roberts' *Rules of Order* was neglected it might have been hoped that the chairman would have the committee accomplishing units of work through the use of planned agendas. Such expectations were not realized. On only one occasion when the secretary of the Chamber of Commerce acted as chairman for the absent health agent was there a semblance of order and form.

Although agenda was not discussed, the group decided that the appointment of a permanent secretary had been neglected. Colbert, attending his first meeting of the fall, volunteered to undertake the job. Minutes were compiled by Colbert and distributed for only that meeting. Grogan wrote and sent out minutes for the meeting he chaired. All other cards and letters of notification and communication, as well as all mimeographed reports and secretarial communiques issued during the study process, were provided by Tracy and his secretary.

After copies of the A.P.H.A. schedules, which had been charged to and paid for by the Community Council, had been distributed and the schedule's contents considered, disagreement arose over how the form was to be completed. Some felt the form was much too detailed; others considered certain sections inapplicable to Salem. There was confusion concerning whether to consider the Salem Hospital an official or unofficial agency. Although the hospital is a private institution, its importance to the community had placed it uniquely, though incorrectly, in the realm of the official.

Dr. Tracy defined an official agency as one dependent upon government for its continued maintenance. Norwood suggested that Dr. Tracy fill in all of the form he could and then pass the rest along to other committee members. Dr. Sims felt that it might be possible for the committee to secure the assistance of a social worker to fill in the entire schedule. Mention was made that perhaps the A.P.H.A. could send someone down to sit in on meetings to take notes and help them when they needed assistance. Finally a decision was made to distribute the various sections to different committee members as follows: Sections A, B, C, D, F, L, M, and N—personnel, facilities, services, public health problems, community health education and staff training, communicable disease control and venereal disease control, water supply and excreta disposal, food control and milk control—were given to Dr. Tracy.

While the above implied a tremendous amount of work, the health agent was assisted in the compilation by one of his public health nurses and the sanitary inspector. Section E, tuberculosis control, was to be shared by Miss Schroder and Dr. Tracy since their agencies both had data that would have to be utilized. Norwood was assigned Section G, maternal health. Mrs. Patterson, with the help of Dr. Morris whose work at Salem Hospital and North Shore Babies Hospital was concerned with certain aspects of the area, was to fill in section H, infant and pre-school health. Carletno was assigned Section I, school health; Section J, adult health, was to be filled in by Drs. Katzenstein and Bradshaw. Section K, accident prevention, and Section O, housing, were assigned to Colbert and Sutorius respectively. Colbert and Dr. Tracy planned to fill in the section on financial support for local health work, section P, since one was intimately involved in the support of private work and the other with public service. A new category, which will be discussed later, Section Q, mental health, was assigned to Dr. Sims. Four members, Grogan, Epley, Gage, and Lassiter, were not assigned specific tasks.

The committee felt that the form could be completed in 11 days by the next meeting on November 17. Preparation for the normal year-end holidays of Thanksgiving, Christmas, and New Year limited the time spent on the project. Although meetings were held on November 17, December 1 and 15, it was not until January 15 that the schedule was complete enough to be discussed, i.e., it took approximately 70 days to complete the task rather than the 11 originally projected.

A master schedule was kept in the health department office, and each member was expected to fill in the sections he or she completed and to copy other reports into their own schedule for reference. Dr. Lassiter was appointed liaison officer to trail and "intimidate" slackers and to do any of the "foot work" other members might require. The three meetings mentioned above served as mediums of clearance and estimates of progress as well as instruments of prodding.

From our staff's primary contact with the self-study committee we were interested in what problem areas the members would see. The segments which are considered the concern of public and private health agencies today have changed as medical and social science have demonstrated their ability to control, to prevent, and to cure diseases that previously decimated men and disrupted economic and social life.

It seemed probable that the areas which would be investigated would depend upon several factors—first, the insight and knowledge of the participants concerning avenues worthy of investigation; second, the availability of information, i.e., statistical and other records; and, third, the freedom of the committee to delve into problems which might prove unpopular with various segments of the structure. With reference to the last area, our staff was equally interested in health areas which the committee touched upon casually and then dropped or side-stepped entirely.

We have previously described and evaluated various aspects of medical care in Salem. The following will indicate the areas touched upon and the problems which were related to them. The A.P.H.A. schedule confined the study to the areas included there. Several sections were left incomplete. Carletno never turned in the material on school health, although he sent word it was being processed. Dr. Tracy, lacking statistical information, neglected Section F—venereal disease control. Drs. Bradshaw and Katzenstein failed to report on adult health, although both Dr. Sims and Dr. Lassiter compiled and gave them figures to be used in their area of concentration. Sutorius compiled none of the data but, using his position as a ward councillor, shifted his responsibility to his paid employee, the health agent. The latter spoke only from casual observation on the subject rather than from careful study. Colbert, assigned partial responsibility for the section on financial support, never completed the area.

During the six meetings which took place in the course of investigation, several health areas were discussed which never appeared in any of the formal reports. Such subjects as free dental care, cost of hospital services, the presence of venereal disease, the problem of alcoholism, and public medical care for pre-school children were mentioned. Some, such as venereal disease, were dismissed as numerically unimportant in Salem; others were dropped in deference to a more pressing need during the general rating of problems.

Reports of findings were given on January 15, 1953. One report was informal; all others were typed or mimeographed. Often the oral discussion following the report was more significant than the report itself. Much of it will be recorded below.

Before the presentation of the reports, Joseph Colbert won the floor and spoke for approximately five minutes emphasizing and reiterating that he felt any report issued by the committee should be a positive report, a creative report, and not a negative report which might antagonize the community. He said, "Let's call this a positive report and report the growth and services of our community agencies." The effect of his statements was cataclysmic. Dr. Katzenstein immediately stated that he could not possibly agree with Colbert's suggestion since it was going to be impossible always to present a positive report. Simultaneously, Dr. Gage agreed with Dr. Katzenstein and emphasized that problems must be brought out, certainly in a positive way, but brought out regardless of whom they might hurt.

While it is impossible to analyze Colbert's motivation, his determined suggestion, which seemingly reversed his past action, indicated perhaps his reticence to antagonize groups within the community which might be affected and with whom he might have to work.

Sutorius was asked to report his findings on housing. Since

he obviously had not fulfilled his obligation, the committee had to rely on as much information on the subject as they could receive from the health agent, who volunteered to help the councillor.

Following the report, Dr. Katzenstein stated that he believed the slum sections in the city should be torn down. He recognized it as a difficult but rewarding program. Mrs. Patterson asked whether the people who were living in substandard housing in Salem could not find other dwellings. Dr. Tracy responded positively. Immediately Dr. Gage suggested that while they might find other housing the cost would be prohibitive and, therefore, these people actually could not provide alternate housing for themselves. Neither Sutorius nor Dr. Tracy had presented any statistical material on the problem but had indicated that this material was not available. Mr. Grogan contradicted the supposition by informing the group that there was "loads of it" listed in a U.S. Census Report for 1950, secured a copy from his office, and pointed out some interesting facts.

Mrs. Patterson's investigation of maternal and child health did not seem to the committee to have uncovered any serious problem. Her conclusions were accepted with optimism: (1) facilities are available for infants, if people want to use them; (2) no statistics of death rates for children under one month are available; (3) there are plenty of free clinics available.

Colbert presented a report on the Salem accident program and concluded that accident prevention was not a problem. He suggested that an accident prevention council be organized to prevent duplication of effort on the part of the numerous organizations involved in the program. Following Mr. Colbert's earlier statements and the group reaction to them some criticism was likely. Several questions were asked concerning various programs carried on by the fire department. Dr. Katzenstein then questioned whether it would be possible to prove that the glowing accident record Colbert had presented was really a good one by comparing it with other communities. Grogan asserted that he felt comparison of statistics would be the next step. Dr. Katzenstein returned with, "We don't know whether we're doing a good job unless we do have a basis of comparison." Colbert became defensive and said that he did not see any reason why they should compare their accident figures with any other community's. He said, "We'll solve our own problems without comparison. There can be no comparison between communities." There was much disagreement with Colbert, and the committee finally decided that comparison was extremely important and that the few statistics which were presented in the report were valueless unless compared with reports of other cities of like size, industry, and street plan construction.

Norwood discussed maternal health in Salem particularly as it was related to hospital programs. Recognizing the availability of prenatal care he emphasized the educational aspects of the problem. Many women, he said, did not know they needed prenatal or postnatal care. Physicians in the community insisted upon this care and, because of the prosperity at the time, women were able to accept the service. Norwood and Dr. Katzenstein felt that in the future money might become scarce and that then a sure-fire health education job would have to be done.

Miss Schroder's report on the tuberculosis situation was accepted without comment except for commendation.

Two reports were of greater interest than the others. Since early September, meeting after meeting reverberated with discussion on various phases of psychiatric services and general public health programs. During the initial meetings between the University of North Carolina staff and community leaders, the problem of better psychiatric services had been mentioned. Time and again, during interview after interview and in meeting after meeting, talk of additional psychiatric services, necessity for an incinerator, improved restaurant sanitation, and the possibility of a new health center was heard.

The early meetings of the study committee were often scenes of conflict over the necessity for better psychiatric services—agency people standing firmly against the loud protestations of the physicians. The early stand of the medical men was based on consultation with Dr. Arnold Goldner, psychiatrist at Salem Hospital, who stoutly maintained the community had an over-abundance of mental health services. It was left to Dr. Pauline Sims, state psychiatrist, to investigate and report the situation.

Dr. Sims' report was excellent. It was positive and yet pointed out emphatically the serious problems the Salem community faced in the field of mental health. She cautiously unveiled the Salem Hospital's psychiatric program. The psychiatric clinic at the hospital was so hard pressed that only cases referred from the in-patient department of the hospital or referred from other out-patient clinics would be accepted.

Dr. Katzenstein, at the end of the report, questioned Dr. Sims in regard to conclusions. Dr. Sims answered, "Very definitely you are not taken care of as a community, but what can I say? There are just not any psychiatrists available. I have been trying to get one in my department to assist me for several years and it is just an impossible situation. While I would like to spend more time in Salem, I cannot." She went on to say that every time she spoke before a group on the importance of mental health programs she received six to twelve new referrals to her clinic which she could not handle. Dr. Sims was the type of woman who was able, by her sincerity and industry, to convince large groups of people of the importance of a program. Her report was accepted with a good deal of comment by the group. Surprisingly, both Dr. Katzenstein and Norwood were seriously convinced of the need for additional psychiatric services.

At the following meeting, Dr. Joseph Bradshaw, who had been absent from the first reporting session, asked in regard to Dr. Sims' report, "Are we going to accept the report on the need for psychiatric services without consulting the hospital psychiatrists?" The rest of the committee pointed out that Dr. Sims had given a very comprehensive report and had convinced them of the need for additional psychiatric services in Salem. Dr. Katzenstein and Mr. Norwood were most insistent and succeeded in getting Dr. Bradshaw to conform to the majority opinion. From that moment there no longer existed any further open conflict concerning this need.

Dr. Bradshaw had questioned the acceptance of the report following a brief discussion with Mrs. Patterson. During an interlude in the meeting, Mrs. Patterson had emphasized the need for additional services. Dr. Bradshaw asked Mrs. Patterson whether she thought that the problem in psychiatric care was due to the lack of psychiatrists. She said, "Yes, it is." Dr. Bradshaw replied, "We know how the hospital psychiatrist feels about this question." His tone seemed to indicate that he expected Mrs. Patterson to support the attitudes expressed by any hospital staff member. Mrs. Patterson's husband was on the staff at Salem Hospital. Mrs. Patterson, however, replied, "I couldn't disagree with him more." With the support of Dr. Katzenstein and Norwood the tension which had always existed during any discussion of this special service disappeared.

The final report, which dealt with areas within the jurisdiction of the Salem department of public health, was given by Dr. Henry Tracy. Tracy's report might be divided into two parts: (1) new or additional public health services; (2) physical plant construction. The health agent pointed out that what the health department really needed was a health center where all of the health agencies in the community might have offices and where a good clinic could be established. He said that this would cost about $200,000, a figure which he considered large. Mr. Grogan remarked that $200,-000 was not very much for health. At that time the health department maintained three or four separate offices housing various facilities. Grogan pointed out that if the health agent would indicate to the city council what the board of health was paying to maintain three or four offices, the Council might come across with a new health center.

Dr. Tracy also expressed the need for an incinerator in order to solve the problem of garbage disposal in Salem.

Since the city lacked new dumping grounds and used no sanitary fill, the problem was becoming acute and the city government would be forced to face it eventually. Dr. Katzenstein commented that the city had been having "incinerator talks" for years. Politics had usually kept anyone from getting anywhere.

Even though the health department maintained a dental clinic which cared for elementary and grammar school children in the public and parochial schools of Salem, Tracy indicated that investigations showed that large numbers of children were being neglected because of lack of sufficient personnel. He recommended that an additional staff member be employed.

The importance of public food handling establishments in the transmission of diseases moved the health agent to request additional sanitary inspectors in order to insure public safety. At the time the study was in progress, the municipality maintained one inspector. Public health authorities recommend one inspector for every 15,000 population, and the population of Salem was 41,000.

The health agent ended his recommendations and results of his investigation by stating that the city of Salem spent approximately $.39 per person per year for public health services. To provide a well-rounded health program according to national standards, a community should spend $2.50 per capita on its public health program. While this is a desirable objective, it is recognized that it is beyond the reach of many communities. A minimum program, however, should not go below $1.50 per capita. Dr. Tracy recommended that the budget of the public health department should be substantially increased to provide Salem citizens with services which approximate minimum standards.

Recurrently, members of the committee suggested that the problem areas indicated by the reports be ranked according to importance. There was little discussion of the probability of success in relation to time and socio-political movement within Salem. Following the first report session in

January, 1953, the group directed the health agent to multi-graph all reports and to distribute them, with a brief questionnaire requesting ranking of problems, to the committee. At the next meeting each member would read his list with reasons for the rating.

While much information required by the A.P.H.A. schedule had been secured, little use was made of the statistical measures of service effectiveness which the form is set up to indicate. Consequently, ranking was based on individual opinion and reflected the influence of the reports as well as personal community experiences. The next meeting was devoted to a discussion of rating. Each person was given the opportunity to present his opinion. Dr. Tracy called on Miss Schroder to present her listing.

Miss Schroder opened her report by saying that she felt education, the aim and objective of the health study, was the most important matter before the community. However, she rated the problems as follows: (1) sanitation of restaurants; (2) additional mental health clinical services; (3) increased dental services in schools; and (4) extension of facilities of the health department to include a building in which the T.B. clinics and other health organizations could be housed.

Norwood in his report said that he saw the following problems before the community: (1) food control or environmental sanitation in restaurants; (2) elimination of dumping through the building of an incinerator; (3) sewage disposal between communities; (4) a health center to coordinate health activities with an adequate staff to run it; (5) the problem of substandard housing; and (6) health education. Norwood said that education should probably rank first because it had been mentioned so often. He referred to Miss Schroder's report in which she had rated it number one. Norwood said he was sure the community was not aware of its facilities and that one thing he had gained from participating in the study was knowledge. He was going to make sure that, in the very near future, the hospital did something about informing the community about its health facilities.

Norwood then said he would rate auto accidents seventh. Eighth he listed mental health. "We don't have adequate services at the hospital, and we would like to be able to meet this problem."

Dr. Katzenstein gave his report. First, he listed health education. He said, "Let the public know what the community is doing. Tie it up with and let them know what clinical services the hospital offers and tell them that if we cannot satisfy their needs we have connections with the Massachusetts General Hospital to provide additional assistance." Second, he felt that the lack of a health center was an important problem which the community had to face. A good health center was needed where people might go for information on tuberculosis, contagious diseases, inspection, hospital care, and so on. Third, he felt the community needed dental hygienists.

Dr. Gage's report was next. He felt that the most important problem facing the community was substandard housing, and second, more adequate free psychiatric care. He said, "On this point I have no criticism of what has been done in the past, but it just is not adequate. I would very much like to hear how the other psychiatrists in town feel, however." Third, he felt that the public health department was inadequately staffed and that more people should be hired. He said that environmental health in restaurants is merely an example of inadequate staffing in the health department. Fourth, he said the public school buildings were in great need of a survey of their toilet facilities. He called attention to the antiquated school buildings in Salem and hoped the Community Council would in the future have a committee on school building perhaps to facilitate a school building program.

Dr. Lassiter went into her report and rated as important: (1) prenatal care and education concerning prenatal care; and (2) garbage disposal by incineration.

Mrs. Patterson gave her report in which she listed the following: (1) more psychiatric care; (2) increased free dental care for children; (3) more supervision of food inspectors (Mrs. Patterson said that she felt the one inspector Dr. Tracy had was not doing enough and that it would not mean much to add an additional member to the staff if he were going to be like this man); (4) less substandard housing; (5) the addition of a sanitary inspector for the health department [this may be considered interesting in light of the fact that she felt the one inspector was not doing enough work]; (6) the need of an incinerator; and (7) the need of a new health center. Mrs. Patterson emphasized the fact that her first and second items were "crying needs" because they affected children. She engaged the group in a discussion concerning the recommendations for education that had been made in two of the reports. Mrs. Patterson said she did not feel that education was a part of the program or purpose of the committee. She said that actually it was the responsibility of each agency to take care of its own publicity. It was important for the hospital and for agencies to emphasize their own services and their own work with the community.

Dr. Lassiter replied, "Well, shouldn't we point out that they need better publicity?" This statement was overlooked as Mrs. Patterson went on to say, "We can't publicize agencies or the hospital." She said that if a company such as Electro had something to advertise, they went out and advertised it through a campaign; she felt that it was about time that hospitals and agencies recognized the fact that they had to do the same.

Dr. Tracy added, "I don't know very much about what the hospital does offer to the community." Miss Schroder said, "If people were educated they wouldn't let their problems go on and on as it is apparent they have been doing in Salem." Dr. Tracy said that he felt the health organizations were not clearing with each other as far as services were concerned. Dr. Katzenstein said, "Well, why can't we recommend that health agencies improve publicity?" Mr. Norwood added it was important that problems get before individuals or groups within the community; it did not really matter *how* you got publicity before them.

Dr. Katzenstein joined in saying that when he was put on the board of health he thought it was the health board's job to publicize health services in the community but that he and the agent had both fallen down in that area. Dr. Tracy then reminded the group that the health department and the T.B. association sponsored a health forum of the air on Wednesdays. He said there would be no reason why programs concerning the services offered by the various agencies in the community could not be scheduled. Miss Schroder said that probably a great many people do not even know very much about the state department of health or the regional office.

Mr. Colbert's report was then read. He listed the following problems: (1) the review and enforcement of sanitary standards in restaurants; (2) the need for a psychiatric diagnostic clinic in Salem; (3) better school health examinations for children; (4) the organization of a city-wide health council to meet monthly to review health problems of the community; (5) the establishment of an alcoholics clinic to serve the area. The last named was already under way, and it was hoped that funds would be secured from the state legislature to carry on an alcoholics clinic somewhere in the North Shore area.

Dr. Tracy then read his report. He listed: (1) better health facilities for the health department as far as space, auditorium, and a clinic were concerned; (2) the reorganization of school health into one departmental jurisdiction; (3) a solution to the problem of substandard housing in Salem; (4) the need for an incinerator; (5) additional trained personnel for the health department. Dr. Tracy said that he thought the health department should be a central health information collecting agency for everyone.

The seven individuals who reported listed 14 problems. Only two of the participants rated the same area, restaurant sanitation, as the most important concern of the Salem community. In general the votes which each of the problem categories received were as follows:

Environmental sanitation of restaurants	5
Additional psychiatric services	5
Community health center	5
Health education	4
Substandard housing	4
Incinerator	4
Increased dental service for school children	3
Reorganization of school health into one department	2
Additional health department personnel	2
Accident control program	1
Prenatal care program	1
Better intercommunity sewage disposal	1
Organization of a permanent health council	1
Organization of an alcoholics clinic	1

Without assembling and counting the votes, the committee members assumed from the lengthy discussions which had followed the presentation of certain problems that environmental sanitation of restaurants was number one, the need for additional psychiatric services was number two, and the suggested community health center was number three.

The perennial question of "Where do we go from here?" again emerged. Dr. Tracy suggested that it was time for the committee to expand its base of operation by inviting a large group of people such as the official family (city government), the newspapers, and health agency executives to a meeting at which the problems might be discussed.

Mrs. Patterson suggested that the only action the committee could take was to present its findings to the Community Council and let it continue the work. She said, "We have done what we have been asked to do as a committee. We have investigated, we have found the problems, and we are now ready to tell the Council about it." Miss Schroder moved that a committee of three or four be appointed to compile a report of findings and recommendations and to present this report to the committee of the whole for approval or revision. Plans would then be made to present the report to the Community Council. After the motion had been carried the health agent appointed Miss Schroder, Mr. Norwood, Mr. Grogan, Mr. Sutorius, and himself to assemble the mass of material into one report.

The compilation of a study report into a meaningful, organized dispatch is far from easy. Such writing should take into account the transition to action which may follow. It should also consider the relative seriousness of the problems uncovered, the relative chances for a successful program, the possible steps which might be taken, and their timing. The committee which had assumed some of this responsibility met three times to deliberate.

For the four and a half months preceding the writing of the report, four members of the committee, excluding James Sutorius, had been drawn closer and closer together. Convinced of the serious nature of their work and assured of each other's amiable intent, first steps in the writing process were taken in February, 1953. Some of the problems were categorized under large sections. For example, housing, collection and disposal of garbage and rubbish, inspection of food handling establishments, and rodent control were classified under environmental sanitation.

Grogan, who took an extremely active part in assembling the report, devoting much time in an already overcrowded day, felt that it would be important to emphasize the difference between the two types of items the committee considered desirable: (1) better programs; (2) improvement of physical plants.

During the three meetings the committee held, the members discussed and reiterated much that had been expounded over a four months' period. They emphasized that, although many of the recommendations entailed projects of considerable size and implication, there was much that could be done on a small scale. Grogan suggested that after the report had been written members of the committee should discuss it with those individuals in the community whose position might be open to criticism as a result of its recommendations. Particularly was Grogan thinking of the report on accident prevention. He felt it would be shameful to have the chief of police, who had probably done everything possible to control and prevent accidents, feel that his work was unappreciated, even criticized. Grogan recommended clearance of each critical item with the individual concerned. This suggestion was never acted upon.

The impossibility of four individuals sitting about a table compiling or writing a report became apparent. During the second meeting, Dr. Tracy was commissioned to draw up a first draft. The committee felt that the report and technical vocabulary therein ought to be correct and asked the University of North Carolina field worker to check terminology. The second step apparent to the group was the rewriting of this technical report in language which would appeal to the layman.

Dr. Tracy was to write the first technical draft of the report within the next few days. The report was then to be typed and carbons distributed to Miss Schroder, Mr. Norwood, Mr. Grogan, and Mr. Sutorius for additions and revision. On February 9, 1953, the committee was to meet again in Dr. Tracy's office to discuss this report. A date would then be set for the meeting of the entire self-study committee at which time approval of the report would be asked and decisions would be made as to final presentation before the Community Council.

Mr. Grogan said that he still envisioned experts coming into the community to discuss what actually was happening there. The use of the State Department of Health personnel as a resource was mentioned from time to time during the course of the several meetings held by the subcommittee to write up the final report. Little mention up to this time had been made during the course of the study concerning resource help from outside agencies.

The report submitted to the subcommittee by Dr. Tracy at the third meeting was an assembly of the recommendations of the various committee members. No introduction or conclusion had been written. The subcommittee felt, after reading the report, that the material did not "hit particularly hard." Grogan said he felt the report ought to be brief, to the point, well organized, and one that would hit the public squarely between the eyes. He felt that the way the report had been set up by Dr. Tracy made it impossible to determine which problem was most important.

Grogan envisioned the report in the following form: (1) an introduction; (2) community programs; (3) physical plant; (4) financial needs; and (5) conclusion. After such an expression of enthusiasm and know-how, the committee suggested that Grogan rewrite Dr. Tracy's report in a popular vein. Grogan volunteered to do so provided he might have the assistance of the secretary of the department of public health.

On February 19, 1953, an abbreviated report, following the outline mentioned above, was presented to the self-study committee in the absence of Mr. Grogan. The report was received rather coolly. Dr. Carlton Gage was critical not only of the brevity of the report but the fact that one man, Peter Grogan, had been responsible for its final form. The Unitarian minister questioned the report throughout the meeting. He said it was not specific enough in pointing up recommendations such as the need for an incinerator, setting up committees to investigate housing in the community, or recognizing the need for health education. Dr. Gage felt the recommendations in the report did not cover the job which the committee had set out to do. He said, "I thought we wanted to get this down into the grass-roots level, and we certainly have not made any recommendations that it be done. An addition should be made to the report indicating that we hoped, as a committee, this report would not die in the Council. There should also be added a sentence which states that it is the responsibility of the community, not merely the concern of the Community Council, to work out the various problems cited by the committee."

Dr. Gage suggested that he felt the time had come to call in an expert to analyze the findings of the committee and thought that perhaps someone should be brought from Harvard to appear before the Community Council in session to analyze the report of the self-study committee. With determination he said that he would like very much to know what the report meant and what areas should be concentrated upon. Gage added, "Although we have good people working on the self-study, and although we have tried to be objective, it is impossible to look at our own study dispassionately." Dr. Tracy responded negatively to Dr. Gage's suggestion and said that it was rather late to call in an expert. Dr. Bradshaw agreed with the health agent.

In an attempt to thwart the negative reaction of the committee toward the report compiled by Dr. Grogan, Mr. Norwood mentioned that another report had been written upon which Mr. Grogan based his material. Mr. Epley, who had returned from Florida, commented that the report as written would "never set people on fire." A motion was ultimately made that the two reports be combined and a new meeting held to adopt the report at a later date.

On February 26, 1953, the eleventh meeting of the self-study committee was held to approve the final report, which was to be presented a week later to the Community Council at its monthly meeting. Dr. Tracy had telephoned all of the people with the exception of Carletno and had received approval from those who were unable to attend the meeting. Arrangements had been made by Joseph Colbert of the Community Fund to have Fred Burrell, reporter for a local paper, cover the Community Council monthly meeting. He suggested further that a series of articles on each of the various phases of the study be published.

The results of the deliberations of the committee, which drew up the study report, indicated the difficulties involved in such procedure. While Grogan's report may have needed elaboration, it was not poorly written. The criticisms which befell it, in the absence of the author, seemed to indicate the inability of the parent committee to relinquish the reins even temporarily at a judicious moment. Certainly, the report would have remained unwritten without the use of a sub-committee.

After nine months the self-study committee was at last in a position to submit a report of its findings to the parent body, the Community Council. The chairman of the self-study committee requested that each committee member attend. At the February meeting of the Council a new president, Mrs. Childs, was elected to replace Dr. Carlton Gage. She in turn had to be informed of the background of the study.

The committee extended, through Mrs. Childs, an invitation to the mayor to be present at the meeting. The interaction between committee members in inviting the mayor and in the selection of a member to present the report to the Council was of interest. Mr. Colbert asked Dr. Gage how he stood with the mayor. Dr. Gage replied that he was considered to be in opposition during the last election. Although he had not committed himself formally, he was a Harrigan [opposing candidate] man. Colbert then suggested that Mrs. Childs call the mayor and ask him to be present. A similar discussion occurred about the choice of a person to deliver the report. The mayor's presence, as well as the importance of wooing the politicians, made the selection of a "middle of the road man" mandatory. Colbert refused to fill the position. Dr. Gage was unpopular with the "pols" and was identified with the old Yankee element in Salem. Peter Grogan, as a newcomer who had won the respect of committee members by his industry and general good humor, was appointed. Dr. Tracy was not considered.

Several days before the Council meeting Dr. Tracy, Miss Schroder, and Mrs. Childs met to plan strategy. Dr. Gage, Mrs. Childs said, had asked her whether she would prepare a statement in case members of the Council attempted to minimize the importance of the report because it was the result of unprofessonial staff work. This was the first manifest sign of possible conflict verbalized by the members of the Council toward the self-study. It was decided that Mrs. Childs would chair the meeting, ask Dr. Gage for a few words of introduction as past Council president under whose regime the activity had been initiated, and then introduce Peter Grogan. The meeting was to be held on March 2, 1953.

On a cold, bleak New England day, the Community Council wedged between the annual meetings of several important welfare organizations the luncheon meeting in which they were to deliberate on the long awaited self-study report. The club room of the Hotel Hawthorne, which the Council used for its meetings, was crowded since nearly one hundred people were present. The mayor, aloof, perhaps critical, certainly on guard, was seated at the head table with Mrs. Childs, Dr. Gage, Mr. Grogan, officers of the Council, Mrs. Schaffer, field worker, and Dr. Cecil Sheps of the University of North Carolina staff, who had journeyed to Salem to observe the partial culmination of almost nine months of self-study.

Mrs. Childs rose, dispensed with the reading of the minutes of the last meeting, and presented the University staff to the assemblage. She then called upon Dr. Gage. The Unitarian minister spoke briefly of the background of the study. He emphasized that the report did not represent criticism of what had been accomplished by government or by private agencies. Rather it pointed out a long-range program. He concluded his remarks by expressing a note of thanks for the efforts of the staff of the University of North Carolina.

Mrs. Childs rose once more and introduced Peter Grogan who was to present the findings of the report. Previously, Colbert had placed dittoed copies of it under each plate.

In presenting the report Grogan did not adhere to the printed form. A tall man with a charming New England accent, the Chamber of Commerce secretary was at his best, amusing and witty, as he attempted to sell the Community Council the report findings.

Grogan opened his remarks by saying, "Before I begin to talk, I've got something to say." This amused the listeners. Grogan suggested that many members who were facing in other directions turn their chairs around, make themselves comfortable, and give him their complete attention. He began "to talk" by mentioning the fact that Joe Colbert had been responsible for arousing the interest of the University of North Carolina in Salem. Grogan said that Colbert wanted to make sure that Salem was spending money properly in the health area, or at least in the area of private health. The University of North Carolina accepted the invitation of the Community Council to make their study in Salem. Grogan said that the University felt "we were a community which was deserving."

The speaker went on to discuss the history of the study, the committee appointments, and other details. He then mentioned the fact that Dr. Henry Tracy had been made chairman of the committee. This was of much interest to our staff since Dr. Tracy was never formally elected chairman of the group. It just became an accepted fact. He mentioned the selection and use of the A.P.H.A. schedule by the committee. It was the feeling of the committee, Grogan said, that facts, not impressions, were needed. Sometimes the facts were available; often it required a great deal of work to get them. Next came an analysis of the material which had been gathered.

Grogan said that the committee talked with all of the key people in various health fields in the community. He stressed that in the period devoted to analysis many "fights" took place between committee members. The committee attempted to iron out those difficulties, but they were not always in agreement. Grogan hinted that perhaps many of the difficulties had not yet been ironed out.

It was the opinion of the self-study committee, the secretary said, that health education was the most important problem the Community Council or the community as a whole had before it. Requesting permission to issue a minority report, he said that as far as he was personally concerned one of the most important problems before the community today was that of environmental sanitation in restaurants.

Grogan was very amusing at this point and mentioned the

fact that during the course of the study he had learned a great deal. One thing that he had learned was a new and fascinating term—environmental sanitation. Food handling is a very important problem in Salem. "We all eat three meals a day. Some of us, like myself, eat four meals a day." He then jokingly added, "Of course, if you eat at the Hotel Hawthorne more than twice a day, you have to eat four meals." Grogan then read from the formal report suggesting an increase in the sanitary inspection staff of the Department of Health in order to do a better supervisory job in Salem and in order to conduct food-handling and manager's courses.

Grogan touched upon the problem of housing, quoting from the U.S. Census report which indicated that there was a great deal of substandard housing in Salem. The committee had never really analyzed the U.S. Census report on housing. Grogan ended the first part of the report with a consideration of accident prevention. Briefly, too, he mentioned the need for additional dental care for the dentally indigent children in Salem. When he mentioned the category, he said that the phraseology might appear different to the group but "this is the way you say it if you want to say it technically right."

The second portion of the report dealt with physical plants. Grogan commented that this was a point in the meeting when the mayor was going to wish he was not present since large government expenditures were usually involved in the erection of new physical plants. Grogan told a joke that he had heard about the mayor. Throughout the presentation of the report he attempted, with a great deal of humor, to lighten criticism of the various sections.

The first measure mentioned was the health center. He said, "It is an effective way of operating if we are going to give the best service we can in the medical area to our people. All services would be housed under one roof." He went on to suggest the construction of an incinerator and mentioned the fact that waste land will soon be nonexistent in Salem.

Since it was now approximately two o'clock, some agency people found it necessary to leave the meeting. Grogan watched the people leaving and remarked, "Well, as soon as you begin to talk about money people leave." There was a great deal of laughter following the comment. Grogan said that as far as private financing of welfare and health services was concerned, Salem was up to the standard for the United States and higher than the standard in New England. He pointed out that an examination of health services would not be complete without an evaluation of local financing.

According to national standards, a community, to provide a well-rounded health program, should spend $2.50 per capita on its public health program. A minimum program should not go below $1.50 per capita. Salem, Grogan said, is spending approximately $.39 per person. "This committee," he said, "recommends that the budget of the public health department should be substantially increased in order to provide Salem citizens with health services that approximate even the minimum standard."

Grogan concluded that what the committee and the Community Council did from then on was important. A great many people, he said, have spent long hours compiling the report. He told the group they had a survey which would have cost a great deal of money if outside help had been used. He indicated that the committee had received a great deal of aid from professional people from within the community and from Mrs. Schaffer of the University of North Carolina staff.

Mr. Grogan concluded his report with the story about the cynic and the philosopher who were sitting on a park bench. The cynic was constantly irritating the philosopher. One day while sitting on the park bench, the cynic grabbed a bird out of the air with his hand. Turning to the philosopher he asked whether the bird was alive or dead. The philosopher thought for a few minutes. He realized that if he said the bird was alive, the cynic would immediately crush it with his hand and the bird would be dead. If he said it was dead the cynic would release the bird and it would fly away and again he would be wrong. Finally the philosopher turned to the cynic and said, "It is as you will it." Grogan then looked about the Community Council seated before him and said, "It is as you will it."

Mrs. Childs took the floor and acknowledged the tremendous responsibility the committee was placing on the Community Council. In response to a query for a motion, Dr. Tracy moved that the report be accepted. John Senter, executive secretary of the North Shore Society for the Prevention of Cruelty to Children, seconded the motion which was carried.

The fate of the self-study committee was then in abeyance. Dr. Gage suggested to the Community Council that the self-study committee either be reappointed as a steering committee or that a new committee be set up. Motions were made and carried that the self-study committee be recognized in the future as the steering committee. The steering committee was to be an advisory body to the various subcommittees appointed in each study area.

As president of the Community Council, Mrs. Childs asked whether there were any suggestions concerning individuals who might serve as chairmen of the various subcommittees. Mr. Norwood then rose and said that the committee had drawn up a list of people whom they would like to recommend to the Community Council for chairmanships. He then read the list. Additions were made to it from the Community Council's suggestions. These committees will be discussed later.

Echoing a former request that the report be submitted to outside agency experts in the field of public health, Dr. Gage suggested he would like to see a large meeting at which the report might be aired before the community in the presence of an expert. Following his suggestion, Claude Downer of the North Shore Children's Friend Society remarked that he felt the various committees should be free to call on experts in their particular fields rather than submit the report to one expert. Miss Schroder conceded to Dr. Gage and moved that an expert be consulted.

Dr. Katzenstein suggested that the report be referred to Dr. Cecil G. Sheps of the University of North Carolina for review. Dr. Sheps was asked to say a few words concerning Dr. Katzenstein's suggestion. He acknowledged the position of the University of North Carolina in the community and emphasized that the study which had been presented had been made by a responsible group. This group had crystallized to their own satisfaction the problems that existed in the community.

Dr. Sheps also said that it was important to make the community understand the findings and the recommendations. He presented several lines of action in connection with securing expert advice: (1) The report could be turned over to one person or to one institution for review as Dr. Gage suggested, or (2) the Council and its subcommittees could be made free to turn in any direction for advisory help. Dr. Sheps strongly recommended the latter. Dr. Lassiter moved that the committees be given the authority to consult resource agencies whenever they found it necessary.

In an effort to take advantage of the favorable newspaper publicity and interest in the self-study, Dr. Tracy and Miss Schroder made arrangements, without consulting other members of the steering committee, for a general community meeting to be held in Salem Town Hall on March 23, 1953. Dr. Tracy called a meeting of the steering committee on March 19, a week before the Town Hall meeting, to discuss arrangements with the group.

The announcement of the forthcoming meeting came as a surprise. Miss Schroder and Dr. Tracy had felt it inadvisable to inform anyone lest their plans be discouraged. They announced to the steering committee that notices had been sent out for the meeting. Approximately five hundred letters were mailed to people in the Salem community. Slight thought, however, had been given to the program. Both Miss Schroder and Dr. Tracy assumed that Mr. Grogan would fill the same role at the community meeting that he had at the report meeting. Unfortunately, Mr. Grogan was unable to attend because of a previous commitment. Likewise Mr. Colbert and several others were unable to fill this position. The job of spelling out the findings to the community at large was placed on Dr. Tracy's shoulders.

Program-wise the pair had arranged to have Miss Ann Koestner, health educator for the state tuberculosis society, discuss how the community as a whole might become involved in the health study. Dr. Paxton from the state health department district office was requested to say a few words, and Dr. Stewart Phills, who had accepted the chairmanship of the health center committee, had volunteered to speak on this area of interest. There had been an attempt on the part of Dr. Tracy to get Dr. Sternfeld from the Harvard School of Public Health to speak. However, he was not available. Later the health agent called Dr. Franz Goldman of the Harvard School of Public Health and asked whether he might suggest someone to speak at the community meeting. Dr. Goldman recommended Dr. Sternfeld. Discouraged, the use of resource aid was abandoned.

The committee discussed the possibility of adequate publicity on such short notice. It was apparent that many members of the committee felt a "trick" had been played on them. If it had not been for the esteem in which Dr. Tracy and Miss Schroder were held within the group, it is certain that there would have been minimum cooperation. Administratively, in an attempt to make the meeting a success, Miss Schroder bore the burden of sending hundreds of notices, printing large signs to be used in the meeting room, and calling dozens of people on the telephone.

Illustrative of the feelings that existed concerning the forthcoming community meeting were some of Mr. Grogan's comments. When the latter had established a certain amount of rapport with the committee, he always expressed his feelings frankly. After listening with trepidation to the obviously unplanned schedule he finally emphasized the importance of utilizing the "right" method of placing the material before the public. "There should be a plan so that when you bring these people together you know what you're going to say; you can't just have them fill out slips." Miss Schroder had planned to recruit membership for various subcommittees from the gathering in Town Hall via the slip method. "So far," he continued, "it is not apparent to me what plans have been made, and I don't think this committee can stand a failure. If I am a member of this committee and don't know what's happening, just imagine how the rest of the people feel!" Grogan added, "I'm just telling you what's on my mind. I don't like to be pessimistic and I can be persuaded that we are on the right track." Both Colbert and Grogan then attempted to set up an agenda. The health agent announced that Dr. Gage would chair the meeting. Just as avidly as Dr. Gage had criticized Grogan's report, the latter insisted that there was no reason for the minister to preside when Mrs. Childs was president.

The mayor's presence was again a matter of discussion. Grogan questioned whether the mayor's attendance was mandatory. Indecision followed. If the meeting were a failure, the mayor's presence would be damaging to the future of the study; if successful, his absence would be unfortunate. Optimistically an invitation was extended to the mayor.

On the evening of March 23, 1953, the doors of historic Town Hall were thrown open for the community meeting. The room had been decorated by Miss Schroder at Grogan's suggestion with yellow and green signs reading in large, bold letters: "Accident Prevention"; "School Health"; "Mental Health Survey"; "Your Community: A Healthy Place, a Safe Place to Live"; "Housing"; "Environmental Sanitation—Incinerator"; "Health Center"; "The Job Ahead"; "A Community Steps Forward"; "It's Been Done Before"; and "Your Town Has Made A Good Beginning." The curtain that had once decorated the small stage had long since been removed, and a covering for the iron frame had been devised of yellow crepe paper which fit into the color scheme of the brilliant posters.

Approximately one-third of those invited attended the meeting, or about 150 of the 500. Miss Schroder, who had undertaken the task of contacting individuals, used several methods. As an active agency secretary for many years she had assembled lists which were intended to reach every segment of the Salem population. All members of the Tuberculosis Association Board were contacted by letter. Membership on this board is acknowledged as a symbol of high social or economic position. The complete membership list of the association as well as the list of participants in the successful city-wide X-ray survey, which had been held several years before, were used. The latter two contained the names of some leaders in Polish, French, Irish, and Italian communities. Every physician and city councillor was notified. Organizations which contributed to the annual Christmas seal drive were sent cards. Many more were contacted by telephone. Two ministers announced the meeting from the pulpit and urged congregational attendance.

It is interesting to note that only five individuals listed as top community leaders—Gage, Lassiter, Phills, Burroughs, and Resnick—were present. Several representatives of the city administration made an appearance—the mayor, three city councillors—Mooney, Suckow, and Sutorius—and members of the fire, police, and health departments. Two members of the board of health—Leder and Katzenstein—were present. The attendance of only three or four members of the upper socio-economic group in Salem showed that the interest of this group was negligible. The major interest seemed to come from agency professionals and agency volunteer people.

Each of the 150 individuals in attendance was equipped with a dittoed copy of findings and a slip of paper which served a dual purpose, that of registration form and volunteer interest commitment in one of the special subcommittee areas. Dr. Tracy opened the meeting, briefly discussed the history of the study, and presented in an uninteresting and uninspiring fashion the study findings.

One of the high lights of the meeting was the introduction

of the mayor. Mayor Corcoran spoke briefly, committing the city to give to the community for a health center the old vocational high school building. This was the first time a representative of the city had made a commitment of this size since the initiation of the study process.

The health agent called on Dr. Gage to describe the findings in connection with psychiatric services. The minister said he hoped that he could interest the group concerning the results of the survey. Always speaking effectively, he conveyed the thought that there is something fine about a community which can determine the facts and look at its problems. He spoke about a school in New York which had sent a team to New England to see whether the section was alive. "Sometimes it's hard to determine whether we are alive. However, when we look at industry and realize that electronics was born here and note that people have become involved in a study such as the one we are considering this evening, it helps, in a way, to justify our contention that we live."

Reverting to his role as minister, Dr. Gage mentioned the concern of his colleagues over the problem of acquiring adequate psychiatric services and requested that some of the people present join in the work of his committee.

Proceeding, Dr. Tracy introduced Dr. Stewart Phills, recently retired chief of staff at Salem Hospital who had accepted the chairmanship of the Health Center Committee.

Dr. Phills opened his remarks by saying that he had had great interest in the social welfare of people in the community and the state for many years. He maintained that it was important today to locate all health agencies under one roof. Pointedly he emphasized that such a center should not duplicate services already supplied by the hospital. He said he had volunteered to chair this committee and that he hoped to investigate the subject thoroughly. Dr. Phills did an excellent job of presenting his topic and his little talk was accepted with a good deal of enthusiasm.

Miss Ann Koestner, the health educator from the State

Tuberculosis Society, was then introduced. As a health educator she was assigned the task of attempting to get people to act. First, she said that the group should take as an assignment the reading of the report which had been mimeographed and handed to everyone present in the hall. Second, she said the group ought to know what their health problems were and know that they could be solved. She commented that the days of legislating health into existence were gone. Miss Koestner said she could tell the group, if she had time, what other communities had done, but she did not feel that such knowledge was particularly valuable. Then she asked the question, "What can *we* do?"

She went on to say that each individual present should get in touch with all the people they knew who could not come to the meeting to tell them what they had missed. "Look over the facts," she said, "and be able to answer questions that people may raise concerning the health study. Look around, see who can help on this program, businessmen, health professionals, so on." Miss Koestner said also there was a typical American pattern for solving problems in typically American communities such as Salem. She suggested that the first step was the formation of committees and requested the group to fill out the slips they had been given with their name and address and the name of the committee or committees of interest to them.

The meeting terminated with a question period in which representatives of the city council, medical profession, agencies, and U.S. Public Health Service were given the opportunity of expression. Some of our notations record the conflict and dynamics of group interaction.

Councillor Lewis Suckow, who had been sitting in the rear of the auditorium, rose and asked a question. "Have we got problems in all 15 areas that were studied?" Dr. Tracy replied, "No, we have problems in only a few of the 15 areas." Mr. Suckow rose and continued, "Where does the $.39 come from? How did you arrive at that figure?" Dr. Tracy said that the State Department of Health gave this figure from a study made in 1951. He turned to Mrs. Louise Sorrell, health educator for the District State Health Department unit, for an affirmation of this fact. Mr. Suckow then asked where the additional money would come from for health services.

At that point, Dr. Max Katzenstein rose to his feet and said he had not been asked to talk but that he would like to make a few remarks. Dr. Katzenstein stated that he felt the community should be ashamed to compare itself with other municipalities, considering the small amount of money it spends for public health measures. "Every time I bring a budget to the City Council, and every time I've asked them for anything the City Council cuts it out." Mr. Suckow responded sharply, "No, we don't! The City Council has never cut anything from your budget!" Bickering between the two continued for five or six minutes. Mr. Suckow was a new member of the City Council. He was mistaken in his statement. Not only was it untrue, but Mr. Suckow certainly should have been aware of the fact that the City Council, earlier that evening, in a budget meeting cut out an additional sanitary inspector which had been requested for the health department budget for 1953-1954. At that point Dr. Tracy broke into the heated discussion and attempted to put an end to it.

A gentleman rose to ask a question concerning housing. Dr. Tracy then called on John Connolly and identified him as a staff member of the housing divisions of both the U.S. Public Health Service and the State Department of Health. Mr. Connolly stated that one-fifth of all the housing in Salem is substandard. This aroused audience interest.

Connolly was asked: "What would you tell us to do?" Connolly overlooked that remark entirely, much to the dissatisfaction of a number of people. James Sutorius of the Salem City Council rose and asked how Salem compared with other communities. Connolly replied, "It is no better and no worse." Lieutenant Newcomb of the Police Department rose and said that Salem had recently had a great tragedy in connection with a fire in a house built before the housing law was put into effect. Connolly inferred that the code was not applicable. Dr. Gage questioned, "Whose responsibility is it to enforce the code?" Connolly stated that there were about six departments in each community involved in the code and that they must work together. There must be some system established to prevent duplication of effort. Mr. Connolly remarked, "Incidentally, cooperation and coordination are the most difficult things to get in the community, and yet they are the least expensive."

Questioning ceased, commitment slips were collected, and many of those in attendance clustered in small groups to discuss the meeting.

Two meetings had been held at which study findings were presented. It was difficult to determine their results. In summary, both meetings aired the report and, through newspaper stories, established the committee system for further specific investigation. Second, each contributed its share of recruits for the seven committees recommended by the study group. Third, steps were taken to broaden the base of action from an exclusive to a more inclusive group. Lastly, the meetings offered an acceptable avenue for the commencement of community action following study.

By April the study committee had served its purpose, had suggested change and further study, and stood ready to act in an advisory capacity. The small subcommittees represented a proven procedure of establishing new groups designed to bring about the changes desired. Placing these new entities on a sound working basis was the next step.

Preceding the report which was made to the Community Council the self-study committee attempted to reinforce its recommendations that substudy committees be set up in each area to initiate further investigation and action. Mr. Colbert and Dr. Tracy, sometimes in sharp disagreement but with the help of the committee, set up a list of individuals whom they felt should serve on the new committees and who were in a position to augment their work. The following were selected and requested to serve either by Tracy, Colbert, or Schroder.

The Committee on Mental Health, Co-chairmen: Claude Downer, Carlton Gage.

Mr. Downer, the director of the North Shore Children's Friend Society, was one of the agency members who had remained firm and positive in his demand for better and additional psychiatric services. Dr. Gage's interests were apparent.

The Committee on Health Education, Co-chairmen: Mrs. Donald R. Patterson, Miss Katherine Schroder.

Both had an interest in the area and were ranked on different levels of Salem society which would prove advantageous in recruitment of workers and stimulation of interest.

Dentally Indigent Children's Committee, Chairman: Mr. Lawrence Furtado.

Mr. Furtado had been president of a Salem service club and had aided in social services to the medically indigent. He had also been active on the Salem Parent-Teachers Association council.

Miss Katherine Norman, a member of the Salem School Committee and a bacteriologist for the State Department of Public Health, was recommended for membership.

Restaurant Sanitation Committee, Chairman: Mr. Peter Grogan.

Supplemented by Mr. Warren Deyton, owner of a local restaurant.

Accident Prevention.

After much discussion concerning this committee it was decided that a request should be submitted to the general agent of the Salem office of the Metropolitan Life Insurance Company to select someone to serve as chairman of this committee.

Incinerator Committee, Chairman: Mr. Martin A. Bernstein, manager of a local theatre and active Rotarian.

Health Center.

Dr. Stewart Phills, who had retired from active participation as chief of staff at Salem Hospital, was suggested as possible chairman of the committee. Norwood tactfully urged that a woman, possibly Miss Schroder, approach the physician with the request. Mr. Ralph Douglass' name was suggested, but the committee decided that, although he was to leave his position soon as president of the board of trustees at Salem Hospital, the expansion of his business enterprises all over New England would prohibit additional activity on a local level.

Following the report to the Community Council, as prearranged, Mr. Norwood rose and read the suggested chairmen of the various committees.

Of those selected to serve as chairmen or co-chairmen, the eight following accepted: Peter Grogan, Martin A. Bernstein, Lawrence Furtado, Dr. Carlton Gage, Claude Downer, Miss Katherine Schroder, Mrs. Donald R. Patterson, and Dr. Stewart Phills.

The community-wide meeting and the Community Council meeting, as well as the suggested agencies and occupational groups recommended for committee appointment by the study report, provided members for the seven committees established. Miss Schroder compiled lists from the commitment slips and from personal contacts of her own and of the health agent. She also contacted and sent membership lists to each committee chairman urging meetings in the near future. Following Norwood's suggestion, Miss Schroder had approached Dr. Stewart Phills to gain his acceptance of the chairmanship of the Health Center Committee. The recognized leader of the Salem medical profession, a meticulous, fastidious man, considered by many to be "one of the last real gentlemen left," Dr. Phills had held power over his fellows for over twenty years.

When Miss Schroder made her request, the physician is known to have replied, "Certainly. I could refuse nothing you might ask." Dr. Phills had worked actively in the Tuber-culosis Association for many years and, as his response during interviews with the University of North Carolina staff in-dicated, had recognized Miss Schroder's dedication to her work and her unselfish response to any request. He could do nothing but accept as long as the request was socially and professionally acceptable.

A total of 84 individuals was committed to committee service. Of those, 27 percent were full-time workers for the local political structure, 20 percent were on the staffs or represented the staffs of social agencies, 16 percent were actively involved in health work as physicians or nurses, and 37 percent were in private business or were civic leaders. Only one chairman of a committee was a representative of the health profession, although all but two committees, acci-dent prevention and incineration, had at least one member from that area. Four chairmen were local businessmen and four chairmen or co-chairmen were employed by social agencies. Business or civic leaders were found on each com-mittee, while the social agencies were not represented on four committees. Although the importance of including represen-tatives from the civil offices was seldom underestimated throughout the self-study, no one from that level was selected as chairman. The only committee without a member of the city administration was health education.

The ethnic character of the subcommittees shows little per-centage increase over the study committee. There were several more Irish, two Poles, one Italian, and one French Canadian. There was only one Jew.

Following the community and the Council meetings and the designation of committees, only three units showed signs of action. The health education committee met twice and attempted with the help of the steering committee to deter-mine its function and plan its activities. This committee con-sisted entirely of women. It was finally decided that the edu-cation committee was to develop a program for keeping the health study before the community and to compile resource files with listings of membership, activities, and the structure and function of all clubs and organizations within the community. The committee, through Mrs. Patterson who was co-chairman of this subcommittee, requested an appropriation of $150 from the Community Council for a series of special articles on the various study areas to be written and published by Fred Burrell, reporter for a local newspaper. A portion of the sum was to be designated for publicity for the Community Fund. Colbert, of the latter organization, had been most influential in suggesting the above activity.

The committee on housing, under pressure from Dr. Tracy, likewise held two meetings. Encouraged by John Connolly of the Housing Division of the U.S. Public Health Service, the group committed itself to the guidance of a group of volunteers which it hoped to recruit for training by the U.S. Public Health Service to study Salem housing. However, United States budgetary cuts prohibited further activity by Federal government personnel.

The health center committee had not met formally, but its chairman, the health agent, and two representatives of the State Department of Health had considered plans for securing the vocational high school building, which the mayor so graciously committed, as its physical site.

In passing, it is interesting to note that a large portion of committee members consisted of men and women active in health or welfare organizations on a professional or volunteer basis or whose business interests, i. e., insurance, real estate, etc., made committee membership desirable.

While several members of the study committee engaged in attempts to project the study to what is called the "grass-roots" level of the community, few concrete steps were taken in that direction. Clearly the term "grass-roots level" is nebulous and evades definition. On occasion, special publics such as P.T.A.'s or men's and women's organizations have been classified as the latter. In direct contrast, individuals in the lowest socio-economic stratum of the community had been recognized as such. In a complex society we may group individuals on the basis of wealth and social standing, or we may throw people into groups on the basis of occupation and rank them from common laborer up to the professional. The type of action to be taken is the determining factor in selecting the particular class or group or public which one wishes to involve.

With urbanization and the increased complexity of medical care, society in general has tended to shift its responsibility for public health programs, planning, and policies, to a small number of professionals and citizens. An attempt to involve individuals whose interests and understanding are far removed from social planning and the making of social policy makes it necessary for the specialist to carry on a mass educational program which may not bring the results desired. Differentiation between the various levels of community leadership so that one may know to which to appeal for a certain type of proposed health activity is an administrative skill which represents a better guide to "community organization" than folklore or the blind course of chance.

It is too soon to determine all of the results of the study activities, since many of the projects must be considered long term. The officers of the Salem Community Council have anticipated an emphasis on this phase of the Council's activities for several years.

CHAPTER 11

Specific Action

I T CAN BE said that the activities of the self-study committee, with its ritualism and observances of proper form,
served as stage panorama for the one major action that followed its work. Its activities provided legitimacy, sanction,
and a background of consideration for the proposal that en-
sued—that of getting a community health center.

To explain the action taken, one needs to understand that
it was beneficial to all concerned. First, it was of real benefit
to the community at large. Second, it aided individual leaders
in their diverse strivings.

On the latter point, it will be observed that Dr. Tracy's
desire for more adequate working quarters was appeased.
The mayor, who had been accused, in some quarters, of being too conservative, could show liberality. Others, by their
actions, could prove the efficacy of their positions of leadership.

The money involved in the action to be described was
readily available. A surplus, no little part of which was due
to increased revenues from the new electric plant, could be
spent without raising questions of prodigality. Nor was a
question of major policy change raised that would have necessitated drawn out clearances and negotiations with those who
might otherwise have opposed the move.

The project was actually put forward on the basis of
"economy" since it required only $50,000 rather than
$200,000 originally and tentatively suggested in relation to
it. It was fortuitous in many ways.

After the appointment of a number of special committees

by the Salem Community Council in the spring of 1953 some action on the recommendations of the survey committee seemed preeminent. Theoretically, movement should stem from group recognition of problems, or a problem, combined with community organization for action. Both qualifications seemed to have been met in Salem.

At the end of nine or ten months of deliberation the self-study committee recommended to the Community Council eight areas of needed health improvement and the possible committee members to study them. From the community-wide meeting additional committee workers were enlisted.

After the report had been made to the Community Council and to the community, responsibility for further study and implementation was shifted to the newly appointed chairmen of eight committees: housing, health education, health center, restaurant sanitation, incinerator, dentally indigent children, mental health, and accident prevention. The self-study committee was reappointed by the Community Council president as a steering and guiding body for the smaller groups. Tracy, as former leader, was appointed chairman of the new steering committee.

In order to determine whether action will be brought to bear upon any suggested work or problem areas, several factors must be considered: (1) the degree of awareness of the people involved in the action program, of those individuals or groups they represent or with whom they come into repetitive contact, and of the community in general; (2) the community positions filled by those on the action committee as well as their role expectation and their attitudes toward the roles of other participants in relation to the committee, the amount of prestige and esteem attached to a position or individual, and the degree of authority or power possessed or exerted by the participants; and (3) the attitudes of power groupings whose interests might be affected by the action.

Within this framework we will consider the health action which took place between June and December, 1953. Undoubtedly, the action itself might have taken several alternative forms. It was possible that all eight committees would begin to function at top speed. It was possible that the Community Council or its leaders might determine several areas of pressing need, as rated by the self-study committee, and focus its attention upon the particular committees dealing with those areas. A third possible line of action was that all forces might be moved to concentrate upon one of the several areas.

During several of the various meetings previously discussed all of the alternative approaches were informally considered. Grogan felt that the easiest problems, those in which success could be obtained with limited effort and within a minimum amount of time, should be attacked first. This, he felt, would make success in difficult ventures more probable. Tracy expressed an interest in attacking only one of the eight problems. Some, he felt, were politically unpopular and might remain so for some time. Other committee members offered no plan, willing to jettison the difficult job of action. Mrs. Patterson attempted to interpret the work of the self-study committee as completed after a report to the Council had been submitted and said that implementation was up to another or other new committees.

Formally, neither the Community Council nor the new steering committee bound themselves to a particular course of action. The attitude of those Council members who were interested in the report was that it represented a long term plan in which the Council might engage from time to time for a number of years. Of the steering committee membership, Tracy and Schroder were most concerned about the next steps.

What should those next steps be? On which segments of the broad health program areas should they work? What community organization problems would be involved? These were difficult questions to answer. Substantial evidence might be found to support any hypothetical interpretation of possible alternatives. The knowledge gained from our focus upon community power structure and intimate day-to-day experiences with the participants in the action system under observation revealed problems involved in anticipated action within the eight study areas.

Six of the eight committees were to deal with problems which required some type of intercourse with the Salem city administration. A seventh, health education, might have, depending upon its emphasis, also interacted with the political structure. The only committee which might possibly have failed to need help in some form from the local government was that of mental health.

Three committees, dentally indigent children, restaurant sanitation, and accident prevention, were to deal with the problems which required continuous supervision and adaptation to change. Improvement of this type of program is dependent upon adequate knowledge of the problems involved. These three were "welfare" problems which usually can be improved or temporarily corrected with small financial outlays. Only one of the three chairmen, Peter Grogan, had had previous association with the self-study. The accident prevention committee was to be chaired by a representative of the local office of the Metropolitan Life Insurance Company. The dentally indigent children's committee was to be chaired by Lawrence Furtado who had been active in service club projects. None of these men, with the possible exception of the Metropolitan Life Insurance representative, could be considered an expert. Their limited experiences would prevent them from instilling other committee members with the enthusiasm and drive necessary for successful operation. Presumably the latter would have to come from the steering committee—probably from Dr. Tracy. Outside direction might possibly limit the success of the projects and place committees in critical "rubber stamp" positions.

The incinerator committee was also to be chaired by a layman—the manager of a local theatre, Mr. Bernstein. The financial problems involved in the project would indicate the contribution that such a leader might make. However, the reasons for building an incinerator were both technical and controversial. It would have necessitated not only a large financial outlay but inter-community cooperation which was at a premium. The local government had considered the project for many years and it had been the object of political manipulation on several occasions. The problem was one that required pressure from the top levels of the community power structure of which Mr. Bernstein was not a part.

The mental health committee, co-chaired by Dr. Gage and Claude Downer, executive secretary of the North Shore Children's Friend, was a committee which one might have expected to be active. Both Gage and Downer had been concerned about the problem for some time and had spoken out against the reticence of the community to act. Such a committee might have provided the lever needed to augment their previous work. Gage had been attending a course on community mental health care sponsored by the State Department of Mental Health. The philosophy of the course seemed to be: move cautiously—good programs take time. It was plausible to assume that this philosophy might permeate the activities of the committee chairmen.

After the careful deliberation and manipulation discussed heretofore, Dr. Stewart Phills was named to head the health center committee. At the community-wide reporting session the mayor had pledged his support in obtaining an old vocational school building for this purpose. The combination of both Tracy and Phills' interest and the possibility of a building in the near future seemed to indicate at least one area of successful action.

It will be remembered that by June, 1953, several important stages had been completed. The Community Council had sponsored a self-study of Salem's health problems. Through its elected officers it had appointed a study committee consisting of Council and non-Council members. From October, 1952, until June, 1953, it received reports of the committee activities. At its March, 1953, meeting the Council voted its acceptance of the report and acknowledged its continued support and interest. In truth one might sincerely question the Council's actual participation in the study.

Basically the study was primarily made because Joseph Colbert of the Community Fund, who had received a letter of inquiry from the University of North Carolina, felt it represented an opportunity for Salem to get publicity. Secondarily, Henry L. Tracy and Katherine Schroder recognized the sudden interest the inquiry aroused on the part of a number of civic leaders as the stimulus necessary to fulfill their dreams of such a study and its end product—a possible health center where all public and private health agencies might work together.

The role of the Community Council, as a representative body, was to give symbolic approval to the project. Its limited participatory activities beyond this are not necessarily a criticism of its potency nor do they support its weakness as an organization. As a Council its manifest function is to act as a clearing house and common meeting ground for representatives of the various community agencies. Likewise as a Council its latent function is to place the stamp of approval or disapproval on various community enterprises. The successful fulfillment of this latent function in regard to the self-study doubtless represented the temporary acceptance or rejection of it by other leaders in the community.

A committee was appointed, a study made and reported upon. New committees were set up. Some acted, others did not. After defining their position in relation to the other committees and making temporary plans for the publishing of a series of newspaper articles, the health education committee became inactive. The severe cuts in the U.S. Public Health Service budget crippled the housing program to such an extent that offers of help in the original form to the Salem committee were withdrawn. This committee became inactive. Apparently activities had come to a standstill. The possibility of further action after the summer months could not be determined. Speculation was far from optimistic.

However, in September the *Salem Evening News* carried

front-page headlines which indicated that at least one committee had been active. On September 26 there appeared, "Salem Health Center Supported by Mayor"; on December 10 there followed, "Prompt City Action Can Establish Health Center"; and climaxed on December 11 with "$50,000 Voted to Set up Municipal Health Center." How did this action reach fruition? Why was this one project successful out of all they said they were going to do or might have done? This is the story. It is a story which involves not only the health and welfare leaders and the city administration but men we have previously placed far up the echelon of community power.

Interviews, newspaper articles dating several years before the self-study, and day-to-day contact with Dr. Henry L. Tracy indicated, in no uncertain terms, that the health agent hoped eventually to convince the city administration and community leaders that a health center was a primary need in Salem. He spoke of it before service clubs. He discussed it informally with local political leaders in and out of power. He recognized the self-study as one possible way of increasing interest in and gaining support for this project. He recommended the establishment of a health center in his report to the self-study committee. Finally, he augmented the appointment of the committee, set up to investigate the need of a center, by aiding in the selection of the strongest, most powerful chairman the community could offer to fill this position—Dr. Stewart Phills.

For at least two months after the community-wide meeting Dr. Tracy and Miss Schroder concerned themselves with the consummation of committee appointments and the temporary activities of the health education and housing committees. By July, an event, which Mayor Corcoran had prophesied, motivated more immediate action. Early deliberations as to possible health center sites in overcrowded Salem narrowed to three areas. All were within several blocks of the center of the city. Two were already in the hands of the local government. The private property and one piece of city property would require a new plant. The other public property was the vocational school building and grounds which might possibly be available in the future. Miss Katherine Norman, an active member of the Salem school board, had initiated plans for the integration of the vocational high school plant and its curriculum into that of the Salem Classical and High School. Appropriations had been made and plans approved for the merger.

By October or November, 1953, the old vocational high school building would be vacant and disposal of its property would be forced on the city council. A decision had to be made concerning its possible renovation as a health center. Previously Tracy had discussed the value and attainability of building a new plant. The opinions varied, splitting down the middle. The probability was certainly much less than the chances of renovating already existing facilities. Tracy determined to concentrate his efforts on the latter.

The action which followed appeared to be a combination of the right organization, proper clearance, compromise, and timing. After making an initial compromise with the decision to utilize an old building, Tracy proceeded to appoint additional members to the health center committee. He emphasized the importance of a lay committee to put the project across. Basically he established three prerequisites for membership. First, they had to "be in a position to be helpful"; second, they had to "have a sincere interest in making a success of the plans"; and third, they had to have "been active in public health activities in the past."

The original committee appointed by the Community Council consisted of Dr. Stewart Phills, members of the board of health, Lucian Gosset, Richard Jones of the North Shore Babies Hospital board, and Russell Perry of the Heart Association. It was felt that others were needed to implement the work. Mr. Jones was involved in a very demanding schedule and he was replaced by Lewis Nelson, retired office manager for the New England Electric Company in Beverly. He was known to many because of his activities in the North Shore annual church canvass. Mr. Nelson was recommended by the North Shore Babies Hospital.

Mr. Michael O'Hara, an official in the local C.I.O. Processors' Union, perhaps the largest single labor group in the area, was added to the committee. In the past he had aided both Miss Schroder and Dr. Tracy in putting across health programs which affected people in the leather industry. He was a member of the Heart Association board, was considered to be politically powerful because of his status in labor and friendship for the Corcoran administration, and was elected to the school committee in the fall of 1953.

Dr. Ronald Allen was invited to membership in view of his professional status as a local physician and his position in the local Heart Association. Robert Fanjoy, secretary of the Heart Association, and Roger Dial, President of the Cerebral Palsy Association, whose organizations hoped to share in the benefits of a health center, were also appointed. In addition, Mr. William Brody, a retired electrical engineer who had been active in temporary work of the housing committee, was added to the list. A final selection was Thomas Barrow, treasurer of Jack Brothers Game Company and president of the Salem Tuberculosis Association.

The functioning of this group did not follow the pattern of the earlier self-study committee. It consisted of an ebb and flow of clearance with various groups and the establishment of a pattern and deference toward certain individuals—all skillfully manipulated by Dr. Tracy.

Action plans involved four groups and two individuals— representatives of the State Health Department, the Salem board of health, the health center committee, the City Council, Dr. Phills, and the mayor of Salem. Tracy planned, informed, and cleared with these groups and individuals until success was assured. Before calling a meeting of the health center committee or presenting the project officially to the board of health, the health agent consulted on the tenability of the proposed center with State Department of Health personnel, Dr. Paxton, the district health officer, and Dr. Rosenberg, director of the inspection of hospitals for the State Department of Health. After inspecting the edifice, both gentlemen expressed enthusiasm over the enterprise. Dr. Rosenberg even suggested that Paxton move the district health office from Wakefield, Massachusetts, to the new building.

Next Tracy presented the plans for renovating the school together with the views expressed by Rosenberg and Paxton to the board of health. This body felt that it should take official action immediately and request the mayor to turn over the plant in question to the board. Tracy, recognizing the probable impotency of such a move, asked that the board serve on the regular citizens' committee. The chairman, Dr. Katzenstein, suggested that Dr. Phills not be bothered with cumbersome details until all plans and specifications were drawn up. Ignoring the suggestion, the health agent made an appointment with Phills because he "felt that Dr. Phills should be aware of my intentions and the intentions of the board and just how he would be involved. Also, to discuss the philosophy concerned with an endeavor such as this and express what each had in mind."

When this meeting was held, Dr. Phills remarked that he had once felt that if a health center were built it should be added to Salem Hospital so that all clinic facilities might be utilized. Tracy agreed in principle but felt that, since the health center would maintain only a screening clinic, it ought to be located at some central point reasonably available to transportation systems and parking. Tracy acquainted Dr. Phills with the plan in regard to the vocational school. The following day Phills and Tracy inspected the plant, and Phills signified that he would be happy to go along with the project favoring the location of the health center in the vocational high school building.

Phills' decision was reported back to the board of health. At their request a Salem architect was engaged to draw up basic structural plans. The board continued to express doubts concerning their membership on a citizens' committee and on Tracy's emphasis on such a group.

On July 23, 1953, Tracy called a meeting of the health center committee. The health agent, city councillor Mooney, Mr. Dial, Dr. Paxton, and Mr. Fanjoy were present. The other members who were unable to attend expressed their desire to help and promised their cooperation at later meetings. Again the health agent had to review the progress made, interpret the project as he saw it, place the burden and responsibility of decision on this group as he had on those mentioned above. Questions were raised concerning the suitability of the old building. Councillor Mooney realistically expressed recognition of the fact that it would be far easier to secure funds to renovate an old building than to build a new one. He also felt that if the building could be made fireproof the city might obtain one-third of the necessary rebuilding funds from the state. The placement of clinics within the building was also a concern of the committee.

With architectural plans drawn from rough drafts submitted by Dr. Tracy and Miss Schroder, Dr. Phills, Dr. Rosenberg and Dr. Paxton had a second meeting, went over these plans, again looked over the building, and approved. It was their suggestion that the committee be informed of their decision. On September 14, 1953, the plans were submitted and approved by the health center committee. Mr. Barrow informed the committee that he was going to recommend that his association (T.B.) join with the health department in moving to the health center. The remainder of the time during the meeting was consumed with plans for next steps.

Questions were posed on the attitude of the mayor toward the project, the amount of money that should be requested, and the method that should be used to present the plans to the mayor. In answer, Mr. Mooney expressed the belief that the mayor was "favorably inclined" and had indicated so at the community-wide meeting in the spring. Dr. Katzenstein suggested that the committee not ask for more than $20,000 although the architect's figures quoted $40,000 to $45,000. The committee finally decided to ask for $40,000. Although several members suggested appointing a committee to see the mayor and Dr. Katzenstein felt that Dr. Phills, members of the board of health, and the health agent should present the project, Tracy's pointed emphasis on the importance of the citizens' committee won out when Mr. Thomas Barrow injected, "Why don't we all go!"

A short meeting was held several nights later, three days before a morning appointment with the mayor, to make final plans. It was decided to change the request for financial aid from $40,000 to $42,000. On September 26, 1953, Dr. Stewart Phills, Dr. Henry L. Tracy, Dr. Max Katzenstein, Everett Leder of the board of health, Katherine Norman of the school board, Councillors Mooney and Franklin, Michael O'Hara, Roger Dial, Thomas Barrow, William Brody, and Lewis Nelson presented the plan to Mayor Corcoran.

Dr. Phills was a key figure in the final decision made for establishing the center. One person who attended the final meeting at which the question of recommending the project to the city council was in balance, described Dr. Phills' participation in these terms:

Dr. Phills was about fifteen minutes late for the meeting. We had all been stumbling around in our presentation of the need for the center and I had the feeling that we were getting exactly nowhere.

When Dr. Phills came in, we were all very relieved. After apologizing for being late, he got right down to cases. He told the committee exactly what was needed and how they should go about getting it. In about fifteen minutes he had the whole group sold. Nobody raised any serious objection after the doctor had spoken.

The respect with which Dr. Phills is held and the fact that he is the person to whom all look for medical policy cues in the scheme of community delegation of authority was obvious.

The mayor acknowledged his sympathy with the proposal and promised his support if he were re-elected. His election was uncontested. The requested appropriation was given another boost when someone arbitrarily mentioned $50,000. Miss Norman reminded the mayor that the city would probably receive a subsidy of $25,000 from the state toward the new vocational high school which could be applied toward converting the old building into a health center.

These initial procedures were followed by informal talks with heads of private health agencies and public addresses before service clubs. Visits were made to health centers in Quincy and Brookline in an attempt to modify the plans if suggestion warranted it. Articles were run in the *Salem Evening News* at appropriate times, i.e., prior to city council meetings.

Early in December, 1953, the mayor sent in a request to the city council for a $50,000 appropriation. Mr. Gosset moved that it be sent to the finance committee for consideration. Fearful that it might be buried in committee, Tracy enlisted the aid of several community leaders to call Mr. Gosset and also asked Councillor Mooney to use his influence on Gosset to bring it out of committee.

On December 10 the proposal was presented to the council by Mr. Gosset who told his colleagues that the conversion and consolidation would take care of housing not only the city health agency but private agencies such as the heart, tuberculosis, and cerebral palsy organizations. "I think," he said, "that the money will be well spent for it will bring clinics and the health department under one roof." Dr. Tracy spoke briefly on the center and the order was carried with a minimum of discussion.

Although the project was a success there were still problems which had to be solved. There was still the question of whether all the private health agencies would take advantage of the new center. Utilization and service policies would have to be discussed and established. The position of the board of health in view of Katzenstein's insistence that it "carry the ball" in all health center activities had to be ascertained. Nevertheless, there was much enthusiasm over the center. The Lions Club was interested in the establishment of an eye clinic within the center guaranteeing $3,000 annually to help defray expenses.

In summary, it would be far too idealistic to assume that the proper organization, clearance, and compromises accounted for the quiescent manner and open purse of the mayor and city council toward the venture. Mayors and city councils are not generous with physical plants or large sums of money. They are noted and elected for the zealous penuriousness they display on such occasions. Realistically there are probably several reasons. Among them are these. The project had the support of an organized group of citizens representing labor, welfare organizations, the medical profession, "Chestnut Street," and even the city council. The group was chaired by Dr. Stewart Phills whose influence and prestige in Salem were undisputed. Noteworthy is the fact that although Phills officially chaired the committee he attended only the meeting called to meet with the mayor. Instead Tracy acted as go-between, clearing and interpreting developments among the committee, Phills, State Health Department personnel, and the board of health.

The availability of a city building is always of interest to a multitude of civic organizations. The vocational school was located in geographic proximity to Chestnut Street and to the Italian district. Rumor had it that the Italian Catholic Church hoped to obtain the building as a social center. The probability of Chestnut Streeters peacefully agreeing to such a move was possible, but merely possible. The cries of depreciation of property values and the amassing of power groups were not unknown in Salem.

The generous offer of the vocational school as a health center eliminated, for an indisputably important function, the religious and ethnic problems which might have arisen if other allocation had been necessary. The presence of a considerable surplus in the city coffers made the problem of financing painless to the council. Without a doubt the health center project could not have been launched at a more propitious time.

CHAPTER 12

Ideas That—Guide?

AFTER A FEW words on social science hypotheses in general, we shall attempt a critical evaluation of the specific ideas that were aimed at setting the stage for the present work.

Hypotheses are generally conceded to be, as the dictionary states, tentative theories or suppositions provisionally adopted to do two things: (1) explain certain facts; and (2) guide in the investigation of others. In the latter case hypotheses are called working hypotheses. The hypotheses utilized in the present study were working hypotheses.

A set of hypotheses in social science investigation gives a frame of reference for study—a rationale for the things done to complete a given study. No study today is quite complete without an initial set of hypotheses. They help to focus the problem under investigation in logical terms. They are useful.

It was stated earlier in this writing, as an hypothesis, that *cultural changes occur with least conflict and confusion along lines of established community patterns.*[1] This statement seemed logical at first sight. It was only after we tried to work out a research design in relation to this hypothesis that we ran into difficulty.

In the first place, "cultural changes," as a phrase, presented a problem. Cultures do not change rapidly—certainly not observably within a year of field research. Or at best, we must admit that we did not have the techniques with which to

1. *Infra*, p. x. Also, since, in the pages to follow, we shall be discussing all the hypotheses utilized in the study, we shall italicize them for ready reference.

226

observe cultural change in the time span allotted to the study. We observed some dissatisfaction among certain ethnic groups related to present cultural arrangements, but this does not prove change. Undoubtedly changes, imperceptible, were going on before our eyes, but we did not see them. We did not perceive them. We might guess that in ten years or twenty years, if nothing in the way of crisis occurred in Salem, the Yankee group would lose more of its present prestige; the Irish group would continue to move up the professional and political ladder; and the Polish group would move into a more prominent position in community affairs. We might say other things about other groups, but it would be guesswork. It would not prove the hypothesis on change.

Secondly, it would have been impossible to begin immediately to do research in terms of the hypothesis, i.e., the observation of change was based upon the assumption that we knew, or should know, the "established community patterns" in order to observe "conflict and confusion" or the lack of it. We were in the community for three months before we felt at all sure that we had a knowledge of even a few of the established community patterns.

Thirdly, we soon recognized that the hypothesis was so broadly drawn, through the use of the word "culture," that we were hampered before we started. Salem's culture is in part internal, part external, and besides, we were not charged with a cultural study as such. We were going to take cultural factors into account, but the general proposition to which we were devoting our efforts was to determine how Salem citizens went about studying health needs. General elements of culture that might be correlated with men's actions in relation to health facilities and personnel were not to be overlooked, but we were not prepared to try to observe Salem culture as a whole.

In brief, the hypothesis was a troublesome one, and we soon found that we rather wished we did not have to deal with it. It became apparent that we could neither prove nor disprove it. We did not, however, discard it. It had value in assisting us to remain aware of cultural factors, and in this narrower sense it helped to guide our research. Perhaps we should be more explicit about the meaning of the word "guide."

Turning back momentarily to our definition of hypotheses, we recall that hypotheses are "tentative theories or suppositions provisionally adopted to explain certain facts and guide investigation." Our hypotheses could not be taken as "social theories," but they were suppositions adopted subject to proof or disproof. They served as guides in at least three ways.

First, the mere fact that they had to be formulated helped to focus areas of study. Secondly, they helped to provide a frame of reference in relation to questions devised to work out specific patterned relationships within the community, and finally, they were read, re-read, and discussed by the staff as the research was in progress.

In a general way, after the research was in progress, the hypotheses did guide the field staff, but they did not bind the staff if they became troublesome, as in the case of the first hypothesis cited. In the field work it became apparent that additional hypotheses needed to be developed that would further the research and, while these were few in number, these field hypotheses were as important as the ones developed preceding the field experience. An example lies in the tentative assumption that materials gathered from the Jack Brothers' Corporation employees would give us some information that would shed light on community leadership evaluations. Or, again, that a study of participation patterns of physicians would round out some of the materials gathered in other areas.

In cautious honesty, however, it must be admitted that it was necessary to remind ourselves, on occasion, that we had hypotheses to refer to, and it took conscious effort to bring them out of the files and re-read them. In this sense we raised the question in the title of this chapter, "Ideas that—guide?" They guided, but they did not bind. They guided, but they did not stand alone in their guidance.

Knowledge possessed by the members of the field team before the study and not formulated into hypotheses also guided the research. Situations in which the researcher found himself provided further guides. And too, the accumulation of data provided still more guides, because the materials raised questions that could not be answered in terms of the original hypotheses. One reaches a stage in community research in which mental patterns are somewhat unconsciously formulated. A Gestalt pattern forms in one's thinking, and forthcoming data are related to this pattern and fitted to it, held in abeyance for further examination or rejected as unrelated material. Thus, for these reasons, if for no others, we raise a question in relation to the function of hypotheses in studies of the nature presented here. And with these things said, let us examine some other hypotheses.

A community can solve most of its health problems itself through action programs if:
  a. *Its citizens have available to them an objective picture of their health situation.*
  b. *Its citizens have a knowledge of other communities' experiences in solving problems, and*
  c. *It has competent, democratic leadership.*

We were unsure of this hypothesis and its corollaries from the beginning of the study. Again, the time span comes into the picture. We do not know, at the present writing, whether or not Salem will be able to solve most of the health problems that were brought out in the self-study. We only know that a definite group of men have got a health center program worked out to the point of blueprints and financial planning. Many of the other programs within the areas of need are in a state of quietude.

The citizens of Salem do have at their disposal a relatively objective picture of their health programs in terms of unmet needs. We are not prepared to say that a whole picture of needs has been presented, but enough items were uncovered in the self-survey to keep the subcommittees, that were formed as a result of the study, busy for some time to come. The fact that only two subcommittees, the health center committee and the education committee, have been active raises some questions in relation to community organization processes that may be dealt with in the next chapter. But here it must be said that an objective picture *alone* does not guarantee action.

Getting a broad picture of community health needs is certainly a logical first step toward action, and the breadth of the study in Salem must be commended. It would be impossible for the average Salem citizen to know, without the kind of study that was made, just what some of the strengths and weaknesses are in his community health programs. Without some close follow-up of the recommendations of the study committee, however, it is doubtful that many citizens of Salem will actually know the contents of the committee report. The education committee has a job to do—a job left relatively untouched by the study committee—that of informing large groups of Salem citizens about the strengths and weaknesses of existing health resources and what resources need to be developed to make all services more adequate.

In relation to the study committee's activities in "getting a knowledge of other communities' experiences in solving similar problems," it must be said that some effort was made in this direction. A trip to Quincy was made by one of the members of the study committee to learn of study procedures utilized by that community. Members of the committee were in touch with state health officials in regard to study procedures and methods. As plans were drawn up for the health center, some contacts were made in relation to how other communities had solved this problem. Study committee personnel did not isolate themselves completely from outside sources of help in the study and planning process. It did use outside help with reserve, however, and somewhat sparingly.

As to "competent and democratic leadership," how does one measure this? We know that the top leaders of the community, as a group, were not involved in the study process, but the persons who were involved appeared to be a cross section of people who were presumed to know most about the subject under study and consideration. The process in the study committee seemed "democratic" enough, if give-and-take is a criterion of democracy at work. If large numbers of people is a criterion of democracy, then the process could not be considered completely democratic, for the vast majority of Salem citizens did not participate in the processes of decision in relation to the recommendations coming out of the study.

But to be completely fair on the question of numbers involved in study decisions, it must be re-emphasized that the *whole community* was invited to hear, on occasion, progress reports of the study and to offer criticisms and suggestions. That the attendance at these meetings was not large cannot be laid entirely to negligence on the part of the study committee. There is a lethargy in our democratic communities that is difficult to explain. We do not know why large numbers of people did not come to the publicized meeting of the study committee and help in the whole process. We can only wonder why they did not and leave the question open for the moment and return to it presently.

The persons who were actually involved directly in the study were ones who, from a role point of view, bore out some of the initial "suppositions" that we held before going into the study. We felt that, *Salem goes about solving its problems related to health in a manner that would conform to its general pattern of problem-solving on a community-wide basis.*

As briefly stated previously, Salem was chosen as a site for study precisely because it was well enough organized, large enough, old enough, and experienced enough, as a community, to go about the process of study without leaning on the University staff for guidance in study development. The staff did not want to be in a position of having to stimulate or encourage the study in any way. Making studies to meet social needs was no new process for many members of the

Salem community. Every member of the study committee had previous experience in similar studies. Each acted, roughly speaking, in conformity with general role expectations for committee members. None had to be told what to do in the formation and operation of the whole committee structure.

As we have seen in the chapters devoted to a description of committee procedures, there was pulling and hauling in getting the committee under way. There was some quiet jockeying for position as the committee work progressed. There was a painful period of defining the function of the committee. There were certain members of the committee who assumed leadership as the study got under way.

The period of defining the role of each member of the study committee and the process of working out definitions of committee function does not mean that the members were inexperienced in such activities. As a matter of fact, the committee gave the opposite impression to the staff member observing them. They were like fire horses who could jump into the harness at a moment's notice. Some of the procedures were familiar to each member. The problem under consideration, making a community health survey, was new to some of them, but none were dismayed by this fact. Most moved in relation to general role expectations that contain within them a certain expertness in attending or guiding meetings.

Community functions are delegated to specific functioning groups in the community. There is an overlap of this hypothesis and the one just previously cited. A part of the "general pattern of problem-solving on a community-wide basis" is related to the fact of delegated responsibilities. We shall presently see that other hypotheses are also interrelated.

In Salem, as in any other community we can think of, there are definite patterns of delegation of tasks. If one is interested in a problem related to commerce and industry, one would normally approach the Chamber of Commerce in Salem to inquire as to the most likely person or persons to help in its solution. In like manner, problems related to schools, politics, physical planning, welfare, and health also have central organizations staffed with professional persons who draw around them lay people interested in various aspects of the operations and functions of the specific organization.

Certain persons within any one of the groupings mentioned over a period of time emerge as "key figures" in the organization. Such persons may be laymen or professionals, but upon entering a community one is usually quickly steered to John Jones or Bill Smith "who knows more about the problem you have in mind than anyone I can think of." Jones and Smith usually do not act alone. They belong to one or another of the many community organizations entrusted by the community at large with specific functions.

In the area of health, the delegated responsibility to "specific functioning groups" is divided among several agencies, as has been pointed out in the chapter on community health organizations. Specific problems relating to tuberculosis, heart disease, vaccination, or any number of diseases, if affecting an individual would obviously be referred to individual doctors, the hospital or the public health department, as the case might be. If the problem was one of group importance, that had implications for the community at large, an individual agency, such as the tuberculosis society, the heart association, or the department of public health might be approached. If the problem involved more than one agency in its solution, the health division of the Community Council would be drawn into planning meetings. Such are the traditional patterns of delegated responsibility in the community. The patterns are not basically different from hundreds of other communities in the nation.

Within this framework of referral, however, the fact that a community council group was available was important. It is quite possible that any of the local agencies might have promoted and organized a community-wide survey of health needs, but in such a situation the individual agency would have been going beyond the general expectations of the community in regard to its specific function. Individual agencies are not expected to coordinate the activities of all other agencies in the community. They may help, but the over-all coordinating task is better lodged in an agency charged with specific responsibility in this area.

Through these modes of delegation, certain persons become recognized as being vested with qualities of expertness that are desirable in the processes of study, negotiation, and activities needed to accomplish goals. Thus, when a study seemed in order, those recognized as experts in health matters were drawn together for consultation and advice.

Doctors, health agency executives, and lay members attached to health organizations were called upon to exercise their traditional roles. It was also recognized at the outset of the community study that more than expert advice would be needed to accomplish the mission of the study committee. If the committee were to function adequately, it needed persons on it skilled in committee leadership.

The secretaries of the Chamber of Commerce and the Community Fund were invited into the committee sessions for their contributions to the study process from the point of view of providing organizational skills. If any of the recommendations coming out of the study were to require publicity, the presence of a member of the press, in this case the local newspaper, would be desirable. Thus, the editor of the local paper contributed by his early attendance at some of the study sessions. In like manner the politicians were represented, also certain members of the community who were presumed to be influential in securing money from private sources should the need for financing arise. In brief, *the members of the study committee followed, in general, their traditional role expectations.*

Because of the technical nature of the problems involved in health agency operations and because there were in existence agencies within the community designated to meet almost any health problem that might arise, it is clear that only a few of those who were instrumental in appointing the study committee thought in terms of involving immediately large masses of the Salem citizenry in the study of health needs. There was talk in several of the early meetings of the self-study committee concerning the desirability of involving grass-roots people of the community, but, in reality, very few people engaged in either the study or in the promotion of activities aimed toward establishing a health center. The committee for study was 13 in number. The public meeting drew fewer than 200 people. The action committee that waited upon the mayor and councilmen was only 12 in number. Thus out of a population of 41,000 in the Salem community, a total of little more than 200 persons, to use a liberal figure, was engaged in the activities of study and action in relation to community-wide problems in health. It would be meaningless to work out the ratio of active participants to the total population, but it can be definitely stated that: *a relatively small proportion of the population was involved in the self-study.*

Rather than dwell upon the implications of the numbers of people involved in the study, at this point, we shall merely say that our original hypothesis along this line was borne out. We believe this was partly true because of another related set of circumstances implied in the above discussion and embodied in the hypothesis that states: *a few leaders will emerge in the study process who will be primarily instrumental in furthering the study.*

The leaders who emerged in relation to the study were those who had the confidence of supporting groups—health agencies, welfare organizations, civic organizations, political bodies, and business groups. The ordinary citizen in Salem is accustomed to delegating passively responsibilities for action in conformity with what is presumed to be his interests. Community leaders have goals in mind before entering into such a study process as we have described here. Some of the leaders that emerged did so briefly. Dr. Bradshaw, for example, was a leader, in a negative sense, in the first few sessions of the study committee's activities. His function was to help, in the interests of the medical practitioner group he represented, to keep the study within bounds. Once he was assured of the limits within which the committee intended to operate, he subsided.

On the positive side of the ledger, Dr. Henry L. Tracy and Peter Grogan assumed leading roles in keeping the study moving. Miss Katherine Schroder stood behind Dr. Tracy throughout the study process. Without repeating the detail of roles assumed by these people, it can be said that without them the committee, as it was constituted, might have foundered. Of these three people, Dr. Tracy and Miss Schroder had specific goals in mind at the outset of the study. Both of them wanted a health center established in Salem. They wanted more than this specific thing, but they had this goal rather clearly in mind. It was to their advantage to keep the committee moving.

Other members of the committee had other motivations, perhaps, for keeping the committee going, but their motivations did not come to the fore as definitely as those of the persons mentioned. The genuine interest in the broader question of civic improvement and of the strengthening of health services for the whole community on the part of all participants cannot be doubted nor overlooked, but it would be naive to say that these motivations were uppermost in the minds of the committee members at all times.

Because of the composition of the study committee, it is hard to say with assurance that: *health organizations had a greater interest in promoting and extending the study than other community groups.* Mr. Grogan did not have a primary "health" orientation or interest. He did not represent a health organization. Neither did other members of the committee. Both Mr. Grogan and Mr. Colbert, of the Community Fund, along with other community leaders, saw the self-study as a way in which to "put Salem on the map." It was understood by many persons that a report of the study would be made available to other communities, and, if Salem did a good job in the study, it would redound to the community's credit.

It seems apparent that the mayor saw that support of at least one of the recommendations of the study committee would offer political advantage. Councillor Gosset, along with other councillors, also supported the idea when the votes were to be counted in relation to the final recommendations on the establishment of a health center.

Even though the group of members devoted to the study was relatively small in number and even if some of the interests of specific members of the total group might be described as relatively narrow, the group, as a whole, was composed of persons who traditionally have "moved things" in the community. This was a fact recognized by all who had any knowledge of the project. It was also a fact recognized by the persons responsible for organizing the group in the first place. The selection of members of the study committee and consequent action committees was no accident. The recognition of the principles of community controls, the decision-making process, and power elements within the community was present from the inception of the study, whether or not these elements were explicitly stated. *Matters of community-wide "policy" in relation to health will inevitably involve the community "power structure," it was said.* And so they did.

Of the 40 persons chosen by others in the community of Salem as top decision makers and power leaders, at least 11 of them can be identified as having had some part in the study and action process in relation to health needs under scrutiny. These 11 were: Mrs. William Wallace Burroughs, Paul Carletno, Joseph Colbert, Richard J. Corcoran, Carlton Gage, Thomas Barrow, Dr. Margaret Lassiter, Russell Perry, Dr. Stewart Phills, Lucien Gosset, and Anna Resnick. The relative positions of these persons within the patterned structuring of policy and decisions within the community have been described elsewhere. The majority of these persons are not top policy makers, but all are leaders in the community.

They have the confidence of relatively large groups of people, and by broad processes of selection they were put forward to serve their community in ascertaining the merits and demerits of health services in Salem in 1953.

Perhaps we should now take the question mark off the present chapter title. The ideas elaborated upon, thus far, and with the exceptions noted, did guide in the investigation of actions taken by Salem citizens. Among other things, they have also helped in summarizing our data. But there were other ideas that guided our investigation that must be touched upon in order to give a balanced account of the whole research process.

As the research staff of the University of North Carolina discussed the problems of seeing action processes in the community, it became apparent that there were underlying assumptions as well as questions in the minds of the researchers involved. Some of the staff had grave doubts that the "self-study" would really be a *self*-motivated study. It was felt that the mere presence of the staff in the community would stimulate movement in relation to the study and might help to precipitate action. We could see no way of measuring this idea with any degree of accuracy. All that can now be said is that we still feel that our presence was a factor in the whole project. We feel certain that our presence was used by several persons to goad others toward action because the community was placed in the limelight—brief as that light may have been.

The research staff was not called upon to organize and guide the study in an active sense, however, and in large measure the study can be classified as a self-study in relation to the survey of health needs. We do not believe that the self-study committee was as thorough in its task as it might have been had the committee seen fit to call upon competent outside resources to help them.

The fact that the research staff was interested in the elements of social structure that were investigated in the early stages of inquiry, e.g., the power structure, prestige factors, political organization, ethnic groups, and social organizations, actually produced a situation in which the staff could not know whether or not the community would have taken these factors into consideration if no work had been attempted along these lines.

Some of these factors—power, prestige, and the like—are often taken for granted by groups whose individual members feel they are well acquainted with them in their particular community. Again, we have no way of knowing whether these factors would have been taken into conscious consideration in the data gathering process had the staff not been present in the community. We feel rather certain that much of the material contained in this writing would not have been put on paper by local investigators. We feel equally certain that we could not have observed the relationships of people in Salem with any degree of assurance had we failed to make the initial inquiry into the areas of social structure mentioned.

Another idea that guided the staff, not embodied in the hypotheses, was that we were going to try to observe the Salem community with as complete critical detachment as possible. This is no new idea, of course, and social investigators are supposed to do just that. It is a task that requires a great deal of working at as one goes along in gathering data, meeting people, and referring data and people to one's preconceptions. We tried to place ourselves, in relation to the persons we met in Salem, in a critical perspective from the beginning of the study.

It was generally known that we would be writing a report of all activities observed. We promised no blanket immunity from revelation to any group or individuals giving us information. We reserved the right at all points to describe events as we saw them. None that we know of disagreed with this basic premise, although it was tacitly understood that we would do nothing to hurt any individuals or groups in Salem by libelous or slanderous remarks. Our basic purpose was to observe such actions as might help us and others to understand community dynamics.

The staff was also convinced that a narrow view of actions in relation to self-study—a view held entirely within the bounds of a conventional study of community organization processes—would yield little new light on actual happenings. Reports on community studies filled with clichés relating to "coordination, cooperation, integration, and success upon success ad nauseam" constituted a pitfall into which the staff did not wish to fall. On the other hand, it was not the intention of the staff to lean the other way and pick flaws in the study process and overemphasize failures. We truly wished to see the process as it was.

To avoid the description of "community organization in a vacuum," the dimensions of economic and political factors were injected into our plan of a study of processes. Thus, the last hypothesis, or guiding idea consciously held by the research staff, may be restated: *The formation of the study committee will be subject to the general economic, political, and social processes that bear upon the parent sponsoring body—in this instance—the Salem Community Council.*

We would say now that the original hypothesis was too narrowly drawn. It was not only the formation of the study committee that was subject to the forces indicated, but the work of the committee and the actions flowing from its work were also subject to them.

CHAPTER 13

Community Organization—Unreality and Reality

COMMUNITY ORGANIZATION for health and welfare services
is a social process involving the measurement of community needs in terms of available community resources,
and from such measurement, developing, extending, modifying, joining, and curtailing agency and organization services
for an adequate meeting of the continuing needs of people.
Community organization thus encompasses two major sets
of behavior: social study and social action. One concept
merges into the other in the practice of community organization.

Community organization, as a social process, also takes
place in a social setting—usually in an organized community.
The way in which a community is socially organized has a
bearing upon the way in which a group measures, modifies,
and changes existing relationships of agencies and organizations.

The techniques of community organization encompass
activities devoted to exchanging ideas, meeting, negotiating,
bargaining, educating, accommodating, and on occasion,
using authority and pressure. These techniques, with others,
are modified both by existing situations and by the social
situation in which they are exercised.

As a community increases in size, various agencies are
formed to meet the needs of its population—recreational,
welfare, health, and other civic needs. In communities that
have grown to 25,000 or 30,000 people and above, one often
finds a council of social agencies or a community council
organized to coordinate the activities of the various agencies.

A council is often charged with the responsibility of trying to eliminate overlapping and duplication of services. Councils usually function through hierarchical committee arrangements. The parent body of a council, from which committees are formed, is a delegate assembly made up of representatives of member agencies. These representatives are most often two in number. Thus, such agencies as Boy Scouts, Girl Scouts, the local Family Service Society, the Department of Public Welfare, Red Cross, the Department of Public Health, the local Nursing Association, the League of Women Voters, the local luncheon clubs, and a host of other community agencies will bind themselves into a loose federation to achieve common goals.

Each individual agency has a unique service to offer the community, yet each is liable to have common interests with any number of other community agencies. In the field of recreation, for example, the Y.M.C.A. program differs, obviously, from that of the Y.W.C.A., but both agencies are devoted to serving young people. Thus agencies having common interests are usually grouped into functional divisions within a community council, e.g., the basic committee divisions of case work, group work, recreation, and health. Representatives from agencies related to these areas of interest get together periodically to discuss common problems and program planning on a community-wide basis. Theoretically, a council provides means whereby a maximum of autonomy and individual initiative resides in the member agencies of a council, but common goals and strengthening of services can also come in for joint thinking and attention.

Most theorists who have written about community organization have liberally used the word "process," a term employed to describe the general movements of people from the inception of a community project to its termination. The process of coming to terms with a problem involves the ideas of measurement, negotiating, meeting, and bargaining mentioned previously. Underlying the assumption of process are several notions.

It is felt by most community organizers and community theorists that if one can just get a broad cross-sampling of people around a table and get them to discuss problems, the problems are well on the way to solution. This phase of community organization process has proved successful enough in practice so that the notion stands upon some base of pragmatic validity. Another basic notion encompasses the idea that conviction on the part of leaders will bring acceptance of large groups of people for any idea promulgated and provide a basis for community-wide support and solidarity in relation to the particular program under consideration. The principle of "selling the leaders on an idea" is often called the "bellwether principle." This too has proved valid in practice. Community chests have successfully exploited the principle over many years.

A third widespread set of ideas in the field of community organization relates to the leadership principle and to the idea of getting people around a conference table. This set of ideas is hard to define in a few words, but behind it lies an assumption that if "proper procedures" and "proper protocol" are followed in terms of "democratic process" all is bound to turn out well in the end. If by any chance a project goes sour, atrophies, or "dies aborning," one need look first of all at what procedures and protocol were followed and determine the causes of failure in poorly defined "process." It is an assumption that procedure is more important than other factors in the situation—even more important than the people involved in the process.

Along with the ideas related to protocol and procedures there is extant a system of self-deception. The self-deception is not necessarily harmfully deceitful in essence, but its practice lies in an area of symbolic reference in relation to community organization projects. Let us put this idea concretely: Often words are used such as "The whole community believes this ought to be done," or, "This project represents the combined thinking of all the agencies in Smithtown," or, "Without the support of the Brotherhood of Junior Birdmen, this project would never have got off the ground."

The speaker who makes a statement such as any one of the above usually does so in public. The system of symbolic reference in public is couched in terms that are generally conceded to be acceptable. One does not air soiled linen in public. But the same speaker, or set of speakers, if asked to give his candid opinion of the same project, might say, in relation to the three phrases above, something like this, "Between you and me, a handful of people put this across, and Mr. Jones was really the prime mover"; or, "One man wrote the report for this project, but everyone agreed that it was a community-wide product—they went along"; or, "The Junior Birdmen have made a good thing out of this project, but frankly they had little to do with it." Technical language is also used to obscure real events. It is said that one must "read between the lines" to get the real meaning of a report, or one ought to "go and see Bill Jones to get the real low-down on what actually happened."

The self-deceptions touched upon here are justified by such phrases as, "I have to live in this town, why raise a lot of questions that would split the town wide open"; or, "One can catch more flies with sugar, you know"; or, "It is the function of a council group to bring people together, not to divide them"; or, "Controversy can be avoided by strategy."

In a piece of behavioral research it is important for the researcher to distinguish between what people say and what they do. Speaking is a part of behavior, but it is only a part. A person's actions may belie what he says, or objective facts may indicate that a man earnestly believes what he says, but in the total situation he is apparently wrong. Many things were said to us in Salem. Many things were taken at face value, but we were also interested in observing a total pattern of action in order to work out descriptions of community actions. We observed a process of community organization, much of which followed the schemata theoretically outlined here, but we observed this process in a larger community setting. Let us now summarize in our own terms of "reality," the process as we observed it.

Salem is less different from other communities than some of its residents think it is. Like other New England communities, it is undergoing a period of profound economic and social change. Some of these changes are readily admitted and appear on the surface. The movement of the largest mill from the community is a fact that cannot be hidden, for example. Nor can the conflicts and antagonisms between ethnic groups be denied by those familiar with the community's social organization. Observable needs related to parking, housing, preservation of historical sites, and the development and redevelopment of tourist attractions and recreational facilities are problems that are under consideration in the process of change and in the realignment of thinking in the community.

But with all of these problems, many of them seen only in part by many members of the community, there is a laggard willingness to face up to them in any broad scale and concerted fashion. We say this with no sense of blame. We believe that those involved in the process of everyday living in Salem are convinced they are doing the best they can within the limits of circumstances as they see and read them. We believe that many see rather clearly "what might be done" in any number of troublesome situations, but the odds favoring failure along many lines seem so great that inertia and waiting for the next crisis seem preferable to ill-timed and under-supported action.

Few persons living in Salem were able to say openly what we are about to say from afar. Self-interest was a dominant value in Salem. It was a value in a complex value system that was in keeping with the community's basic social organization—a system that represented a balance of many conflicting interests. Within the community, self-interest was bound up with acceptable terminology, related to broader interests, and thereby socially tolerated.

The readily identifiable values existing in the Salem culture did not differ, by and large, from the most obvious ones of the greater American culture of which the community was a part. Actually, many of the ideals of American culture found expression in Salem and the New England area long before the vast majority of other American communities came into being. The bedrock values relating to freedom, opportunity, independence, and fair play were still fundamental elements of the larger value system.

Along with the virtues of these expressions—expressions of the long-range goals and cultural expectations of the people— the principles of the Yankee trader were in evidence. Thrift, bargaining, working for advantage, and bettering one's self were also values understood by the community elders and passed on as virtues to the young. As with other American communities, progress was a keynote, and progress to many meant monetary, social, and power advancement. Most people of Salem with whom we talked expressed these ideas in one way or another examining their own thoughts about the social situation in the community.

Such phrases as: "jockeying for position," "putting the screws on," "turning on the heat," "enlightened self-interest," "selling out," "the build up," and "for the good of the organization" are all terms related to the proposition of individual or group advantage and advancement. They are as much a part of the culture as the higher sounding phrases related to freedom and the like. Persons in Salem understood clearly that one may be dedicated to the advancement of self, groups, or causes. If one was not too blatant in the advancement of himself, this type of advancement was socially sanctioned.

It was learned by all that advantages accrue to those who have a broad base of support within the social structure of the community. The historical expression, "In unity there is strength," had been taken literally by group after group in the community. Group solidarity enhanced the opportunities of its members in Salem. This was understood by all even though it may not have always been stated openly. There was tacit agreement as to the desirability of strength within one's own group, or, in conflict situations, there was recognition of the fact of strength of group opinion both within one's own group or in others, whether this fact seemed desirable or not.

Every organized group had stated or unstated long-range goals that were in conformity with the basic value statements of the larger culture. Democracy, freedom, and the like were a part of the public pronouncements expressed in relation to any given issue. The members of various groups who made such public pronouncements, whether they were instructed to do so by their groups or whether they did so on their own, were expected to enhance the prestige and standing of the group by their statements. That such statements might not have always expressed the exact nature of events was forgiven on the grounds of a larger interest being served. Let us illustrate this by looking over a newspaper release related to "monument of vision and action." Without citing the total release, but only sections of it related to the history of the Salem project, we shall make our point.

When [Salem's new health center is] completed and set in operation early in the summer, [it] will stand as a monument to the vision and determination of civic-minded citizens who evaluate community betterment in terms of action rather than wishful thinking.

All of which brings to the fore the Salem Community Council, and in particular the man who founded it, Joseph Colbert.

Soon after coming to Salem, as executive director of the Community Fund, Colbert brought together the groups with allied interests in education, health, welfare, and recreation to exchange ideas and discuss kindred problems.

Then, in the spring of 1946, the Salem Council was organized, primarily to provide a means by which all agencies dealing with health and community well-being would work together....

Among the Community Council's charter members were Dr. Henry L. Tracy of the Salem Health Department and Dr. Carlton Gage, the latter an ardent social worker and past president of the Society for Prevention of Cruelty to Children.

In their respective fields they had long recognized the need for a better community health program and facilities to coordinate the work of the various agencies. The answer, obviously, was a health center. They recognized the Community Council as the medium to awaken the public to the need. . . .

[There follows a description of the committee set up to study the need.]

After months of work the committee compiled its report embodying a series of recommendations, among them the proposal that municipal and private health agencies be centralized in one building.

In September, learning that the school building on Broad Street was to be vacated, a committee representing the Community Council called on Mayor Richard J. Corcoran and requested that the school building be allocated for use as a health center.

Mayor Corcoran told the group that he was impressed and gave them assurance of full cooperation. . . .

Going on to other endeavors, Colbert makes the observation:

"In this continuing process designed to make for community betterment, first consideration must be given to urgent problems, all of which demand complete and prudent analysis in terms of current conditions.

"In dealing with the problems of the present," he added, "we must look beyond to the future, keeping our effort geared to an embracing long-range program that will not stop at better community health, but will prove of benefit to all who live and work here, and which will bolster the structure of this city's economy."

A picture of Mr. Colbert accompanied this piece. The article was written by a reporter on the paper with whom Mr. Colbert had a close working relationship. There were those in the community who said that the story gave too much credit to Mr. Colbert and the Community Council. It is not our intention to discredit the statements made. In essence they are true. They do not, however, tell the whole story.

Actually, as indicated in our discussion of the work of the study committee, Colbert did not assume a very active role in the committee's deliberations. It is also true that the role of the Community Council, as an organization, was minimal.

It is furthermore true that other articles written in the same paper on earlier dates gave credit to various individuals and groups in the community in relation to the successful conclusion of the community center project.

As in every civic undertaking, there were several individuals, representing a variety of organizations, who "wished to get in on the act." This desire springs, undoubtedly, from a variety of motives, but public statements, such as those cited in the news accounts above, stress group and community solidarity. They are made "for the good of the organization" and are acceptable. They help to build prestige for the organization and enhance its functional advantage in community affairs. The article on the Community Council apparently was aimed at such an end. The self-interest in the release was socially acceptable within the value structure of the community.

Value systems of other interest groups were also served by the action taken in relation to the health center. Some were latent, but as real as if they were manifest. We will merely mention a number of them to highlight the point of self-interest.

The value of thrift was evident in the situation. The city fathers and those close to the distribution of tax funds solved the problem of a center in an economical fashion. The use of an old building—a building erected for an entirely different function than that of providing for health services—cost a fraction of a sum that might have been necessary if the possibility of getting more adequate quarters had been explored. We are not prepared to say that the building chosen is inadequate to the task of providing for the services needed in Salem. In comparison to some health centers in smaller communities, we would cast some doubt on its adequacy.

If Salem were freer of another value that binds it, the value of community self-sufficiency, outside sources of advice might have given the community a better measure of adequacy in the development of the center than we feel the community had by relying almost entirely on the judgment of persons within it who were guided by the values of short-term gains.

The city administration benefited by the expenditure of the relatively modest sum involved. Action by the administration satisfied two groups, namely, those who wanted betterment in relation to a civic endeavor and those taxpayers who wanted any actions taken by the administration to be in keeping with the value of thrift.

It is not our intention to belabor the point of self-interest in terms of ethical considerations. Selfishness is just as "wrong" in Salem as it is elsewhere. Right or wrong it was inextricably interwoven into the social fabric of the community, and disregarding it or disguising it in terms of community betterment does not help one to a basic understanding of community forces. Self-interest is at the crux of the bargaining process in many community ventures.

Enlightened self-interest, group preservation, self-improvement, and group improvement were all powerful motivating forces in Salem. The clusters of values around these central ideas were relatively stable and slow to change. As values they were often in conflict with ideas related to charity and altruism. Actually, some of the agencies of charity and altruism served as vehicles for the self-interest and advancement of individuals—not openly and blatantly, but as a latent function of any organization embodies elements of prestige accrual for the benefit of its members. We need not argue the old question of whether or not there is any such thing as "pure" altruism. We do know that whether or not a man wishes to gain prestige by being known as a charitably minded person, by his acts he gains prestige by identifying himself with the larger good of a group or his community.

In the scale of values within the community of Salem, some organizations have more prestige than others. Organizations of the highest prestige are not, in general, the most active in promoting social change. As has been pointed out, organizations like the sewing circles, the Essex Institute, and the Marine Society were high prestige organizations, and obviously one of the central functions of each of these organizations was to give stability to existing relationships within the community rather than organizing people within and outside their membership for new ways of doing things. The members of such organizations were devoted to doing things in the tried-and-true, traditional way. Acts within these organizations were prescribed by well-established rituals, formal rules, and recognized but unwritten standards. Such organizations were voluntary in nature, that is, they had no overt power of enforcing their actions upon others.

At the other extreme of organization in Salem's civic life stand the political groupings. While the rules of conduct were formal and prescribed, in many ways, there was also a latitude of action allowed and sanctioned in this area that set the political groups apart from other community groups. While the social forces that apply to all citizens in Salem were operative in relation to politicians, the persons elected to office did have overt power, and their decisions were binding upon all citizens so long as their power was exercised within the rules of reason that might be upheld by courts of law and that were in keeping with community sanctions and tolerance.

Between the higher prestige organizations and the legal organizations in the community, the voluntary organizations, such as the health and welfare agencies, had a place. Some of these agencies had more prestige than others, and therefore they had more general influence. Yet, they did not have authority and were dependent upon persuasion for attainment of their goals. The Community Council of Salem had considerably less prestige than many of the civic agencies and no authority. As an organization, it was at a distinct disadvantage in relation to either the other prestige organizations or the political groupings. But it was not altogether without advantage as an instrument of social change. Its advantage, as seen in the Salem self-study, was one of symbolic reference.

The close-knit prestige groups, as pointed out, were not

instruments of change. The political groups may have been suspect by many, if they moved too quickly on any issue or project. Generally speaking, the political groups moved when they were activated by a body of citizenry rather than being self-motivated. In such a situation it becomes necessary to bring into being social groupings that are not so bound by tradition, on the one hand, or suspicion on the other, so that they can move in relation to new alignments of community forces.

A community council, in theory at least, represents a meeting ground for diverse interests, but interests that may be working toward some common goal. A community council is usually thought of as being nonpartisan in its make-up. It is altruistic in its stated values, and it is usually devoted to a goal of social action rather than the keeping of tradition.

The stated purposes of the Salem Council fit rather well with those just mentioned, but as an organization the Council was weak. It had not been in existence for many years. Its members were not used to meeting together. It did not have within its membership some of the most influential citizens of the community, nor many of the lower status groups. It was peopled, in the main, by professional health and welfare workers. Only a few of these people took the Council seriously as an action organization.

It was rather generally recognized by many in the community that if things were to get done, it would not be the Council, as an organization, that would act. On the other hand, the self-study was sanctioned by the Council, and the final report of the study committee was made to the Council. The Council served, in this instance, as a symbolic reference.

No single health agency would have had the sanction for doing a community-wide study. If one agency, such as the public health department, had initiated a community study on its own, it is quite likely that many of the other organizations would not have "gone along." But, by putting the study into the Community Council framework, other agencies and groups felt that the sponsorship was broad enough that they could cooperate in the venture. The Council organization served as a symbol of cooperation by many of the civic organizations.

As the study progressed and as the study committee sought sanction for its findings, the Council was referred to as a sponsoring agency. Most of the time, however, and at points of action referred to earlier, the Council was not considered. It had neither the prestige to make it influential nor the authority to make its decisions binding. This fact did not deter those who were interested in the promotion of the health center. The Council was used for what it was worth— the value of symbolic reference. Perhaps in this the citizens of Salem were being realistic.

In observing the movement of the group and individuals interested in the establishment of a health center, it was obvious that there was an awareness of the "processes" of community organization described in the opening paragraphs of this chapter. There were relatively few false moves, retreats, or slip-ups in the action process. The time for action was apparently propitious and none quibbled too much about form and procedure. There was a clear recognition of the need to utilize prestige persons, technical persons, and those politically oriented in reaching the objective sought. This driving straight for a goal characterized the work of the action committee in contrast to the study committee—a type of committee that all too often is found in the best run community councils.

Within the action process related to getting the health center, one also finds a single agency, the public health department, and an individual within that agency, the health agent, vitally concerned with the outcome of the issue. It became apparent to some, during the process of study, that Henry Tracy had his eye on the school building as a possible health center—and many had their eyes on Henry Tracy. Dr. Tracy was well liked in many quarters, and none were willing to deny the legitimacy of his aims as they became known. He was extremely cooperative with everyone. All would agree that he had taken the proper formal and informal steps to achieve his ends—ends that would achieve community goals. He actually "carried people along with him" in a very effective and astute manner. He recognized his own position in relation to many factors—political, economic, and social—and many were happy to have had a part in helping toward his goal. All of this was done, of course, in the name of the community for the "benefit of all who work there" and "to bolster the structure of the city's economy."

This process of community organization was real enough. Some of those engaged in it, particularly Henry L. Tracy, said to us on occasion, "We are not following a pattern set down in the textbooks relating to how things should be done, but this is Salem and you have to take into account a lot of factors, political and otherwise." The apology stemmed partly from the fact that many in Salem knew that the processes described here would be published. We think that the apology was unnecessary. We also recognize that it was only half meant. There is, however, a principle of community organization in the statement. No community ever follows the textbooks, and every community that successfully executes a project does it in its own way taking into account its own unique factors of social, political, religious, and economic organizations. Difficulties are liable to arise when this principle of local uniqueness is violated.

In looking back over the Salem situation and trying to formulate some ideas that might be summarized as guides or aids to other communities that wish to study health needs, one hesitates to do so because of the differences between individual community structures and organizations.

While it is true that the action committee achieved a goal that it sought, there is some evidence, at the time of this writing, that many of the recommendations made by the study committee may not be carried out soon. There seemed to be few people in the community as enthusiastic as Henry Tracy to work at them. Thus the results of the community-wide study may not be community-wide in translation.

The processes of community organization are not automatic. Far from it. Many of them are not accepted generally. The very fact that they are geared to social change frightens some people off. The relatively new place in the scheme of things of the Council in Salem made the organization more ineffective than otherwise. The fact that the basic organization of the Council tended to break down some of the existing barriers between groups may be looked upon as desirable in theory, but in practice it threatens many groups in the Salem community. No, the processes of community organization are not automatic—not as automatic as the processes of other group organizations in the community. To be made operative, community organization needs constant stimulus from an established organization. Salem lacks this, since its Council is nominal rather than actual.

In Salem the lack of professional staff on the Council militated against the continuity needed to keep projects alive through the kind of prodding that is necessary in moving community groups to action. While paid professionals in a council do not guarantee continuing support of any given project, there is more likelihood of sustained interest by them in keeping projects alive after reports are turned in by study groups.

Even in the best organized councils, however, the same forces of social lag and lethargy are at work as were observed in the Salem case. Often there is not a clear understanding of the social, political, and economic alignments that make action difficult if not impossible. Groups devoted to self-study tend to take these forces for granted, or if they are known, even in part, expressions concerning them are rarely made publicly. The outside expert is often in a much better position to assess the strengths and weaknesses of organizations than those who have become accustomed to group alignments and allegiances. From the inception of the Salem self-study, it was apparent that there was an over-involvement of professional people on the study committee in ratio to laymen, and there was little involvement of some of the top leaders of the community. There was much talk about involving grass-roots people in the study, but this was never done. The majority of people in Salem were given a health center by a very small group.

By using the Community Council as a symbol of concerted community action, the study committee, and finally the action committee, disregarded the presence, within the community, of several large interest groupings that have been considered throughout this writing. From observations of other communities engaged in the processes of study and action, Salem does not appear too different in its oversight of such underlying groups. The oversight merely casts some doubt upon the usual community organization statements related to "the *community* did this or the *community* did that." A whole community rarely acts on a given issue or project. The real question in analyzing action is, "Just who did act?" and in this writing we have attempted to show actions in this perspective.

The risk that self-study groups run in narrowly defining their areas of study should be touched upon before closing our narrative. We have indicated repeatedly that social structures related to health are not unrelated to other structures of prestige, power, and politics of the community. We are not at all sure, from reading reports of other self-study groups, that it is possible for local groups to see the relations between these elements, or if they do see them, that they will be put down. Thus, solutions to problems that require large segments of community support, or that require fundamental change in social alignments, may go begging for want of breadth of analysis.

We must say that the fear expressed from the inception of the study in relation to a discussion, at the community level, of the controversial topic of public medicine denied others in other communities the opportunity of benefiting by such discussion. Without this type of discussion at the local level of national life, it is difficult for our national legislators and policy makers to come to sound decisions. The implication in one of our original hypotheses that problems of health can best be solved by communities coming to conclusions through self-study is denied if groups in local communities refuse to tackle controversial questions. We doubt that many communities are prepared to come to grips with some of the heavily charged questions, but, if they do not, doubt must be cast upon the efficacy of the method of self-study.

Salem did not appear ready to undergo quick change in relation to its social arrangements, nor was it prepared to engage in basic controversy over its distribution of medical costs; that is, the persons with whom we had contact did not appear ready for these things. Nor do we believe that lessons in the catechism of community organization will change the basic structure of the community. Community organization offers a good deal in the way of a rational approach to meeting problems, but the social system of Salem subscribed to no single rationale, and as a whole, it had many non-rational elements within it. At best, the agencies and individuals that could have made the processes of community organization operative were so bound with restrictive and conflicting sets of values that long term processes of accommodation, negotiation, and compromise needed to precede any action.

As a social system, the community of Salem has been in operation longer than the great majority of American cities. In spite of the pulling and hauling of conflicting forces within it, it is evident that the community will prosper in the future as it has in the past. Mills, commercial enterprises may come and go. Leaders, too, will rise and have their hour, and some of them will despair and look backward to the day of their grandfathers and great-great grandfathers. Some may not like the ways of the new leadership nor the names of persons who keep the town alive. These things pass to another new phase of history. Those who have ears to hear the beat of history may listen to the drums of a military band practicing on the Salem Common each Monday night during the summer months. With their eyes they will see—those who wish to see—the crowds of proud relatives watch this band made up of young men whose fathers and grandfathers came to Salem from Poland. They symbolize many other groups in their pride of community—for it is their community and they will finally do with it as they will.

Bibliography

BOOKS AND DOCUMENTS

American Council on Race Relations. *To Secure These Rights in Your Community. A Manual for Discussion, Fact Finding and Action in State and Local Committees.* Chicago: The Council, 1948.

American Public Health Association. *An Official Declaration of Attitude of American Public Health Association on Desirable Minimum Functions and Suitable Organization of Health Activities.* New York, 1941.

Atchley, Mell H. *Community Study Guide. A Study of Community Resources and Activities.* Gainesville: The University of Florida Press, 1951.

Carr-Saunders, A. M. and P. A. Wilson. *The Professions.* Oxford: Clarendon Press, 1933.

City of Salem. *Annual Report of the Board of Health.* Salem, Massachusetts: Newcomb & Gauss, 1950-53.

Colcord, Joanna C. *Your Community—Its Provision for Health, Education, Safety, Welfare.* New York: Russell Sage Foundation, 1947.

Committee on Administrative Practice. *Evaluation Schedule for Use in the Study and Appraisal of Community Health Programs.* New York: American Public Health Association, 1947.

Committee on Administrative Practice. *Health Practice Indices 1947-48.* New York: American Public Health Association, 1950.

Cox, Oliver Cromwell. *Caste, Class, and Race.* New York: Doubleday Company, 1948.

Davis, Kingsley. *Human Society.* New York: The Macmillan Company, 1950.

Ehlers, Victor M. and Ernest W. Steel. *Municipal and Rural Sanitation.* New York: McGraw-Hill Book Company, Inc., 1950.

Ensminger, Douglas. "Diagnosing Rural Community Organization," *Cornell Agricultural Extension Bulletin 444*, May 1939.

Firey, Walter. *Land Use in Central Boston*. Cambridge, Massachusetts: Harvard University Press, 1947.

Goldmann, Franz. *Public Medical Care*. New York: Columbia University Press, 1945.

Hiller, E. T. *Social Relations and Structure*. New York: Harper and Brothers, 1947.

———. *The Strike, A Study in Collective Action*. Chicago: The University of Chicago Press, 1929.

Hiscock, Ira V. *Community Health Organization*. 4th ed. New York: The Commonwealth Fund, 1950.

Hunter, Floyd. *Community Power Structure*. Chapel Hill: The University of North Carolina Press, 1953.

Kaufman, Harold F. "Prestige Classes in a New York Rural Community," *Cornell Agricultural Extension Memoir 260*, March 1944.

Kimball, Solon T. and Marion Pearsall. *The Talladega Story*. University: University of Alabama Press, 1954.

King, C. M. *Organizing for Community Action*. New York: Harper and Brothers, 1948.

Lynd, Robert C. and Helen M. Lynd. *Middletown*. New York: Harcourt, Brace and Company, 1929.

———. *Middletown in Transition*. New York: Harcourt, Brace and Company, 1937.

Merton, Robert K. *Social Theory and Social Structure*. Glencoe, Illinois: The Free Press, 1949.

Miller, Paul A. *Community Health Action*. East Lansing: The Michigan State College Press, 1953.

Mott, F. D. and M. I. Roemer. *Rural Health and Medical Care,* New York: McGraw-Hill Book Company, Inc., 1948.

Ogden, Jess and Jean Ogden. *Small Communities in Action*. New York: Harper and Brothers, 1946.

———. *These Things We Tried*. Charlottesville: University of Virginia Extension, 1947.

Peabody, Andrew. *What the Physician Should Be*. Cambridge, Massachusetts: Bigelow and Company, 1870.

Phillips, James. *The Essex Institute Historical Collections*. Salem, Massachusetts. Vol. XC, January 1954.

Roucek, Joseph S. (ed.). *Social Control.* "The Nature of Social Control," by H. C. Brearley. New York: B. Van Nostrand Company, Inc., 1947.

Salem Board of Health. Minutes of the Board. Salem, Massachusetts: Unpublished, 1799-1953.

Salem City Council. *Revised Ordinances of the City of Salem, Massachusetts, 1952.* Charlottesville, Virginia: Michie City Publications Company, 1952.

Sanders, I. T. (ed.). *Making Good Communities Better.* Lexington: The University of Kentucky Press, 1950.

Smillie, Wilson G. *Public Health Administration in the United States.* New York: The Macmillan Company, 1949.

Southern Regional Council. *Your Community Looks at Itself, A Manual For the Home Town Self-Survey.* Atlanta, Georgia: The Council, 1951.

Sower, Christopher and Associates. *Community Health Action in Central County.* East Lansing: Social Research Service, Department of Sociology and Anthropology, Michigan State College, June 9, 1953.

Stern, Bernhard J. *Medical Services by Government.* New York: The Commonwealth Fund, 1946.

———. *Social Factors in Medical Progress.* New York: Columbia University Press, 1927.

Swanson, C. E., J. M. Newcomb, and E. L. Hartley (eds.). *Readings in Social Psychology.* "The Effect of Public Housing Projects Upon Interracial Attitude," by Morton Deutsch and Mary Evans Collins. Rev. ed. New York: Henry Holt & Co., 1952.

Veblen, Thorstein. *The Theory of the Leisure Class.* New York: B. W. Huebsch Co., 1922.

Warner, W. Lloyd. *American Life, Dream and Reality.* Chicago: The University of Chicago Press, 1953.

——— and Associates. *Democracy in Jonesville.* New York: Harper and Brothers, 1949.

——— and Paul S. Lunt. *The Social Life of a Modern Community.* New Haven: Yale University Press, 1941.

——— and Leo Srole. *The Social Systems of American Ethnic Groups.* New Haven: Yale University Press, 1945.

West, James. *Plainville, U.S.A.* New York: Columbia University Press, 1945.

PERIODICALS

Bales, Robert F. et al. "Channels of Communication in Small Groups," *American Sociological Review,* 16 (August 1951), pp. 461-68.

Bierstedt, Robert. "An Analysis of Social Power," *American Sociological Review,* 15 (December 1950), pp. 730-38.

Brooks, Maxwell R. "American Class and Caste: An Appraisal," *Social Forces,* 25 (December 1946), pp. 207-11.

Burney, Leroy E. "Community Organization—An Effective Tool," *American Journal of Public Health,* 44 (January 1954), pp. 2-3.

Bauer, Louis H. "The President's Page," *The Journal of the American Medical Association,* 151 (January 31, 1953), p. 350.

Close, Katherine. "Back of the Yards," *Survey Graphic,* 29 (December 1940), pp. 612-15.

Coutu, Walter. "Role-Playing vs. Role-Taking: An Appeal for Clarification," *American Sociological Review,* 16 (April 1951), pp. 180-87.

Davis, Kingsley. "A Conceptual Analysis of Stratification," *American Sociological Review,* 7 (June 1942), pp. 309-21.

Dunbar, Willis F. "Let's Appoint a Committee," *Social Education,* 7 (March 1943), pp. 121-23.

Fichter, Joseph H. and William L. Kolb. "Ethical Limitations on Sociological Reporting," *American Sociological Review,* 18 (October 1953), pp. 544-50.

Gross, Neal. "Social Class Identification in the Urban Community," *American Sociological Review,* 18 (August 1953), pp. 398-404.

Hall, John and D. Caradog Jones. "Social Grading of Occupations," *The British Journal of Sociology,* 1 (March 1950), pp. 31-55.

Hall, Oswald. "The Stages of Medical Career," *The American Journal of Sociology,* 53 (March 1948), pp. 327-36.

———. "Types of Medical Career," *The American Journal of Sociology,* 55 (November 1949), pp. 243-53.

Hollingshead, August B. "The Concept of Social Control," *American Sociological Review,* 6 (April 1941), pp. 217-24.

———. "Selected Characteristics of Classes in a Midwestern Community," *American Sociological Review,* 12 (August 1947), pp. 386-88.

Hollingshead, August B. "Trends in Social Stratification: A Case Study," *American Sociological Review*, 17 (December 1952), pp. 679-86.

Journal of Social Issues, V (Spring 1949).

Komarovsky, Mirra. "The Voluntary Association of Urban Dwellers," *American Sociological Review*, 11 (December 1946), pp. 686-98.

Merton, Robert K. "Bureaucratic Structure and Personality," *Social Forces*, 18 (May 1940), pp. 560-68.

Mills, C. Wright. "The Middle Classes in Middle Sized Cities," *American Sociological Review*, 11 (October 1946), pp. 520-29.

Minnis, Mhyra S. "Cleavage in Women's Organizations: A Reflection of the Social Structure of a City," *American Sociological Review*, 18 (February 1953), pp. 47-53.

Murphy, Albert J. "A Study of the Leadership Process," *American Sociological Review*, VI (October 1941), pp. 674-87.

North, Cecil C. and Paul K. Hatt, "Jobs and Occupations: A Popular Evaluation," *Opinion News*, 9 (September 1947), pp. 3-13.

Salem Evening News. Salem, Massachusetts (1890-1954).

Seeman, Melvin. "Role Conflict and Ambivalence in Leadership," *American Sociological Review*, 18 (August 1953), pp. 373-80.

Taft, Ronald. "Social Grading of Occupations in Australia," *The British Journal of Sociology*, 4 (June 1953), pp. 181-87.

Useem, John, Ruth Useem, and Pierce Tangent. "Stratification in a Prairie Town," *American Sociological Review*, 7 (June 1942), pp. 331-42.

Winslow, C. E. A. "The International Appraisal of Local Health Programs," *Milbank Memorial Fund Quarterly*, 15 (January 1937).

Index

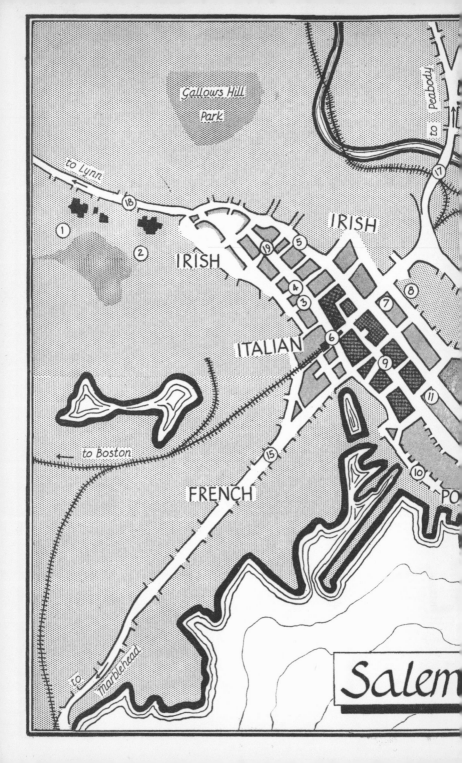